on the
urban scene

on the urban scene

edited by

morton levitt
university of california at davis

ben rubenstein
marlboro college, vermont

published for the
American Orthopsychiatric Association

Wayne State University Press
detroit 1972

These papers were originally presented at the 47th Annual Convention of the American Orthopsychiatric Association.

Published simultaneously in Canada by the Copp Clark Publishing Company 517 Wellington Street, West Toronto 2B, Canada.

Library of Congress Cataloging in Publication Data

American Orthopsychiatric Association.
    On the urban scene.

    "Papers . . . presented at the 47th annual convention of the American Orthopsychiatric Association."
    Includes bibliographies.
    1. Orthopsychiatry—Congresses. 2. Minorities—United States—Congresses. 3. Community mental health services—United States—Congresses.
I. Levitt, Morton, 1920-   ed. II. Rubenstein, Ben O., 1914-   ed.
III. Title.
RC327.A46 1972   616.8'9   72-1440
ISBN 0-8143-1478-3

---

contents

II. the community

III. roles and goals

introduction

I

One tatami is the length and width of a person lying down. A friend of mine in Tokyo says that in today's society, with its overpopulation, the natural space that a person can acquire without fighting or making unnatural efforts is three tatami—one for himself to lie down in, a second for his companion, and a third for them both to breathe in.

Yoko Ono in the *New Yorker*, 8 January 1972

Jane Jacobs' book, *Death and Life of Great American Cities*, has attracted a fair amount of controversy. Although I have never read a copy from cover to cover, I have read parts of it, followed its history in its epic journalistic struggles with Charles Abrams as reported on and off in the *New Yorker* in recent years, and have often heard it discussed at pleasant weekend cocktail parties in one part or another of this country. I discovered from this diverse observational platform that Mrs. Jacobs is opposed to city planners who come in and scientificate neighborhoods, that she steadfastly warns all to avoid "cataclysmic money" (money that comes with many strings attached to it, usually from the government), that she is much taken with the older verities; that is, communities made of old, small buildings which serve a variety of purposes and have many friendly storekeepers and knowledgeable policemen about, and, finally, that the large numbers of people to be found in Mrs. Jacobs' ideal community, not merely at fixed hours but at different times of the day and night, contribute in a most positive way to the safety of all involved. Thus it may be seen that there is a friendly haze that reflects on such a community, the kind of yellowish color that surrounds Florence when seen from the hills of nearby Fiesole. The whole prospect is so simple, so engaging, that it seems hard to know why it can't or won't work.

I had reason to review the Jacobs thesis when I walked through one of America's special communities last year. I had stopped in Berkeley en route to San Francisco, my traveling companion had an errand to accomplish, and the prospect of a walk down the tree-shaded streets of that old university town was pleasant. I started up Telegraph Avenue on a sunlit afternoon just as the University of California was girding up for its summer session. It is not a place I know well; I've seen it either from the terraces of houses up the hill, where the view of the campus joining the bay and the three bridges which lead to the city make an unforgettable sight, or from the Sproul Plaza, where University business occasionally takes me.

The ground-level perspective is different but not less interesting; the colorful student dress and unending parades expressing grievances of one kind or another are the nether side of the city's ambience. As I walked that day, there were many signs of the conjunction of these two vistas for the upper part of Telegraph is made up of citadels of middle-class life—doctors' offices and banks— and the bright, attractive, and well-dressed were out in large numbers. Only as I approached the campus did the environment change. There were more street people, the business establishments were more exotic, and hip boutiques and bookstores became commonplace.

I stopped at a large corner bookshop, bought a couple of books, and started back the way I had come. As I passed a parking lot a short distance down the street, a young woman exited from a side door (a restaurant or cleaning store?) and started to walk toward the street. She was decently attractive, and being an old girl-watcher, I observed her as I walked. Her steps slowed, and I saw five black youngsters watching her from across the parking lot. They ranged in age from eight or nine to eighteen or nineteen, and when they saw that the girl had noticed them, the eldest stamped his foot as if to start in pursuit of her. The girl reacted by starting to run, and, with loud shouts, the five took after her. The girl ran to me as I stood watching the strange tableau and asked, "Will you please help me?"

In a moment, we were surrounded by the five boys who kept shouting to the girl that they were going to rape her. I firmly told the group to "let her alone," and, in the silence that followed, we hurried across Telegraph and began to walk down the other side of the block. Once again, and with a noticeably more sullen quality, we were surrounded by our five tormentors. Their plans for the girl were being expressed in more graphic terms, and I had become a partner in her crime, whatever it was. Alternately running in front and bumping us as we passed, and then tripping us from behind by hooking our heels, they began to demand my wallet and watch. Through it all, I kept repeating in some kind of crazed chant, "Come on, get away, you're all crazy, let the girl alone, just let us alone, move on."

After a bit, there were some whispers behind us, and then I heard the click of a switchblade. A moment later, we were proceeding down Telegraph Avenue in Berkeley at six o'clock in the evening just as before, except that a knife blade was now held at my back. Thoroughly frightened by this time, I began to look around for a store or a building or even a friendly passerby, on foot or in a car. There were no stores open, and I was afraid to enter an empty building lobby pursued by five delinquents. The people on the street avoided our eyes and walked in wide circles around us, and not a single car even slowed.

There we were, a frightened young girl, white-faced and perspiring, a terrified middle-aged man, muttering a crazy litany, and five "street children" carrying a knife and making sexual threats in angry shouts. All walked down the main street in Berkeley, California, in broad daylight, and no one was willing to regard this tatterdemalion gang as anything other than, what?—a family walking home from a happy frolic on the campus?

Perhaps the exercise began to pall; perhaps they were uncertain about the relationship between sexual assault and a watch and/or wallet and couldn't make a choice—this argument did indeed go on. Perhaps my tactic of refusing to stop at all costs finally paid off; I really don't know. We were approaching a side street, and a car turned into a driveway temporarily separating us from our captors. We quickly rounded the corner and entered a small courtyard which fortunately was surrounded by high bushes. The youngsters ran up and back a few times in an angry search, and then slowly drifted away.

After several minutes, we walked down the street to the girl's house. She said "thanks"; I shook my head sadly and walked off. (What does one say? Maybe *New York* with its omnipresent suggestions for terrified city-dwellers has covered this emergency, but I can't recall its advice.)

II

Everywhere's somewhere, and everywhere's the same, really, and wherever you are is where it's at. But it's more so in New York. It does have sugar on it, and I've got a sweet tooth.
John Lennon in the *New Yorker*, 8 January 1972

This morning's newscast brings happy news from the East. Congressman Edward I. Koch of Manhattan's Seventeenth District has come forward with a stopgap proposal for those folk who dwell in his neighborhood. Anyone who wants to can get free police whistles at his local office. Then when dog-walking or television-viewing is interrupted by a premonition of wrongdoing somewhere in the hustings, the wily citizen simply blows loudly on his nickel-plated police whistle. Others who hear the sound are enjoined to immediately put down their drinks, phone the police, and then blow their own whistles. Whether it's the mind-blowing impact upon the would-be criminal of several thousand whistles shrilling from a high-rise, or whether the police respond more smartly to hundreds of phone calls occurring within a few seconds of each other, the indisputable fact is that muggings and other larcenous acts have decreased somewhat during a trial period.

Still, crime is to be found on all sides in the city streets, and few people are moved to do very much about it. Behavioral scientists, appalled as were all civilized people, by the senseless murder of Catherine Genovese in Queens in 1964, have tried to understand how at least thirty-eight people who admitted hearing prolonged screaming on the street assumed that someone else would be impelled to intervene. Writing in the *Nation* (Vol. 25, 1964) shortly after the incident, Milgram and Hollander speculated that Miss Genovese's "random" (my word) screaming—"her cries for help were not directed to a specific person; they were general"—allowed a collective paralysis to develop since "no particular person felt a specific responsibility."

Borrowing an idea from systems analysis, the term "overload" has been offered, and city life is described as consisting of a continuous series of encounters with overload. The consequence is the deformation of human responsiveness, and what often results is a determined movement toward anonymity. Social responsibility is the major loser and is usually well rationalized by principles surrounding respect for others' privacy.

In a remarkably simple experiment, P. G. Zimbardo arranged to leave a car for a three-day period in both New York City and Palo Alto. To encourage a belief that the automobile was abandoned, the license plate was removed and the hood was raised. In the city environment, the car lost all of its moveable parts in twenty-four hours and was reduced to its metal chassis by the third day. Surprisingly, much of the vandalism occurred during the day in the presence of the usual groups of people on the street, and many of the participants in this destruction of property were both white and middle class. *The car abandoned in the Bay Area suburb was left intact.*

Reviewing the city scene in comprehensive fashion in a recent issue of *Science* (March 1970) Stanley Milgram cites a study by Altman, Levine, Nadien, and Villena which was designed to determine how city people compare with their small-town cousins in offering aid to strangers. The investigators (two males and two females) individually knocked on doors, explained they had lost the address of a friend who lived nearby, and asked for permission to make a phone call. As might be expected, females were admitted more frequently than males, but each of the experimenters did at least twice as well in the towns as they did in the city. A striking finding was that in the city, 75 percent of all efforts to talk were accomplished by shouting through closed doors; in the towns, about 75 percent of the respondents opened the door.

Citing a large body of impressive data, Milgram concludes that an organizing theory must start with the external factors in city life, such as numbers, crowds, and heterogeneity. The individual "experiences these factors as overloads at the level of roles, norms, cognitive functions, and facilities. These overloads lead to adaptive mechanisms which create the distinctive tone and behaviors of city life."

III

A boy sat under the Anheuser Busch, The rain, 'twas
coming down in Schlitz. He rose a sad Budweiser boy,
Pabst yes, Pabst no, Pabst yes.

Jimmy Durante

In 1960, something over fifty million Americans lived
in only sixteen urban areas. If all these high density
agglomerates were put together, they would be smaller
than Cochise County in Arizona. Bad times on the farm
have accelerated the country-to-city trend in recent
years, and many rural types are now replacing the middle
class in the city as the latter group flees to the suburbs.
Nowhere is the trend as visible as on the eastern
seaboard where those who leave the cities soon urbanize
the suburbs, and then are forced by their own disenchantment to move further out into the country.

Soon the developers are once again there with
services and shopping centers, and it fails to surprise
when we learn the northeastern New York-New Jersey
urban sprawl has almost fifteen million people and in
one sense at least can be considered the largest "city" in
the world.

While creature comforts are assuredly one of the large
motivating forces in the movement away from cities,
there are certain ideological explanations for the suburbia
cum country renaissance. As a people, we seem to
believe strongly in the benefits of small towns, small
societies, and small governmental units. The vision of the
New England town meeting dances invitingly, and much
is made of the strong sense of community identity which
can be found in those who "live out."

There are, nonetheless, some demonstrable facts
which must be faced. Most people live in or near cities,
almost all work in cities, irrespective of where they live,
and those cities seem to be suffering from a social
variety of blight as witness the titles of recent books: *A*

City Destroys Itself, Sick Cities, The Withering Away of Cities, Crisis in Our Cities, Metropolis in Crisis, and dozens of others. The most cursory reading of any daily metropolitan newspaper makes clear the scope of urban distress. High on such an index are racism, traffic problems, crime and associated police corruption, pollution, increasing taxes, urban blight, declining school quality, busing, prostitution, noise, and literally dozens of other evidences of the difficulty of living in a city.

Many of these issues relate to the crisis surrounding civil rights. Communities suffering from racial riots commonly experienced a white outward migration, and it comes as no surprise that the 1970 census showed that almost one-fourth of all metropolitan areas were peopled by blacks. However, the sanctity of the suburban retreat was broached by a January 1972 federal court decision in Richmond, Virginia, which ordered integration between predominantly white suburban schools and black schools in central Richmond. Some critics of this move have already suggested a counter tactic, a natural integration of races in schools which would result from building low income housing in suburban areas. Thus the suburbs will soon become like the cities, and without debating either the complex merits of that proposal or the questionable consequences of attitudinal legislation, it seems certain that some of those now living in the suburbs will once again move further out, or reverse the trend by coming back into carefully guarded enclaves in the central city.

What is rapidly becoming apparent is that traditional descriptions of the city are no longer relevant. We now speak of urban areas which extend many miles beyond the city borders and which differ from each other largely in terms of names on road signs. It is no longer meaningful to speak of the city, the suburb, and the countryside, since a new kind of urban society which is largely independent of the city has come into being.

There are those who contend that so-called "city problems" are not problems of city living at all, but instead are consequences of a rapidly developing and complex social situation which somehow defies territorial limits. This idea is challenging since it tends to separate social pathologies from an often fallacious city etiology. Viewed this way, crime, poverty, drugs, mental illness, and other of the cancers of life which are commonly attributed to city living can be found throughout the nation; their impact upon the city is worsened only by numbers and is largely unrelated to etiology.

There is another conceptual danger which must be faced. That is the notion that mental health professionals can, through virtue of their special expertise, transform the nature of urban life. Perhaps it was this thought which led David L. Bazelon to issue the following warning in his presidential address to the American Orthopsychiatric Association at its 47th Annual Meeting in 1970:

> When poverty, or racism, or crime is labeled a mental health problem, the label tends to make all of us think of the problem as an illness to be cured by experts in illness. In a society that develops a pill for every complaint, people are only too eager to find the pill that will put an end to poverty, war, injustice—the pill that will allow them to avoid the consequences of their accustomed pleasures while they go on with business and pleasure as usual. Lest the members of Ortho lend themselves to that fruitless and dangerous quest for the pill, I urge you to consider the limits as well as the promise of the mental health professions on the urban scene.
>
> When society turns to these professions for the crystal ball that will predict crime, or the magic potion that will dissolve social tensions, the most valid response is to proclaim the limitations of their art. Difficult as it is to question one's own usefulness, in this case it may be the most useful action.

That meeting was devoted to the urban scene, and the papers which make up this volume represent the most timely yield from that seminar. No burning issues are settled here, but the tone is sober, concerned, and philosophic throughout. Will the reader come away as anything save a "sad Budweiser boy"? In the words of that venerable social chronicler, Jimmy Durante, "Pabst yes, Pabst no, Pabst yes."

Morton Levitt,
Davis, California

I. minorities and expatriates

The Irrelevancy of Traditional Mental Health Services for Urban Mexican-Americans*
E. Fuller Torrey†

The psychiatric flower of the sixties, the community mental health movement, is starting to wilt. Heralded as a bold, new approach and as the third psychiatric revolution, it is wilting because it is neither of these things. It is not a new seed at all, but rather just a cautious tinkering with the *status quo*, a transplant from the psychiatry of the forties and fifties. And, as such, it is irrelevant for many segments of the American population.

The Mexican-Americans are a case in point. There are five million Mexican-Americans in the United States, constituting the country's second largest minority group. In California, 10 percent of the population is Mexican-American. Contrary to the popular stereotype, the majority of them do not live in rural areas but in towns and cities. Traditional psychiatric services, including community mental health centers, are irrelevant for them. This paper will attempt to document this irrelevancy.

The city of San Jose and surrounding suburban Santa Clara County provides a useful case study. It is a fertile, pleasant valley at the lower end of the San Francisco Bay. Due to the expansion of industry, its population

*This essay appeared in the *Stanford M.D.* 9:2-7 © 1970 in slightly revised form under the title "Mental Health Services: How Relevant for Urban Mexican-Americans?" Reprinted by permission.

†For invaluable assistance with this project, I am indebted to Rosa Miller, Robert Campos, and Clifford Barnett.

has quadrupled since the Second World War. One million people currently live in the area, of whom 10 percent are Mexican-American. The county is affluent; in fact, if it were an independent nation, it would be the 43rd wealthiest nation in the world. Certainly a modern prosperous county like this should be able to provide adequate medical, psychiatric, and social services for its population. If it cannot, what county can?

Traditional psychiatric services in the county center around 150 psychiatrists and psychologists in private practice, 120 psychiatric beds in general hospitals, Agnew State Hospital, and the Santa Clara County Community Mental Health Center complex. The last community mental health center opened its main center and four satellites in 1966, funded by building and staffing grants from the Community Mental Health Centers Act.* Late in 1968, a fifth satellite opened, erroneously called the "East Valley" Center—it is, in fact, located in downtown San Jose and not in the East Valley.

The Santa Clara County Community Mental Health Center complex more than adequately meets the specifications of the act. The center's staff of 120 psychiatrists, psychologists, and social workers provides not only the five essential services (inpatient, outpatient, emergency, day hospital, and consultation) required for funding, but additional services of training, diagnostic, precare, and aftercare as well. In terms of fulfilling the requirements of the Mental Health Centers Act, it is well above average; in terms of fulfilling the needs of a significant minority of its constituents, it is hopelessly inadequate.

Looking at utilization rates, a survey of patient visits to the central center during 1968 showed only 4 percent to be Mexican-American. This is under half of what would be expected. Even at the "East Valley" Center,

*Another satellite, the South County facility, receives funds differently. Since the area it serves includes only 3 percent of the county population, it will not be included in the figures.

opened specifically to improve services for Mexican-Americans, only 11 percent of all patient visits during its first nine months were made by Mexican-Americans. A similar underutilization of both inpatient and outpatient psychiatric facilities by Mexican-Americans has been shown by Karno and others in Los Angeles (Karno 1966, 1969; Yamamoto, James and Palley 1968).

Based on need, one would expect Mexican-Americans to overutilize mental health services rather than underutilize them. Their need is indicated by such stress indicators as the numbers of juvenile delinquent referrals, welfare recipients, and neglected and dependent children, all of which are disproportionately high in the Mexican-American parts of San Jose. One predominantly Mexican-American school district has proportionately six times as many children in mental retardation classes as a solid Anglo school district (Joint Venture in Mental Health 1968). One would also expect Mexican-Americans to have a disproportionately high incidence of mental illness since many of them are poor (Hollingshead and Redlich 1958) and since many are undergoing acculturation (Tyhurst 1951).

Reasons for irrelevancy

It is clear, then, that the mental health needs of the urban Mexican-American population are great, that traditional psychiatric services are present, and that the Mexican-Americans are underutilizing the services. These services are irrelevant for the following reasons:

They are irrelevant because they are inaccessible.

The central mental health center is on the opposite side of San Jose away from the main concentration of Mexican-Americans. This location was selected so that the center would be adjacent to the county hospital. To reach the center, a housewife who lives in East San Jose must travel an hour by bus. This is assuming, of course, that she can find and afford to pay a babysitter to look after her children for the half-day she will be away. With the opening, in late 1968, of the "East Valley" Center in downtown San Jose, things have improved somewhat— the bus ride now only takes half an hour.

There is no valid reason, however, to explain why a mental health facility has not been opened on the east side of the city. The area is widely known to have the greatest needs and the fewest medical, psychiatric, and social work facilities. A 1968 survey of mental health facilities divided the county into eight districts. The East San Jose district had none of the 150 psychiatrists and psychologists in private practice in the county, none of the 28 diagnostic, outpatient, and counseling agencies, none of the 14 day-care and partial hospitalization facilities, none of the 6 psychiatric emergency services, none of the 4 rehabilitation agencies, and none of the 10 consultation and re-education facilities (Joint Venture in Mental Health 1968). In brief, the district was, and still is, totally devoid of any kind of mental health facility. It has even been designated by the state government as the neediest catchment area in the entire State of California.

Most of this information was known when the locations of the satellite centers were decided upon. It was also known that East Valley expected the largest population growth in the county. Yet the satellite centers were placed in more affluent areas. Political considerations, bickering between county and city health departments, and certain members of the board of supervisors deliberately blocked the allocation of a satellite to the area where it was most needed.

They are irrelevant because of language considerations.

A person's first language is extremely important to him. It becomes even more important when he is upset and when he wants to share his feelings with others. It is a common observation that individuals often lose their second language altogether when they become mentally ill.

The majority of Mexican-Americans in San Jose are bilingual; Spanish is the language for home, and English is the language for elsewhere. A significant minority of them speak little or no English.

If a Mexican-American wants to use the traditional mental health facilities, however, he had better speak good English. Of the total county staff of 120 psychiatrists, psychologists, and social workers, only five speak any Spanish. There are no bilingual signs in the central center, a marked contrast to the county hospital next door, where all signs are bilingual. The message is clear: traditional mental health services are for English speakers.

They are irrelevant because they are class-bound.

Several studies during the past two decades have shown how traditional mental health services are irrelevant for the lower socioeconomic class. It has been shown that the poor are less likely to be in therapy, remain in therapy a shorter time, are given more severe diagnoses for similar symptoms, are treated by less experienced staff, and are treated by short-term and somatic therapies that the mental health establishment considers to be less valuable (Hollingshead and Redlich 1958; Prince 1968; Riessman and Pearl 1964). In one particularly revealing study of mental health pamphlets, it was found that 90 percent of the ideas expressed in them were directly associated with middle-class values (Gursslin, Hunt, and Roach 1964). The middle-class values cited are, for example, adjustment, conformity, thrift, respectability, control of emotions, and future orientation. The authors observed "we must conclude that the mental health movement is unwittingly propagating a middle-class ethic under the guise of science." (Gursslin, Hunt and Roach 1964)

Mexican-Americans certainly represent a large segment of the lower socioeconomic class in San Jose. The median household income for the 17 census tracts with the heaviest Mexican-American population is $5,400. By comparison, the median household income for the 12 census tracts that make up Palo Alto is $10,000. These figures are for households; in addition, the number of the household members, among whom the income must be divided, is considerably larger in East San Jose than in Palo Alto. And Palo Alto is not the wealthiest part of Santa Clara County; most people characterize it as middle class in comparison to some other areas.

There is also evidence that Mexican-Americans, like other lower-class patients, remain in therapy for a shorter period of time in San Jose. During the first nine months of operation of the "East Valley" Center, Mexican-American patients were seen, on the average, 2.6 times. Other patients were seen, on the average, 5.8 times. Similar patterns have been described for Mexican-Americans in mental health facilities in Los Angeles (Karno 1966).

They are irrelevant because they are culture-bound.

Work in the fields of cognitive anthropology and linguistics over the past twenty years has established conclusively that cultures divide up the world differently. For instance, the Hanunoo in the Philippines divide all colors into just four—"blackness," "whiteness," "redness," and "greenness." Their word for "redness," for example, subsumes the colors that we call red, orange, yellow, and maroon. If you show a Hanunoo man a yellow and an orange paper, he will tell you they are the same color. He may differentiate them by saying one is "more-redness" or "weak-redness," but they will still be the same color for him (Conklin 1955). Many other studies have verified the cultural relativity of perceiving and classifying (Allport and Pettigrew 1957; Frake 1961; Segall, Campbell and Herskovits 1966).

The fact that cultures divide the world differently would seem to have important implications for psychotherapy. How can a therapist use psychotherapy on a person from another culture whose categorization of the world differs? A recent anthropological work that clearly documents this difficulty is Carlos Castañeda's excellent study of a Yaqui Indian medicine man—*The Teaching of Don Juan: A Yaqui Way of Knowledge* (Castaneda 1968).

In an attempt to document these differences in San Jose, I administered a questionnaire to three groups of people—

a. 10 psychiatric residents at Stanford University;
b. 10 anthropology graduate students at Stanford University;
c. 20 high school students at a school in San Jose. Of these 7 were black, 7 were Mexican-Americans, and 6 were Anglos.

Directions for the questionnaire were given verbally and were also printed on the top of the page as follows:

I am trying to understand how people think about being well and being sick. You can help me by taking the 10 words which are listed below in alphabetical order and dividing them up. Divide them into at least 2 but no more than 5 boxes. A box can contain as few as one word. Divide them in whatever way seems most logical to you. There is no right or wrong way to divide them—just the way that makes the most sense to you.

For example:

		might be divided as follows:		
blue	red			
cold	slow	blue	cold	fast
fast	yellow	red	hot	slow
hot		yellow		

Here are the 10 words to divide:

compulsive	neurotic					
crazy	normal					
depressed	religious					
frightened	tired					
hears voices	withdrawn					

The subjects were told not to put their names on the paper; I was able to identify the papers for division into groups by the way in which I collected them.

In spite of methodological shortcomings of the study, the results suggested differences in categorization of symptoms between cultures. For instance, the words "crazy" and "hears voices" were associated by 90 percent of the psychiatric residents, 60 percent of the graduate students, and 48 percent of the non-Mexican-American high school students. Only 16 percent (1 out of 7) of the Mexican-American students associates the two words. Such a difference may indicate greater religious belief among Mexican-American students (although only 1 out of 7 made the association between "hears voices" and "religious") and/or it may reflect greater tolerance for hearing voices in the Mexican-American community. In either case, it is clear that an Anglo psychiatrist and a Mexican-American student share less of a frame of reference than the psychiatrist does with a graduate student (a common source of "good" psychiatric patients).

Another example illustrating the cultural differences in categorization was the association of "frightened" with some combination of "crazy" and "hears voices" by

86 percent of the Mexican-Americans; only 20 percent of psychiatrists, and no graduate students, made the association. This may well reflect the pervasive cultural belief among Mexican-Americans in *susto*, a syndrome of anxiety and depression thought to be caused by a severe fright (Kiev 1968; Rubel 1964).

Anecdotal material reinforces such evidence. During a recent home visit to an anxious, depressed Mexican-American housewife, I attempted to explore the origin of her symptoms within the context of her obvious domestic difficulties. Toward the end of the interview, I offered her a mild tranquilizer to alleviate her anxiety. She nodded politely, but I knew I had not gotten through. I then went back into the symptoms and discovered that she was convinced they were the result of *susto*. After I assured her that the tranquilizer was especially good for *susto*, she brightened up and smiled. Obviously, my medicine could not help her until I understood what was really wrong with her.

There is an increasing abundance of evidence in this direction that points to cultural differences in how the world is viewed. The differences include concepts of disease etiology, classification of symptoms, goals of therapy, and cultural values. The belief in *susto* among Mexican-Americans, for instance, has been well documented by studies showing that over half of Mexican-American housewives believe in it strongly (Holland 1963; Martinez and Martin 1966). The net effect these differences have on attempts to do cross-cultural psychotherapy is profound. They contribute, in fact, to making traditional psychiatric services irrelevant for those who do not share the same cognitive "set."

They are irrelevant because they are caste-bound.

Traditional mental health services are inextricably bound to the dominant, ruling caste of Anglos in the minds of Mexican-Americans. Although this overlaps both the distinctions of class and culture mentioned above, it differs in implying a more rigid segmentalization of society with hereditary positions of dominance and submission. These positions implicitly are part of the divine order and dictate such things as social intercourse and occupation as well as the use of mental health facilities. Caste goes beyond income level and value systems; it is The Order of Things.

Just as surely as the blacks in our society have been treated as a lower caste, so have the Mexican-Americans. They receive reminders of this fact every day. The recent remarks of a juvenile court judge at the trial of a 17-year-old Mexican-American boy accused of incest illustrate this point:

> The county will have to take care of you. You are no particular good to anybody. We ought to send you out of the country—send you back to Mexico. You belong in prison for the rest of your life for doing things of this kind. You ought to commit suicide. That's what I think of people of this kind. You are lower than animals and haven't the right to live in organized society—just miserable, lousy, rotten people.
>
> There is nothing we can do with you. You expect the county to take care of you. Maybe Hitler was right. The animals in our society probably ought to be destroyed because they have no right to live among human beings. If you refuse to act like a human being, then, you don't belong among the society of human beings. [San Jose *News* Sept. 27, 1969]

These remarks are unusual only in that they became part of the court record and received publicity. Until recently, Mexican-Americans have been used to hearing them. This, after all, has been The Order of Things.

Inevitably, the mental health facilities set up by the Anglo caste became associated with perpetuating this order. A widely-circulated story in the Mexican-American community concerns the fate of three Mexican-American county employees who went to Washington for the Poor People's March. Upon their return, they were ordered to have psychiatric examinations by their superiors. The welfare department frequently orders psychiatric examinations for recipients; if welfare recipients can be classified as psychiatrically disabled, they are taken off the general welfare rolls. If they refuse, their check is withheld. Little wonder that most Mexican-Americans look upon psychiatry as just one more way to degrade them.

They are irrelevant because Mexican-Americans have their own system of mental health services.

Realizing that Mexican-Americans in San Jose have problems, and that they underutilize the traditional mental health facilities, I assumed that other mental health services must exist. One possibility was that they relied upon the community "caretakers" described by Lindemann (1965) and Caplan (1964)—public health nurses, welfare workers, the clergy, teachers, probation officers, police, etc. It was the traditional reliance on this group, in fact, that led the architects of the Mental Health Centers Act to include community consultation as one of the five essential services.

It quickly became apparent that while the community "caretakers" might be mental health resources in Wellesley, Massachusetts, they served no such purpose in East San Jose. With significant exceptions (especially a few Catholic priests), this group is identified as part of the Anglo establishment and avoided whenever possible. In fact, to go to the police with a problem would be accepted as *prima facie* evidence by Mexican-Americans that the person *must* be crazy.

There are two mental health resources that do serve the Mexican-American community very well, however:

Curanderos—these are the traditional healers of Mexico and Latin America. Despite vigorous denials by most Mexican-Americans, they still exist, and are widely used by older Mexican-Americans. Because of fears of persecution by the police, the medical society, and tax agents, they are almost impossible for an Anglo to gain access to.

In order to determine how important *curanderos* are in providing mental health services, I interviewed 7 Mexican-American patients from San Jose confined at Agnew State Hospital. All had been diagnosed as schizophrenics. I found that 3 of the 7 had been treated by *curanderos*, and a fourth had been told to go to one because she believed that she had been bewitched by her husband's mistress. One of them had been treated by a *curandero* a total of nine times, and used the *curandero* as his main mental health resource between hospital admissions. He felt he was greatly helped by these visits.

Mr. R. is a *curandero*. He lives with his wife in a modest but well-kept house in East San Jose. There is no sign outside. He sees 5-10 patients a day for a wide variety of reasons including physical illness, social and domestic problems, and divining the future. His fee is whatever a patient wants to give. His techniques include suggestion and practical advice (obtained from his contacts with the spirits), as well as occasional herb medicines from Mexico. For instance, when my research assistant went to him with simulated depression secondary to domestic problems, he saw her three times and mixed reassurance with practical and symbolic suggestions. For example, he took a picture of her husband to "work on" and at the same time told her how to act with him. There are good accounts of Mexican-American *curanderos* elsewhere (Kiev 1968); the point here is that they *do* continue to exist as a mental health resource within the Mexican-American community.

There is another group of people who often call

themselves *curanderos* but who are not mental health resources. These are fortune-tellers. One of them, a woman who advertises herself as a *curandera* on her business card and offers "advice on love, health, and business," speaks practically no Spanish. All of the fortune-tellers with whom I've had contact had starting fees of between $5 and $10, and were concerned mostly with extracting as much money as possible from their patients. They should not be confused with true *curanderos.*

Mental health ombudsmen—are a group of community leaders to whom people turn with their problems. They are more important than *curanderos* as mental health resources among Mexican-Americans in San Jose. In some cases, these individuals overlap the political leadership as well. Their role at times is similar to the all-understanding ward bosses of the past, who were politically important but who also served as listeners, advisers, legal counsel, social workers, and referees for individual and domestic problems of all kinds.

In East San Jose, I have identified about twenty such individuals. They are the people named when you ask a Mexican-American the question: "If you had such-and-such a problem, who would you go to?" All of them are Mexican-American (Allport and Pettigrew 1957). They include both sexes. Most have regular jobs, and supply mental health services during their off-hours. None of them would consider accepting payment for their services. Many of them are aware that what they are doing is "psychotherapy" in the Anglo frame of reference. Most of them tend to specialize in certain types of problems. They see the entire range of mental health problems, except for psychoses, which they usually send to a hospital or the community mental health center. When asked why they do not treat psychoses they say because the person is "really sick."

An example of an ombudsman is Mr. J. He is a middle-aged man who is outgoing, warm, positive, sensitive, and energetic. During the day, he works as a blue-collar worker; during evenings and weekends, he often sees adolescents with drug and/or school problems. He averages three calls a week. Usually, they come to his home, but sometimes he makes the visits. He provides support and practical advice in his attempts to solve the person's problem. He often takes books out of the library on psychology and counseling in an attempt to improve his ability to help people. He has had opportunities to join the Anglo establishment in a "community liaison" capacity, but fears that he would lose his credibility within the Mexican-American community if he did.

Another example is Mrs. P. She is a quiet but warm middle-aged woman who gives freely of her own feelings and conveys confidence. She has worked intermittently for several Anglo agencies, and has averaged three calls a week for primarily domestic problems over many years. She usually visits the home. She has allowed me to come with her on several calls. The problems included a mentally retarded girl's reported disruption of a family (she was being scapegoated), a woman with anxiety and obsessive thinking, a woman with multiple sclerosis and mental deterioration, and a couple with severe marital discord.

Mrs. P. describes her technique as listening and ventilating: "I listen mostly. Then they often feel better. Sometimes they understand what's going on better just by telling me. I also encourage them to express their feelings. They're scared to. I tell them I know it will be hard at first." Some of Mrs. P.'s empathy is a product of her own past domestic difficulties. At one point, she sought traditional Anglo psychiatric help. Its failure typifies the reason why she is a major mental health resource for the Mexican-American community: "I couldn't talk to him. All he ever did was ask me about things way in the past. My problem was in the present. I couldn't talk to him at all."

Discussion

This indictment of traditional mental health services for Mexican-Americans is not meant to be an attack on San Jose and Santa Clara County specifically. They simply provide a case study with which to examine the irrelevancy within a context. Actually, I believe that Santa Clara County has an unusual number of intelligent, sensitive, well-intentioned mental health personnel, many of whom are aware of the problems outlined.

The irrelevancy began at a higher level. It began at the very conceptualization of the community mental health centers. It began when the architects of the act unconsciously and ethnocentrically perpetuated the dominant-class, dominant-culture, dominant-caste model of mental health services. This works as long as the mental health centers are serving Wellesley or White Plains or Palo Alto. But it is irrelevant when they are to serve Roxbury or the South Bronx or East San Jose.

There are currently 299 community mental health centers in operation and 450 funded. By 1980, it has been projected that the number will be 2,000. It is imperative that we learn from our early experiences and modify the model to make it relevant. Otherwise, one of the moving hopes of the Mental Health Centers Act—to make mental health services available to everyone—will turn out to be a bitter illusion.

Looking at the case study under discussion, what kinds of changes might be made in order to make the mental health services relevant?

Control.
The control and money for mental health services should be firmly in the hands of a board from the

Mexican-American community. It should be evident from the problems of class, culture, and caste outlined above that anything short of this measure will merely perpetuate the irrelevancy. As things now stand, general tax funds—including those paid by Mexican-Americans—are being used to build and maintain mental health services that are irrelevant for Mexican-Americans. In other words, residents of East San Jose are having to help pay for mental health services for Palo Alto, and get nothing in return.

It should be realized that Mexican-Americans may conceptualize and deliver mental health services quite differently than we are accustomed to. For instance, they might fuse them with social, educational, legal, or public health services. They may decide to merge them with services under the Model Cities Program. Or they may decide to politicize them and work on the problem of police relations. The remarks of the judge, cited above, would certainly be a good starting point for changing community self-esteem, so vital to mental health. We should encourage them to conceptualize mental health services in whatever way makes sense to them. Our own model may be fine for Palo Alto, but it was not derived from any divine order.

Professional qualifications.

The services should be delivered by those who are capable of performing the services, not by someone with a certain number of degrees. There are many excellent indigenous therapists in East San Jose who should be the ones delivering the services. I have spelled out in detail elsewhere some of the theoretical justifications for their use (Torrey 1969, 1970, 1971).

An initial start in this direction has occurred within the last two years. A program using "aides" in mental health, welfare, and probation was started by Santa Clara County as part of a "new careers" program. It has had excellent leadership by a psychologist, and the initial results are very promising. It is not yet clear whether it will be more than tokenism, however. Such programs should be given top priority and expanded, and an effort should be made to attract the indigenous therapists in the community who are already doing the job.

These are the underlying conceptual issues that need to be experimented with and changed. To do less, such as putting up a few Spanish-language signs in the central mental health center, is simply to put a band-aid on a broken arm from the Mexican-American point of view. The services will be used when they are relevant, and they will be relevant only when they are set up by the Mexican-Americans themselves.

Bibliography

Allport, G. W. and Pettigrew, T. F. 1957. Cultural influences on the perception of movement: the trapezoidal illusion among the Zulus. *J. Abnorm. Psychol.* 55:104-113.

Caplan, G. 1964. *Principles of preventive psychiatry.* New York: Basic Books.

Castañeda, C. 1968. *The teachings of Don Juan: a Yaqui way of knowledge.* New York: Ballantine.

Conklin, H. 1955. Hanunoo color categories. *Southwest J. Anthro.* 11:339-344.

Frake, C. O. 1961. The diagnosis of disease among the Subanun of Mindanao. *Amer. Anthro.* 63:113-132.

Gursslin, O. R., Hunt, R. G., and Roach, J. L. 1964. Social class and the mental health movement. In *Mental health of the poor,* eds. F. Riessman, J. Cohen, and A. Pearl. New York: Free Press.

Holland, W. R. 1963. Mexican-American medical beliefs: science or magic? *Ariz. Med.* 20:89-102.

Hollingshead, A. B. and Redlich, F. C. 1958. *Social class and mental illness.* New York: Wiley.

Joint venture in mental health. 1968. Report of the Ad Hoc Comprehensive Mental Health Planning Committee for Santa Clara County, at San Jose, California.

Karno, M. 1966. The enigma of ethnicity in a psychiatric clinic. *Arch. Gen. Psychiat.* 14:516-520.

Karno, M. and Edgerton, R. B. 1969. Perception of mental illness in a Mexican-American community. *Arch. Gen. Psychiat.* 20:233-238.

Kiev, A. 1968. *Curanderismo: Mexican-American folk psychiatry.* New York: Free Press.

Lindemann, E. 1965. The health needs of communities. In *Hospitals, doctors and the public interest,* ed. J. H. Knowles. Cambridge: Harvard.

Martinez, C. and Martin, H. W. 1966. Folk diseases among urban Mexican-Americans. *J. Amer. Med. Assoc.* 196:161-164.

Prince, R. 1968. Psychotherapy and the chronically poor: what can we learn from primitive psychotherapy. In *Social change, poverty, and mental health,* ed. J. Finney. Lexington: U. of Ky.

Riessman, F., Cohen, J. and Pearl, A., eds. 1964. *Mental health of the poor.* New York: Free Press.

Rubel, A. J. 1964. The epidemiology of a folk illness: susto in Hispanic America. *Ethnology* 3:268-283.

Segall, M. H., Campbell, D. T., Herskovits, M. J. 1966. *The influence of culture of visual perception.* Indianapolis: Bobbs.

Torrey, E. F. 1969. The case for the indigenous therapist. *Arch. Gen. Psychiat.* 20:365-373.

—————. 1970. Mental health services for American Indians and Eskimos. *Community Mental Health Journal* 6:455-463.

—————. 1971. *The mind game: witchdoctors and psychiatrists.* New York: Emerson Hall.

Tyhurst, L. 1951. Displacement and migration. *Amer. J. Psychiat.* 108:561-568.

Yamamoto, J., James, Q. C., and Palley, N. 1968. Cultural problems in psychiatric therapy. *Arch. Gen. Psychiat.* 19:45-49.

The Mainstream—Where Indians Drown*
Charles W. Archibald, Jr.

I offer a solution to a substantial portion of the so-called "Indian problem" of economic dependence and psychological crippling that continues under the present federally administered policies. The dependency policy was preceded by earliest attempts at physical annihilation of the Indian, then isolation of the reservation system of today, followed by attempts at assimilation through relocation in urban centers, where practice of the traditional Indian ways was virtually impossible. For the future, the current official policy for increasing Indian involvement in policy making and service delivery is feared by many Indians as a mask to be swept away, to reveal termination of the special wardship relationship that has existed, equated by the more dependent with abandonment and hence death. My solution is not new to progressive Indian leaders but it may be startling to the average American. It is offered with the humbling awareness that I am generalizing for 700,000 tribally recognized American Indians in 25 states, who speak more than 75 Indian languages and dialects.

Marked differences exist in the traditions of Indians living only a few miles from each other, yet they retain common values that sharply set them apart from non-Indians. Lack of awareness of these Indian characteristics

*This essay appeared in slightly revised form in *HSMHA Health Reports,* 86:489-494 (1971) Public Health Service, U.S. Department of Health, Education, and Welfare.

37

has resulted in the prevalent belief of the urban dweller —be he deeply sympathetic to, guilty about, or disgusted by the plight of the Indian—that the Indian problem can be solved by "getting them into the mainstream," a sentiment which presumes that Indians better themselves by incorporating the white man's social values, economic philosophy, and family life style.

The experience of Indians in the past twenty years in relocating in major urban centers is antipathetic to their basic beliefs—an increasing number of "urbanized" Indians have come to reject the white man's conventions, despite intermarriage, vocational change, or diverse social preference (Ablon 1965). I suggest that by being receptive to the hopes of Indian leaders for the economic development of their tribally governed communities— enough to attract investment capital, to shift federal funds from doles that foster crippling dependency to "seed" money that could free the Indians to live apart with dignity.

Background

The ancestors of these native Americans—representing one of the three major identifiable minorities in the United States today along with the blacks, formerly known as American Negroes, and the Chicanos, formerly known as Spanish-Americans or Mexican-Americans— probably entered this hemisphere from Asia about 25,000 years ago and, by 10,000 years ago, had migrated to the southern tip of South America (Agogino 1970). The oldest identifiable tribe today is that of the Hopi Indians of North-Central Arizona, who were functioning 500 years before Columbus arrived much as they function today. It is believed that over one million Indians inhabited this country at the time of Columbus' arrival. Their capacity to survive, adapt, and change, despite a variety of hardships, is well known. That their number had diminished to an estimated 243,000 by the late 19th century, primarily the result of war and disease, will forever be a scar on the white man's conscience.

Although efforts of the Public Health Service (Nowak 1969) to bring modern medical techniques to the Indians have resulted in an increase in the birth rate more than double that of the general United States population and have increased their life expectancy at a rate 3 times the national average—still 6 years short of the average non-Indian—it is a mistake to think of the pre-white man Indian as a helpless victim of his physical environment. Indians taught the first colonists the values of close family life, the techniques of successful farming, folk healing, and how to exist by hunting live game. They gave us their discoveries of cocaine, quinine, novocaine, witch hazel, and many other drugs. In the 400 years that physicians and botanists have been examining and analyzing the flora of America, they have not discovered a medicinal herb unknown to the Indians (Kennedy 1969).

While most health professionals realize the power the medicine man possessed through psychological techniques, few may know about the sophisticated, dream psychotherapeutic system that the Iroquois used 200 years before Freud (Hurst 1969). They believed then, as thousands privately do today, that to be sick is to be out of harmony with nature, and that only medicine men trained in the folk arts of the tribe could diagnose their sickness and effect a cure.

Is it any wonder then that the white man is resented? He has forced changes on the Indians by legislating against their old, traditional ways of survival. He has broken treaties of self-authorship when these treaties have become inconvenient. How hollow ring the reassuring phrases of those original treaties between the United States Government and the sovereign Indian nations. The treaties promised freedom from harassment and a fair share of the wealth of their former territorial holdings "as long as the grass is green, and the rivers flow, and the sun sinks in the West."

Life style and beliefs

Those who "think Indian" retain the primitive world view (Redfield 1957), recognizing an important and precious relationship between man, his fellowmen, nature and his gods. They believe that man is part of an independent harmonious whole, a cog in the larger order of his community and nature and, hence, without individual or independent career. The average American can at best appreciate only the beauty of nature, for his philosophy and theology focus on man's relationship with man and with his gods, bypassing the possibility of any interaction with his natural surroundings.

This handicap clouds the tourist's first view of an Indian community for, in being struck by the physical signs of poverty, he fails to appreciate the wealth of a people who are still attuned to the beauty of nature and who feel a rapport and spiritual attachment with the land they inhabit. The uncleanliness of a dirt floor in a Navajo hogan can prevent a tourist from recognizing the rich warmth of the human relationships in an extended family. To the same tourist, the material possessions of the reservation Indian seem so sparse that he cannot understand how a sense of loyalty and generosity could permit an Indian community to survive on so little. Can he not see, beyond the overcrowded homes, the revered presence of grandparents who, as passers of tradition, play an important part in raising the children? Can he not see, beyond the idleness and despair of these people, the fierce sense of individual pride and strong expression of autonomy and freedom?

The culture of the American Indian is characterized by an interest in people rather than in things, a strong feeling of belonging, a need to share with others, a dignity in harsh circumstances, a nonexploitive love of nature, and the measure of a man not by what he has or looks like or says but by what he is. These values, to which Americans are so often blind, make middle-class Americans—in contrast to Indians—seem culturally deprived (Kennedy 1969).

Indians in the city

With this thought in mind, consider those Indians who, regarding the reservation as an economically under-developed area, have felt forced to abandon the degree of security and social control their communities repre-sented (Ablon 1964) and have met the encroaching white culture on its home ground—the large urban center.

A few Indians have always left the reservation for a time for schooling, military service and, particularly, for job opportunities, often spurred on by non-Indian teachers and preachers who have considered tribal ways to be unqualified impediments and have, unhesitatingly, equated relocation in the white man's world with suc-cess. World War II moved large numbers of Indian servicemen to within commuting distance of the cities for training, and attracted others to defense industries. Twenty or more years later, many of these people became the Indian leaders who welcomed new arrivals—those coming to the cities for schooling, railroad employ-ment, and adult vocational training programs, especially the voluntary relocation program of the Department of the Interior's Bureau of Indian Affairs (now the bureau's Employment Assistance Program).

This program was initiated in 1952, when ten field relocation offices were established in major cities throughout the country. By July 1970 a total of 86,985 American Indians had migrated from their reservations to seek "stable employment and a new life" (Bureau of

Indian Affairs 1970). The cultural shock of leaving primary relationships and a folk society to enter a complex industrial order whose basic values violate many premises of Indian life was, for many, an overwhelming experience (*Navajo Times* 1969). During the early years of the relocation program, 75 percent returned to the reservation. As emphasis shifted from immediate job placement to training, the proportion dropped to 35 percent.

Here was "marginal man," clearly caught between two cultures. While he retained a basic distrust of white men, he had been conditioned by the federal government to turn to them for money, services, and sometimes even emotional support (Maynard 1969). True egalitarian relationships with whites occurred infrequently, even for long-time Indian city dwellers, although they might work side by side with the white men to improve social conditions for other Indians who were constantly arriving.

While the chief reason for relocating was the wish to find steady employment, many Indians hoped to escape personal and family problems as well: heavy drinking, dependent relatives. But their problems were magnified under new pressures. Relocation demanded initiative and independence of thought and action in contrast to the conditioning of wardship on the reservation (Ablon 1965). They had been taught by their elders that one's possessions were of value only to the extent that they were shared. Budgeting and saving were foreign to them. Since time was a continuum from birth to death, time schedules were irrelevant, and deferring economic goals for an extended period of education was little appreciated.

They listened to relocation counselors explain why they must conform to be accepted. Although they observed how members of middle-class urban society had come to see themselves as objects to be shaped to fit the requirements of a complex modern culture and to be changed to meet goals holding promises of rewards, they could not accept themselves internally as malleable entities (Ablon 1964). In the city, they were billed for services they had always received free, and a slight illness or job layoff was enough to send them back to the reservation, fully aware that, following the initial joy of reunion, they would be faced with little chance for economic development.

Some Indians have adjusted to urban ways, but close questioning often discloses that they have not internalized the new ways and that their basic "Indianness" has not been destroyed (Ibid.). While they can master the techniques needed to manipulate their environment, 75 percent of them say they would return to their communities immediately if comparable employment opportunities were available. They feel they can survive in an alien culture, but they do not agree with the non-Indian evaluation that adjustment is success.

Indians normally do not seek friendships with whites in cities (Ibid.). Traditionally, they look upon whites with suspicion. They do not trust their motives, they have a sense of potential dependency on them, and they fear rejection by the whites if they fall short of the Caucasian definition of success. This feeling contributes to a characteristic reticence to discuss personal matters with non-Indians, which may appear to some to be disinterest, hostility, or dullness. From experience, counselors have learned to counter in part with an attitude that invites discussion and to suggest choices rather than presume always to know the best answer (Leon 1967).

The Indian's natural tendency to seek people most like himself should be accepted, and whites should be content to support these efforts rather than to encourage early participation in non-Indian social and recreational groups. This is in contrast to well-meaning efforts of non-Indians who try to help the Indians feel at home by too quickly introducing them to urban recreational gatherings, particularly with secondary cultural-change goals.

Even the pan-Indian organizations have attracted only a small percentage of city-based Indians. They have influenced some briefly, but it is difficult to determine whether they are a cohesive force for the development and maintenance of Indian culture in the city, a structural defensive mechanism, or a terminal phase in the assimilation process. Their focus is still on the Indian nation as a separate people and on the traditional home areas as locations of choice.

Adjustment—the best way?

Ultimately, the solution would seem to be independence, or at least, equal dependence with other Americans on the federal government for broad services —but not abortive termination (of federal responsibility for land, education, welfare, and health, etc.) that would deny legal and moral commitments to most Indians.

Where oil, uranium, and other natural resources have been found in ample portions on Indian land, standards have been raised far above the subsistence level. The Navajos, for example, have proven their ability to invest wisely in an independent future. Unlike many tribes that made per capita payments that were instantly dissipated without changing the people's living standards, the Navajo tribe has invested in schools, economic development, and training opportunities that offer a long-term payoff to the community. Geographic isolation is the Navajos' greatest value and also their greatest handicap, since it limits delivery of health, education, and welfare services that could raise their standard of living.

Where poor climate exists, where scenic beauty is lacking, where accessibility is difficult, and where Indians are unable to relinquish their incapacitating dependence on the federal government's paternalistic aid, some groups may have to be maintained on society's disabled list for a long, long time.

For most tribal groups, there is a sense of expectancy as tribal plans are formulated in conjunction with concerned governmental agencies to use the economic potential of their communities. Manufacturing and recreational possibilities are being surveyed that will not endanger the life style of the people (Kelly 1967). With anticipation of the number of people that will be needed to run hotels, restaurants, community centers, historic ruins, wildlife preserves, schools, courts, tribal headquarters, and a host of other settings, young Indian people are being sought, selected, and trained to assume positions of leadership in their home communities. Despite earnest efforts to train them as close to home as possible, relocation will often be necessary. But this will be relocation with a difference, because the goal will be in line with their choice to live and work for and among their own people.

Helping people to help themselves has achieved far better relations abroad for the United States than outright doles—again confirming the folk wisdom that "the poor will never forgive you for what you do for them." We have introduced modern technologies to the underdeveloped peoples of the world without presuming to change their traditional folkways. It would seem that this lesson could be applied to our dealings with the first Americans of this country.

We cannot undo the wrongs of our forefathers toward this land's natives, who welcomed them with a spirit of sharing as brothers and then were trampled as impediments to progress. As long as the Indians live, we will be reminded of this wrong while they retain their pride and dignity amidst humble circumstances that would threaten the emotional stability of most of us.

The right to be different

The rising rates of problem drinking and suicide among the Indians show that something has been wrong with our approach (Dozier 1966). Can we accept the right of the Indian to be different—enough to invest in the "new" Indian, who will tell us what is best for him and asks for our trust and support as he attempts to make the most of limited economic resources?

Huxley, in his *Brave New World,* predicted that the time would come when the world would be a sterile and efficient tribute to man's willingness to sacrifice freedom of deed and expression for freedom from responsibility, and that vacations for most would be sought only through mind-altering drugs. It was his hope that the Indian communities would retain their potential to recharge our successors with basic human principles, if only as a reminder of what used to be. To do this, their communities cannot be treated as amusement parks, manned by skeleton crews of caretakers and concessionaires. Their lands must be cultural depositories of a viable people.

The possibility of achieving this can be fostered by asking what the American Indians are really like as a people and what can be done to help them achieve a more comfortable co-existence. The need for a new approach particularly responsive to their economic objectives is long overdue. For each community, we must determine the material and psychological orientation of the Indian people, and then, with them, seek solutions within the framework of the Indian way.

We cannot make up for past mistakes nor can we defend policies that suggest the Indians are less capable or less deserving of the best of our technology to achieve their goals merely because they patiently resist the efforts of the dominant society to absorb them. Let us revitalize and teach the real traditions of the Indians to our children before these traditions are lost, to the detriment of all of us.

Bibliography

Ablon, J. 1965. American Indian relocation: problems of dependency and management in the city. *Phylon* 26:362-371.

—————. 1964. Relocated American Indians in the San Francisco Bay Area: social interaction and the Indian identity. *Human Organization* 23:296-304.

Agogino, G. A. 1970. Man's antiquity in the Western Hemisphere. *Indian Historian* 3:49.

Bureau of Indian Affairs. 1970. Annual statistical summary, 1970. U.S. Government Printing Office, Washington, D.C.

Dozier, E. 1966. Problem drinking among American Indians: the role of sociocultural deprivation. *Quart. J. Stud. Alc.* 27:72-87.

Hurst, J. 1969. A resurgence of the Indians' cultural pride. *San Francisco Examiner* July 18.

Kelly, W. H. 1967. Social and cultural considerations in the development of manpower programs for Indians. Paper presented at National Conference on Manpower Programs for Indians, 16 Feb. 1967, at Kansas City, Mo.

Kennedy, E. 1969. American Indian days. *Keresan* 3:2.

Leon, R. L. 1967. An emotional and educational experience for urban migrants. *Amer. J. Psychiat.* 124:381-384.

Maynard, E. 1969. That these people may live: a report of the Pine Ridge Community Mental Health Program, South Dakota.

Navaho Times. 1969. Oct. 2:2.

Nowak, J. 1969. What's happening with the Indians. *HSMHA World* 4:29-32.

Redfield, R. 1957. The primitive world and its transformations, Chap. 4, *The primitive world view and civilization*, pp. 84-110. Ithaca: Cornell.

Mental Illness Among Puerto Ricans in New York: Cultural Condition or Intercultural Misunderstanding?*

Joseph P. Fitzpatrick and Robert E. Gould

An abnormally high rate of schizophrenia has been observed among Puerto Ricans in New York. No satisfactory explanation has yet been found for this. Some scholars attribute it to features in the culture of Puerto Ricans that may leave them vulnerable to schizophrenia. Other scholars attribute it to the effect of migration and the shock of uprooting. It is very possible, however, that the high rates may be the result of intercultural misunderstanding: behavior that is understandable within the context of Puerto Rican culture may be interpreted by non-Puerto Rican authorities as schizophrenic. Furthermore, the problems of providing adequate mental health services to the poor create special difficulties for the Puerto Ricans since they are the poorest of all groups in New York City.

Official data for 1967 indicates a rate of first admissions for schizophrenia to New York State civil mental hospitals of 102.5 per 100,000 for Puerto Ricans, in contrast to a rate of 34.5 per 100,000 for the population at large (New York State Department of Mental Hygiene 1967). This rate has increased considerably since Benjamin Malzberg (1956, p. 264) found a rate of 91.4

*This paper is based on a Task Force Paper prepared for the Joint Commission on Mental Health for Children, 5454 Wisconsin Avenue, Chevy Chase, Maryland, 20015. The authors express their gratitude to their collaborators, Marta Fernandez, Research Associate; and William Contois, Anthony Croce, Natalie Hannon and Joseph Polka, Research Assistants.

per 100,000 Puerto Ricans in the period 1949-51. Malzberg repeated his study on the basis of 1960-61 data. He still found a high rate of first admissions for schizophrenia for Puerto Ricans, 85.3 per 100,000, in contrast to the much lower rate for non-Puerto Ricans, 37.4 per 100,000 (Malzberg 1965, p. 34). The 1967 study also showed a substantial rise in the incidence of alcoholic psychoses and a significant increase in other psychiatric conditions.

Malzberg made no attempt to explain the high rate of schizophrenia among Puerto Ricans in 1949-51. The objective of his study was to alert New York State to the anticipated increase in psychiatric disorders if the rapid influx of Puerto Ricans into New York City continued. He did observe that the high rates were probably related to the experience of migration, to language difficulties, occupational problems, and the fact the Puerto Ricans were segregated in parts of the city marked by high rates of mental and physical illness.

Puerto Rican culture and mental illness

Surprisingly little study has been done about mental illness in Puerto Rico. The classic anthropological study published by Julian Steward (1956) makes little mention of it; neither does Sidney Mintz's remarkable life history of a poor sugar cane worker (1960). Although the study of family life by J. Mayone Stycos (1955) has no reference to the problem, Stycos does provide excellent insights into family strains and personality characteristics that could provoke mental disorder. The first large-scale systematic study of mental illness (schizophrenia) in Puerto Rico was published by L. H. Rogler and A. B. Hollingshead (1965). They found that schizophrenia was the most common form of mental illness among 1,500 Puerto Rican patients at the only public mental hospital in Puerto Rico. They estimated that at least 10,000 other psychotics were living with their families and not yet committed to hospital care. The population of Puerto Rico in 1958, when the field work for the study began, was about 2,300,000. If the estimate of Rogler and Hollingshead is at all accurate, it indicates a high rate of psychotics in the Puerto Rican population.

The Rogler-Hollingshead study is a sociopsychological study of 20 families in which either or both spouses were schizophrenic. The study found little or no difference in the experience of childhood and adolescence between those who suffered from schizophrenia and those who did not. However, at an identifiable period in the life of the schizophrenic, a convergence of cultural strains and socioeconomic pressures had apparently led to the psychotic break (Rogler-Hollingshead 1965, p. 173 *ff*).

The cultural strains identified by Rogler and Hollings-head, and by others, are as follows:

1. Contradictions in the values that govern male behavior may lead to anxieties in the man about *machismo*; contradictions in feminine values may, in the woman, bring about a martyr complex or excessive fear resulting from being cloistered (Green 1960, p. 37).
2. Problems centering on the mother-son relationship may lead to frustration in the son and difficulty in overcoming dependency on women or in establishing an adequate love relationship with a wife; severe depression may develop in women who seek to respond to an idealized female role (Ibid.; Landy 1959).
3. Authority patterns are strong in Puerto Rico, and, if they become excessive, they may generate hostility against authority figures (Maldonado-Sierra and Trent 1960).
4. The keen sense of personal dignity *(dignidad)*

and the emphasis on respect *(respeto)* may build up a potential for violence (Lauria 1964).

5. The overwhelming burden of poverty and the accumulation of problems of the poor may make the difference between mental health and mental illness (Lewis 1966). A specific form of hysteria called "the Puerto Rican syndrome" is mentioned by many authors. This is called the *ataque* by Puerto Ricans. It is a tendency to resort to a hyperkinetic seizure at a time of acute tensions and anxiety (Rothenberg 1961; Marina 1961).

Several of the families studied by Rogler and Hollingshead resorted to spiritualism as a form of psychotherapy to cure the schizophrenia or to give the victim a new role to play as one who could establish contact with spirits. In an earlier article, Rogler and Hollingshead (1961) presented an excellent analysis of the function of spiritualism in Puerto Rican society, and concluded that it serves as a form of folk psychiatry that has a dual purpose: it prevents the labeling of the person as "crazy" by attributing the disturbance to the activity of spirits; it also marshals the support of a group around the person to alleviate accumulated tensions. In this way, spiritualism proves to be a form of psychotherapy that has no built-in disparities among participants—all are from the same socioeconomic class. The spiritualist session creates a primary group setting in which the abnormal behavior is given a meaning acceptable to the community.

With the exception of the Rogler and Hollingshead work, the studies mentioned above investigate the particular etiology of certain types of mental illness. They do not direct attention to the high incidence of schizophrenia, nor do they seek to explain why it is much higher among Puerto Ricans than among the population at large.

Mental illness and migration

When attention is directed to mental illness among Puerto Ricans in New York, the experience of migration immediately enters the picture. The process of uprooting, of adjusting to a new and strange—and possibly hostile— way of life, has always been noted as a source of disorientation and mental disorder. The stress may become great enough to lead to a breaking point. Studies (Murphy 1955 and 1965) of migration and mental illness focus on three hypotheses:

> 1. Mental illness is a major factor in causing people to migrate, i.e., intense psychological distress prompts people to seek relief by moving.
> 2. Stress due to migration causes mental illness in vulnerable persons.
> 3. Mental illness is related to an accidental association between migration and age, social class, or culture conflict.

The second hypothesis is the most widely accepted one, and the one generally applied to explain high rates of mental illness among Puerto Ricans. However, a number of practicing psychiatrists in New York City, in personal interviews with the authors of this article, held that the first hypothesis must be seriously considered.

No study comparable to the Rogler and Hollingshead study has been made of the Puerto Ricans in New York. In the Midtown-Manhattan Study, Srole and his co-workers (1962) studied 1,911 adults, 20-59 years of age, in a limited geographical area of New York City, in an effort to explore the relationship between a selected number of social and cultural variables and the mental health or illness of the persons interviewed. There were 27 Puerto Ricans in the sample: 23 first generation, and 4 second and third generation. The study ranked the population in terms of mental health according to a set of categories ranging from "well" to various levels of "impaired." The Puerto Rican population appeared more "impaired" than those of any other ethnic group (Ibid., pp. 290-291). Srole and his associates hypothesized that this may have been due to the extreme poverty of the Puerto Ricans. But when socioeconomic levels were held constant, twice as many Puerto Ricans on the lowest socioeconomic levels were found to be "impaired" than those of European background on the same socioeconomic level. The study found an unusually strong attachment to place of birth among Puerto Ricans and concluded that the high rate of morbidity was probably due to their geographical isolation from the main concentration of their fellow countrymen.

Beatrice Berle (1959), in her study of 80 Puerto Rican families in New York City, was primarily concerned about physical illness and its impact on the families. In the course of her work, she also discovered a high incidence of personality disorder although relevant factors in these personality disorders were largely unknown. She made two important observations: 1. Disturbed persons are generally examined and treated apart from the total context of everyday family life. 2. Many of the poor families displayed extraordinary capacity to cope with cases of personality disturbance (Ibid., pp. 157-171). She emphasized the need "for the development of better local facilities for the management of mental defectives and disturbed individuals in their homes and neighborhoods." (Ibid., p. 171). For example, after a lengthy description of the *ataque* (Ibid., p. 158), Berle indicates that this is a culturally expected reaction to situations of serious stress, and that Puerto Ricans manage it as an ordinary occurrence. For someone not familiar with the cultural background, the *ataque* could be interpreted as a symptom of more serious mental disturbance.

Berle urged that the study of mental illness among

Puerto Ricans be kept in social and cultural perspective. She insisted that if Puerto Rican behavior is not examined in the total family and neighborhood setting by someone who understands the culture of the people, there is danger of misdirected diagnosis.

These are the only two studies that involved a sizable sample of Puerto Rican people. Other studies, much more limited in scope, may be summarized as follows:

1. The comparative studies of Malzberg and Srole et al., based on statistical data, offer no satisfactory explanation of the unusually high rate of schizophrenia among Puerto Ricans. However, the elements of poverty and lower-class status are crucial in this respect, both in view of the tensions created by poverty among Puerto Ricans in New York, and, more importantly, in view of the difficulties in delivering mental health services to the poor. This point, that directly · touches the problem of unusually high admissions to mental hospitals, will be discussed later in this paper.

2. Cultural sources of mental illness among Puerto Ricans are indicated by some of the smaller studies. Strengths and weaknesses are revealed in the cultural traits of *respeto*, which is extremely important in the process of socialization, and of *machismo*, which is central to the role of the male in the culture of Puerto Ricans. *Respeto* governs a wide range of interpersonal relationships and is important in controlling hostility and in maintaining tranquility. When thrown out of balance, *respeto* can lead to problems of violence through an excessive concern for *dignidad*, the dignity of the person, or as a consequence of continued repression of hostility. *Respeto* can also lead to problems with authority (Minuchin et al. 1967, p. 238).

3. *Machismo*, in poorly defined situations, such as

those arising when people migrate to a strange culture, can lead to anxieties in men and to fear and suspicion in women. Dependency of men upon women appears as a source of ambiguity and tension (Ibid., p. 239; Opler 1967, p. 37; and Fernandez-Marina, Malonado-Sierra, and Trent 1958, p. 179).

4. Recourse to spiritualism and the Pentecostal sects can serve as a means for relieving anxiety. By redefining the nature of the problem, and by maintaining community acceptance and support, this relief can keep a person functional in society (Minuchin et al. 1967, p. 240).

5. Family strengths are found in apparently disorganized situations. *Respeto* can lead to great confidence and security in interpersonal relationships; a sense of fatalism may act to spare a person from a sense of guilt. A sense of authority provides strength against disintegrating forces (Ibid., Ch. 5).

A central theme common to the above studies of mental illness among Puerto Ricans is that cultural change due to migration results in inter-generational conflict between parents and children, uncertainty due to uprooting, and isolation within the new culture (Trautman 1961; Elam 1965; Gould 1965). Within recent years, however, the attention of social scientists seeking to explain mental illness has been shifting from an emphasis on culture to an emphasis on social class. This development raises the question of whether the high incidence of schizophrenia among Puerto Ricans or their high rate of admission to mental hospitals may be related to their style of life as poor people, and their treatment as poor people, rather than to their Puerto Rican culture. This conceptual and theoretical shift may be very important in relation to the mental health experiences of the Puerto Ricans.

Mental health and the poor

For many years, scholars and practitioners have been aware that mental illness, officially defined, is much more common among people of lower socioeconomic status than among people of higher status. The Mishler and Scotch (1963) review of the literature summarizes data as early as that W. J. Nolan published in 1917 concerning first admissions for dementia praecox to New York civil state hospitals in the years between 1909 and 1916. Nolan found a heavy concentration of patients from lower occupational categories. Every study since has confirmed this finding. The Hollingshead and Redlich study (1958) is a landmark. After controlling for sex, education, marital status, and religion, they found that lower-class status is significant not only in terms of the higher incidence of mental illness, especially schizophrenia, but also in terms of the diagnosis (psychosis rather than neurosis), and the treatment of the illness (organic and custodial treatment rather than psychotherapy).

The meaning of this correlation has been challenged in recent years, partly on the basis of methodology in an article by Dohrenwend (1966), but much more seriously in a wide range of publications such as those collected by Frank Riessman and his associates (1964), which raise some fundamental questions about the definition of mental illness and the difficulties created for the poor by the way in which the delivery of mental health services is organized.

Since most of the Puerto Rican population are in the lower class on socioeconomic status indices, the problem of defining mental illness among the poor becomes relevant. It is likely that the problem is not one of the relationship of Latin or Puerto Rican culture to mental illness, but of the relationship of class position to mental illness in the United States. Although the problem of a middle-class mental health establishment related to lower-class patients involves problems of a cultural gap between the way of life of the affluent and the way of life of the poor, the recent discussions about class are directed more sharply to problems of organization, official definition of mental illness, and political management of mental health services. A review of this question is relevant to the question of mental illness among Puerto Ricans.

The poor people in the study of Hollingshead and Redlich are very similar to the poor people whom Herbert Gans described in *The Urban Villagers* (1962) or whom Walter Miller (1958) described in his studies of the poor. Although in the latter studies none of the subjects is Puerto Rican, in some cases there are strong resemblances to the poor people whose style of life is characterized by what Oscar Lewis calls the "culture of poverty"(1966). In view of this, Hollingshead and Redlich suggested that some of the differentials in incidence, diagnosis, and treatment of mental illness might be functions of the class differences between the professional personnel in the mental health enterprise and the poor.

In a classic article years ago, Kingsley Davis (1938) called attention to the fact that a serious bias was present in the mental health field in the treatment of lower-class people by middle- and upper-class professionals. He indicated that the professionals defined the situation in their terms, and, according to those definitions, the poor were considered maladjusted. However, in the viewpoint of the poor, much of the behavior in question was considered an understandable response to the life situations they had to face.

Robert Gould (1967), in a more recent article, detailed the treatment of a blue-collar worker to indicate the problems that traditional middle-class psychiatrists had in treating emotional problems of the working-class population. He outlined modifications that were necessary for the psychiatrist who could not identify with the markedly different life style of such patients, but who hoped to understand the nature of their problems, and, thus, to treat them effectively.

Dohrenwend's careful and scholarly critique of the methods of the Midtown-Manhattan Study suggests the same thing. The value of this study was the information gathered about untreated mental illness. As noted above, indications of mental illness were much higher for the Puerto Ricans in the study than for anyone else. Dohrenwend retested the research instruments of the Midtown-Manhattan Study and discovered that the differential in symptoms of mental illness may have been due to a bias built into the methodology. Differences in psychological symptomatology may reflect group differences in ways of expressing distress and differences in cultural approval or disapproval of various kinds of behavior. In any event, Dohrenwend concludes it cannot yet be legitimately inferred, from the respondents' answers to the questions of the Midtown-Manhattan Study, that pathology is actually present.

A much more abundant and outspoken literature has called attention to the problems that are built into the class structure of our society. The extreme position is taken by Thomas Szasz (1961) who claims that the definition of forms of behavior as symptoms of mental illness not only structures the population in terms of the definitions, but actually provokes an increase in the very kind of behavior it is trying to correct. In one conceptual and cultural framework, a form of behavior (e.g., hysteria) may make sense and win the sympathetic response of family and friends; in another conceptual and cultural framework, it may be defined as a symptom of mental illness and may lead to confinement, treatment in a mental institution, and the crippling of a person by labeling him as "crazy."

A more moderate, but in one sense more serious,

criticism is found in the analysis of the structure of mental health services as found in Bredemeier (1964). Briefly, he sees mental health services as a vast institutional structure, established by professionals with the interests and definitions of professionals in mind. Actually, the system is largely irrelevant to the fundamental problems of the poor. The poor are seen in artificial circumstances (the clinic or office); their difficulties are discussed in a vocabulary and within a conceptual framework that has no relevance to their world; and they are involved in a treatment process that often damages them through the use of labels that demean them and their communities. By seeking to treat the "mental disorder" in isolation from other problems, the system may hopelessly complicate the life of the poor person in the process. Within this structure, from beginning (diagnosis) to end (possible confinement), the poor person fares badly. Unable to protect himself, he sometimes ends up in a worse state than the state in which he began. When the high incidence of mental illness among the poor is examined in this context, it takes on quite a different meaning.

This self-criticism of the professional community is reinforced by popular protest, such as the rise of the black power movement, and by developments in the anti-poverty programs in the United States. At the 1968 convention of the American Orthopsychiatric Association, Dr. Thomas H. Linton referred to mental health services in the United States as "a chaotic and corrupt system"; and he stated, "There are few professionals in the mental health field who are unaware of the chaos, disorganization and professional exploitation which deeply and tragically scar our work in this field" (Leo 1968). Meetings frequently address themselves to the power structure of mental health services; the "mental health establishment" has become in some contexts almost a term of opprobrium.

Structural analysis of problems such as mental disorder or delinquency perceives the problem in a framework of social organization and the possession of means of accesss to strategic social, economic, or political power. It sees many aspects of the way of life of the poor as legitimate alternatives in American society, or as imaginative and resourceful efforts to cope with difficulties that often result from a society functioning in favor of the interests of the affluent. These forms of behavior are frequently defined either as deviant or as symptoms of mental disorder. Whether forms of behavior are legitimate alternatives, methods of coping with social inequities, or actual indications of mental disorder, those in control of the mental health facilities determine the definition, the methods, and condition of treatment. They can confine those who are weak or segregate them for treatment. They can apply the system favorably to cases they understand, or unfavorably to those they do not understand. What is crucial for the poor is the fact that they have no access to strategic control. They cannot exert political power for the protection of those forms of behavior that they consider legitimate; their coping behavior may bring them into conflict with the system; and they are helpless either to compel the system to operate in their favor, or to resist it when it operates to their disadvantage.

As a result, community action programs in recent years have sought to teach the poor to define their interests, to marshal the political strengths they possess, and to negotiate from a position of strength about the organization of systems—such as those of mental health—and the conditions under which the systems will best serve the needs of the poor. The activities of Saul Alinsky, one of the most controversial of the community organizers, are described by Anderson (1966) and Sanders (1965). Alinsky is convinced that only when the poor can wield power from a position of strength will they have a sense of dignity and the ability to enjoy a more human existence. He claims that this achievement in itself would correct some of the conditions that now provoke mental illness. Applied to mental health problems, such power would also enable the poor to protect themselves against definitions, diagnosis, and treatment that might operate to their disadvantage.

Forces already at work in the Puerto Rican community of New York (Fitzpatrick 1968, p. 179*ff*) are moving in a political direction. As they move more strongly, they will directly affect the manner in which mental health services become related to the needs of the Puerto Rican community.

Conclusion

In the absence of adequate statistical analyses that would permit more reliable assessment of the high rate of schizophrenia among the Puerto Ricans, and in the absence of clinical evidence that would explain it, is there evidence that it may be related to the problems in the organization of mental health services just described? Is the problem really one of a high incidence of illness, or is the high rate of admission a result of the malfunctioning of mental health services? It does not seem possible to answer these questions at this time. But these questions must continually be present in all future research about mental illness among Puerto Ricans.

Everyone in the mental health field in New York City is concerned about the acute shortage of trained Spanish-speaking personnel in mental health clinics and facilities. Lack of communication is a continual hazard to the Puerto Rican. Furthermore, understaffing and overcrowding result in excessive caseloads, rushed and routine diagnosis, hasty treatment. These problems add to the already present danger of error in diagnosis and treatment. The response to this condition has generally

61

been a call for more staff and more Spanish-speaking personnel. But if the problem involves a misapplication of basic concepts of mental health and illness, the remedy requires more than personnel; it calls for a different definition of the entire situation.

The Comprehensive Community Mental Health Centers, which are being inaugurated currently in New York City, are an effort to bring mental health services more conveniently to the community that needs them. These will increase the convenience of the delivery of service, but if they simply coordinate services in one place as they are now given, they may not answer the challenge that has been raised in the criticism of the structure of the mental health enterprise. Community mental health centers will not be without their problems. Lincoln Hospital in the Bronx, New York, has been a pioneer in bringing mental health services to the poor in their own environment and in their own style. But the recent strike at the Lincoln Hospital Center (Fraser 1969) is an indication of the difficulties that surround the attempt to maintain a proper balance between community control and professional skills.

The validity of the argument that the high incidence of mental illness among Puerto Ricans is a consequence of the definition of mental illness and the structure of mental health services can be tested only over time. In a remarkably innovative program at Gouverneur Hospital in New York City, a special "Behavioral Sciences Unit" had 891 cases under care during the first six months of 1967, but only 4 cases were hospitalized. Were such a program extended, and were it to have the same effect on admissions to mental hospitals, the statistics for admissions to mental hospitals given at the beginning of this paper would be substantially altered. This still leaves unanswered the more fundamental question about the actual state of mental health or illness among Puerto Ricans, apart from the rate of admissions to mental hospitals. Both for the sake of the Puerto Rican citizens and for the sake of the mental health enterprise, it is important that these issues be explored without delay.

Bibliography

Anderson, P. 1966. Making trouble is Alinsky's business. *New York Times Magazine* Oct. 9:28-31.

Berle, B. 1959. *80 Puerto Rican families.* New York: Columbia.

Bredemeier, H. C. 1964. The socially handicapped and the agencies: a market analysis. In *Mental health of the poor,* eds. F. Riessman, J. Cohen, and A. Pearl, pp. 98-109. New York: Free Press.

Davis, K. 1938. Mental hygiene and the class structure. *Psychiatry* 1:55-56.

Dohrenwend, B. P. 1966. Social status and psychological disorder: an issue of substance and an issue of method. *Amer. Sociol. Rev.* 31:14-34.

Elam, S. L. 1965. Acculturation and learning problems of Puerto Rican children. In *School children in the urban slum,* ed. J. K. Robert. New York: Free Press.

Fitzpatrick, J. P. 1971. The meaning of migration. In *Puerto Rican Americans: the meaning of migration to the mainland,* ref. ed. J. P. Fitzpatrick, pp. 179-184. Englewood Cliffs, New Jersey: Prentice-Hall.

Fernandez-Marina, R., Maldonado-Sierra, E. D., and Trent, R. D. 1958. Three basic themes in Mexican and Puerto Rican family values. *J. Soc. Psychol.* 48:167-181.

Fraser, C. G. 1969. Community control here found spreading to the field of health. *New York Times* March 9:42.

Gans, H. 1962. *The urban villages.* New York: Free Press.

Gould, R. 1965. Suicide problems in children and adolescents. *American Journal of Psychotherapy* 19:228-246.

——————. 1967. Doctor Strangeclass or how I stopped worrying about the theory and began treating the blue collar worker. *American J. Orthopsychiat.* 36:78-86.

Green, H. B. 1960. Comparison of nurturance and independence training in Jamaica and Puerto Rico, with consideration of the resulting personality structure and transplanted social patterns. *J. soc. Psychol.* 51:27-63.

Hollingshead, A. B., and Redlich, F. B. 1958. *Social class and mental illness.* New York: Wiley.

Landy, D. 1959. *Tropical childhood: cultural transmission and learning in a rural Puerto Rican village.* Chapel Hill: U. of N.C.

Lauria, A. 1964. *Respeto, relajo* and interpersonal relations in Puerto Rico. *Anthropological Quarterly* 37:53-67.

Leo, J. 1968. Chaos is charged in mental health. The *New York Times* March 24:92.

Lewis, O. 1966. *La vida: a Puerto Rican family in the culture of poverty in San Juan and New York.* New York: Random.

Maldonado-Sierra, E. P. and Trent, R. D. 1960. The sibling relationship in group psychotherapy with Puerto Rican schizophrenics. *American J. Psychiat.* 117:239-243.

Malzberg, B. 1956. Mental disease among Puerto Ricans in New York City, 1949-51. *J. Nerv. Ment. Dis.* 123:262-269.

─────────. 1965. Mental disease among the Puerto Rican population of New York State, 1960-1961. Albany, New York: Research Foundation for Mental Hygiene, Inc. (unpublished).

Marina, R. F. 1961. The Puerto Rican syndrome: its dynamics and cultural determinants. *Psychiatry* 24:79-82.

Miller, W. B. 1958. Lower class culture as a generating milieu of gang delinquency. *J. soc. Issues* 14:5-19.

Mintz, S. 1960. *Worker in the cane.* New Haven: Yale.

Minuchin, S., Montalvo, B., Gerney, B. G., Jr., Rosman, B. L., and Scheimer, F. 1967. *Families of the slums.* New York: Basic Books.

Mishler, E. and Scotch, N. 1963. Sociocultural factors in the epidemiology of schizophrenia. *Psychiatry* 26:315-351.

Murphy, H. B. M. 1955. *Flight and resettlement.* Switzerland: United Nations Educational, Scientific and Cultural Organization.

─────────. 1965. Migration and the major mental disorders. In *Mobility and mental health,* ed. M. B. Kantor, pp. 5-29. Springfield: Thomas.

New York State Department of Mental Hygiene. 1967. (unpublished data).

Opler, M. K. 1967. *Culture and social psychiatry.* New York: Atherton.

Riessman, F., Cohen, J., and Pearl, A., eds. 1964. *Mental health of the poor.* New York: Free Press.

Rogler, L. H. and Hollingshead, A. B. 1961. The Puerto Rican spiritualist as a psychiatrist. *Amer. J. Sociol.* 67:17-21.

─────────. 1965. *Trapped: families and schizophrenia.* New York: Wiley.

Rothenberg, A. 1964. Puerto Rico and agression. *Amer. J. Psychiat.* 120:962-970.

Sanders, M. K. 1965. Professional radical. *Harpers* 230:37-47; 231:52-59.

Srole, L. et al. 1962. *Mental health in the metropolis: the midtown Manhattan study.* Vol. I. New York: McGraw-Hill.

Steward, J. 1956. *People of Puerto Rico.* Urbana: U. of Ill.

Stycos, J. M. 1955. *Family and fertility in Puerto Rico.* New York: Columbia.

Szasz, T. 1961. *The myth of mental illness.* New York: Harper §.

Trautman, E. C. Suicide attempts of Puerto Rican immigrants. *Psychiat. Quart.* 35:544-554.

Mellaril or Medium, Stelazine or Seance?
A Study of Spiritism as it Affects Communication, Diagnosis, and Treatment of Puerto Rican People

Beatrice Purdy, Renee Pellman, Sarah Flores and Harvey Bluestone

Three thousand years ago, Saul, overcome by his fears of the Philistines, called on a medium at Endor to evoke the spirit of Samuel to tell him what to do (I Samuel, 28:5-25). Three months ago, Maria Santos called on a medium on Bathgate Avenue in the Bronx, to evoke the spirit responsible for her migraine headaches and the strange ephemeral figure that appeared in her window.

The belief in spiritualism spans the centuries and has claimed among its adherents the famous and the unknown. Many of us may believe that the advent of psychiatry should have been sufficient to displace or dismiss the occult from serious consideration in the treatment of mental disorders. However, this assumption is challenged daily by many of the patients whom we see in our work at the Bronx-Lebanon Mental Health Center.

This clinic, located in a deprived section of the Bronx, serves a population of over 200,000. Approximately half of these people are Puerto Rican and have migrated recently or have lived here for some time. In working with this particular patient load, we have been forced to ask ourselves whether a patient, such as Maria, is really a schizophrenic, as diagnosed, or a medium in training, as she claims—or both? Do her prescriptions filled in the clinic pharmacy produce results as good as those "prescriptions" bought in the spiritualist's "pharmacy"—the *botanica*—and are her therapist's techniques as effective as the medium's seances and consultations?

Maria is a believer in spiritualism, or more precisely, spiritism, as defined by the Frenchman, Hippolyte Rivail, commonly known by his pseudonym, Allan Kardec. It was his theory of spiritism that was adopted in Puerto Rico in the 1800s, that still flourishes there, and that is practiced today in New York City with various modifications and adaptations (Bram 1957).

This paper will attempt to define and investigate spiritism in the Puerto Rican culture as evidenced by the patient population of the Bronx-Lebanon Mental Health Center. By describing the day-to-day practices of spiritism, by surveying the literature, and by referring to descriptive case studies, we intend to show how spiritism is utilized both as an adjunct to psychiatry and as a substitute method of "treatment." We will demonstrate the need to evaluate and redefine our criterion of pathology as it affects diagnosis, treatment, and goals for these patients.

Various books and articles on Puerto Rican life include picturesque descriptions of seances and indications of the widespread belief in spiritism among all classes of Puerto Ricans (Lewis 1965; Minuchin et al. 1967; Wakefield 1960). However, there is very little written on how the belief in spirits is related to the acceptance and use of psychiatry. Even less information can be found pertaining to the effectiveness of spiritism as a "treatment" method.

Probably one of the most comprehensive discussions of how spiritism is used as a coping method by Puerto Ricans is incorporated in a study on schizophrenia by Lloyd Rogler and August Hollingshead (1965, pp. 243-260). This work clearly illustrates the stigma of being *loco*, the term usually attached to a psychiatric patient by the lower class, and the use of the medium as a folk psychiatrist. Joseph Bram (1957), in his paper on spiritism, traces the development of the belief in Puerto Rico and its co-existence with psychiatry in the Puerto Rican's search for a cure of his mental ills.

In reviewing psychiatric journals of the past ten years, we found only one article that dealt with spiritism as it relates to clinical work in the city (Fisch 1968).

In order to obtain a better understanding of spiritism, the authors attended several seances and visited some of the thirty local *botanicas*. A *botanica* is a store that sells the herbs, dolls, and special water used in the practice of spiritism.

In a well-stocked store, one can buy attraction oil (guaranteed to do what its name implies—attract the person desired) and an oil that performs the opposite service, incense, powders, good-luck charms, candles, statues of the saints, prayer leaflets, rosaries, and medals.

The many botanicas located in the area of the clinic indicate the widespread demand for their products. There are over thirty botanicas within walking distance of the clinic, and some are so crowded that customers are given a number for their place in line. The numerous ads placed in the Spanish papers, the flyers attached to car windshields or dropped in mailboxes further attest to the vitality of the entrepreneurs.

According to Kardec "the fundamental principle of . . . *Spiritism* is the relation of the material world with spirits, or the beings of the invisible world. . . . the spiritist theory is . . . based on the existence in us of a being independent of matter, and that survives the body" (1857, pp. 21-24). In other words, the dead survive as spirits who can communicate with us and can also take on the form of another person. In certain cases, they can be perceived by the senses of "sight, hearing, and touch" (Ibid., p. 32). There are both good and bad spirits, and they can be the source of aid or the cause of a variety of complaints ranging from marital problems to delusional thinking.

The medium is a person who has a particular affinity with the spirits, and can evoke them more readily than can other people. Therefore, he or she can exercise a certain amount of control over the spirits, and can influence their effect on a person. The mediums practice in two ways—through private consultations, and in seances or meetings. How they carry out their work will depend on whether they wish to do good or evil. The *brujos* (male witches) or *brujas* (female witches) are spiritists who work with evil spirits. These are the ones who will put a "hex" on a third party. According to local practitioners, this element of Puerto Rican spiritism is really a corruption of the basic Kardec philosophy, and is due to an assimilation of various practices from sources such as African voodoo. Most Puerto Rican spiritists work for good.

Important aspects of the consultation are the *despojos* (to shed) and *santiguos* (blessing). The *despojo* is a mode of exorcising all of the bad effects of the spirits by passing the hands around the head and body of a patient. The *santiguos* is a blessing given by touching the affected areas of the patient. A person with stomach pains, for example, will have the stomach rubbed with a mixture of *florida* water (scented alcohol) and other ingredients such as ashes or salt, depending on the type of spirit causing the pain.

Consultations are on an individual basis. The group sessions or seances are formal meetings and take on the appearance of a church gathering. A typical seance is composed of neighborhood people, in groups of from fifteen to forty, gathered in a storefront chapel, in a tenement apartment, or in the back room of a *botanica*. The group will include all ages, and as many men as women.

The person in charge is the president of the table, or chief medium. He is surrounded by his eight or ten assistant mediums, many of whom vary in their powers and some may still be in training. The mediums sit around a cloth-covered table that holds containers of water and candles, surrounded by statues and pictures of various saints, photographs of well-known personages, and a variety of memorabilia.

The seance begins with the entrance of the mediums, clothed in white, before the silent congregation. There are prayers and readings from Allan Kardec and other spiritual or philosophical writings. The lights are then dimmed, and the mediums perform *despojos,* passing their arms about their heads, calling on protector spirits to guide and safeguard them.

Then, with twistings of the body, moaning, and heavy breathing, they open themselves to possession by the spirits that trouble the various members of the attentive congregation. When possessed, the mediums, one at a time, call upon the person in the congregation who is being troubled by the possessing spirit. What follows is a dialog between the spirit, speaking through the medium, and the person; the conversation can best be described as a confrontation between good and evil. The spirit relates the symptoms and the reasons he is causing them. The other mediums assist by interrogating the spirit, restraining him when necessary, and joining the congregation in prayers in his behalf.

One such treatment may be sufficient to dispel the spirit. Otherwise, the "patient" may be given certain prescriptions and told to return either for further treatment in the group or in private consultation. The meeting is concluded with more prayers and a *despojo* to protect all present from any evil that may still be lingering from the evening's visitors.

Sexual identity plays no determining role in mediumship—there are male and female practitioners. In our visits to seances, we noted more female mediums acting as assistants, with men performing as the president, or chief medium.

Individuals may receive the first presentiment that they have spiritual faculties either as children or as adults. Usually, they develop through a testing period, which means an acceptance of various sufferings, which are seen as part of the road to full development. There are "schools" for mediums, where they are taught to discern the spirits and to test out whether or not they receive the vibrations and feelings that are proof of their psychic power.

A medium's abilities are judged empirically. He must produce results for his clients if he is to be known as a possessor of true faculties. Contrary to medical practice, a patient does not relate his symptoms to obtain a diagnosis; it is the medium who tells the patient his symptoms, and it is the patient who confirms or denies the truth of these statements. This is proof of the medium's power to evoke the spirits, and discern those acting on this particular patient.

In our investigation, the mediums we met ranged from a young man employed full time as a factory worker, to an ex-priest, to a building superintendent. They also included housewives, mothers, single youths, and the educated as well as the uneducated. Their attitudes toward psychiatry varied from one of cooperation to one of hostility. In relating to psychiatry, their basic premise is that the problems of material origin are the realm of the physician; the problems with a spiritual basis belong to the medium. It was never possible to get a clearly defined set of rules to determine when, for example, a patient suffering with auditory hallucinations might more correctly be treated by a psychiatrist than a medium. We were told by one medium that this could be determined by the vibrations he felt in the person's (or spirit's) presence and that one "just knows."

We had offers of consultations for our clinic cases from one young medium who was willing to give up his vacation time to spend it in the clinic with us. Another medium, more hostile to psychiatry, called a spirit to possess him, and the spirit in turn clearly attributed to the mediums the primary efficacy, because they "have a special gift from God, the special affinity with the spirits."

We have selected five case vignettes of clinic patients to demonstrate how spiritism is used as an additional treatment method for emotional problems. The cases are merely descriptive; at this time, no intensive studies concerning the patients have been done. A more detailed paper is planned as a follow-up to this introduction.

Of the cases chosen, one was diagnosed as a psychotic depressive reaction, one an anxiety neurosis, one an hysterical personality, and two as schizophrenia. As far as we can tell, most of these patients were "cured" of many of their symptoms by a medium. For some of these patients, medication or "pills" from the mental health center were totally unacceptable. Some of the reasons given were fear of addiction, ineffectiveness, and damaging side effects, such as hair falling out. Some took our pills in addition to their other prescriptions. However the prescriptions given by the medium were used more faithfully.

In relating this material, we, like Allan Kardec, "address ourselves to those who are reasonable enough to suspend their judgement in regard to what they have not yet seen, and who, judging of the future by the past, do not believe that man has reached his apogee" (1857, p. 39).

Case I

Juanita Martinez is a 28-year-old woman, separated from her husband and living with her two children. Mrs. Martinez's problems were "nerves, insomnia, feelings of depression, hearing voices and seeing shadows." She cried frequently, displayed psychomotor retardation, and expressed feelings of worthlessness. She was bothered by pains in her head and felt dizzy. Her chief worry was a six-year-old son who had had a "spell" the previous year and had stopped walking and talking. Her acute depression began at the time that her husband had abandoned her and the children.

The diagnosis was *psychotic depressive reaction.* Stelazine and Elavil were prescribed.

During the course of her clinic visits, Mrs. Martinez revealed her belief that strong spirits were against her, and had all "her roads crossed." She believed her troubles had begun after her neighbors put a hex on her and spread strange powder at her door, thus promoting fights between herself and her husband, causing him to leave. Then, she lost out on a housing project apartment at the last minute, and, lastly, her son became ill after the hex. The son was examined at various hospitals, and the mother claimed the doctors could find no cause of the The son was examined at various hospitals, and the mother claimed the doctors could find no cause of the illness.

After a series of missed appointments, Mrs. Martinez reappeared at the clinic to explain why she had not come and to say that she would not need to come any more. She was consulting with a medium who was really helping her and told her she did not need the clinic's assistance. This medium, using a photograph of her son, was giving the son *despojos* or blessings. Following a series of these treatments, the son began to cry for one of the first times and seemed to recognize the mother when she visited him. Mrs. Martinez also began to feel her own mind clear and claimed that her "roads were becoming uncrossed." She had a letter from the clinic recommending her for a housing project blessed by the medium and had just been informed that she would soon have an apartment. She felt our pills had helped her to sleep but that the medium was uncrossing her roads.

Case II

Rosa Morales is a 44-year-old woman who lives with her husband and four children. Her problems were "nerves, insomnia and nightmares." The patient described morbid fantasies of people hanging and of the dead returning from the grave. She was anxious and irritable with her husband and children. She was also bothered by the shadow of a tall Negro man that she claimed she had seen on and off since childhood. During her first clinic visit, she reported that she envisioned him during marital relations. Consequently, she was fearful of sex and having marital problems.

The diagnosis was *anxiety neurosis.*

This patient was treated regularly for three months, and Valium was prescribed. After a month of treatment, she declared her sexual problem solved and attributed this to visits to a medium who had evoked the spirit of the Negro man who was bothering her. The spirit admitted that he was at fault. In his earlier existence, he had been wronged by a lover. Following the exhortations of the medium, this spirit promised to bother her no longer, and he had not. The medium had also given her some prescriptions, which she followed faithfully. These consisted of burning candles, saying certain prayers, and washing her floors with a mixture of ammonia and herbs, scrubbing from the back rooms to the door. She then washed the floors from the door to the back rooms with beer, and sprayed the walls with *florida* water. Though the image of the spirit did not bother her any longer, some of the bad dreams had recurred. She attributed this to the fact that she had not been able to get back to the medium for further treatments. She related that she had stopped taking the medication prescribed by the clinic because she feared that she would become addicted and that it might be causing her hair to fall out, as suggested by the medium.

Case III

Magdalena Cruz is a 29-year-old woman, living with her husband and three children. She had been hospitalized at the medical service after an "attack" on her way to work. She was referred to the mental health center following consultation in the hospital. Her problems were facial contortions, feeling blood on her lips, and visual and auditory hallucinations. Prior to this attack, she thought people were touching her and she had palpitations and a "weight" on her heart. She feared that she would faint and then die. Diagnosis was *hysterical personality*. Mellaril was prescribed. During the two months that she came to the outpatient clinic, her various somatic complaints continued; soon, however, she was able to return to work and stopped coming to the clinic.

Mrs. Cruz felt that her real problem was well explained by her building superintendent, who was also a medium. She had called to him to help her one day when alone and fearful in her apartment. He, himself, saw shadows in the mirror and began to cry. He then explained that the shadow in the mirror was her mother (who had died ten years ago). Her mother, a spirit, was in need of purification and hence was attached to her daughter until sufficient prayers would release her. The spirit was sad and fearful and in pain, and was giving these same feelings to her daughter.

Case IV

Josephine Cortez is a 31-year-old woman who had been living in this country for a year and a half prior to her first clinic visit. She was referred from the medical service following hospitalization for a kidney infection. Complaints were negativism and anorexia. She was disoriented and talked circumstantially. She had various somatic complaints, including weight loss, lump in the inguinal region, stomach and back pains, and "sleeping too much." Speech was scattered and at times incoherent. Auditory hallucinations were present.

The diagnosis was *schizophrenia.* Although Stelazine was prescribed, Mrs. Cortez refused to take the medication. Her explanation of her illness was that she had been all right until shortly before leaving Puerto Rico. A close friend there began to suspect that she was having an affair with the friend's husband and, because of her jealousy, had put a hex on her. This explanation was given to her by a medium whom she had consulted in the Bronx. The medium also gave her certain prescriptions.

He had advised her to drink mint with cinnamon for her stomach pains; and to boil herbs in water, add it to bath water and then soak in the water for her backache. According to the patient's report during her clinic visits, both of these prescriptions worked and, when last seen, she claimed to be free of both stomach pains and backache. To keep the bad spirit from bothering her further, she placed a small glass of camphor under her bed each night.

Case V

Filomena Garcia is a 26-year-old woman living with her four children. She has a history of one state hospitalization for postpartum psychosis. When seen initially, she ranged from being highly excitable to being extremely depressed. In addition to being emotionally unstable, she was forgetful and circumstantial, and her ideas were not logically related. She claimed internal injuries caused when a policeman allegedly attacked her, and his voice still bothered her at times.

The diagnosis was *schizophrenia*, and Mellaril was prescribed.

The patient refused medication, saying she was not *loco*. She said that the only reason she came to the clinic was for help in getting back a stolen wallet and for a letter to present to court stating that she was "not crazy."

After three visits to the clinic, she revealed why she did not really want psychiatric help, and refused to take any medication. As she put it, "To heck with the pills, I know what's wrong with me, I won't be cured by pills." She then stated she was a medium and knew that something was going on within her but that this was her time of testing, and no psychiatry could help. She knew she was a medium because she had been able to give good advice to many people who consulted her.

As indicated, each of these patients suffered from some form of auditory or visual hallucination. Or, in Kardec's terms, each patient was possessed by spirits "appreciable by the senses of sight, hearing, and touch."

In spite of the fact that the patients were receiving psychiatric treatment concurrent with "spiritual" treatments, cures or symptom abatement were attributed by the patients primarily to the medium, except the last case, where mediumship itself was the source of the problems.

To what then can we attribute the apparent success of the mediums as opposed to that of the mental health professional? Patients do not see the mediums with any greater regularity than they attend the clinic; they usually seek help solely during times of immediate crises. As illustrated by our case vignettes, results attributed to the mediums appear, to the patients, to be faster, more conclusive, and certainly more dramatic than those of the mental health center.

Medication is another consideration in this dilemma. For many of our Puerto Rican patients, drugs immediately produce images of the narcotics addict, who is hated and feared. Patients do not understand the differences between the various drugs, and are terrified of becoming addicted. Mental health workers need to take the time with their patients for a careful explanation of the purpose and effect of all medication prescribed.

Finally, and what we believe to be the most salient reason for the success of the medium, is the revulsion for the word *loco*. *Loco* is an appellation feared by almost all Puerto Ricans. Here is where the medium, with his firm belief that "spirits" cause most or all problems, can be more effective in dealing with Puerto Rican patients than the professional. It is, of course, far less painful to blame a spirit for bizarre behavior than to relate the cause to oneself, or to admit to being *loco*. The mediums are, after all, the peers of their patients, and they themselves hear voices and see images. Also, such phenomena can even be a mark of distinction among peers, because of the suggestion that the person in question is developing spiritual faculties. There is also a group spirit engendered when the same neighbors come together regularly in a familiar community setting, rather than in a clinical atmosphere.

Professional mental health workers may be seen by these patients as punitive authorities who sit in judgment and attempt to categorize their patients into slots that are reprehensible to them. The professional therapist may understand the diagnosis, but the patient does not, nor do the traditional approaches to treatment always hold much meaning for him.

The medium is able to label the problem immediately, to provide an acceptable explanation for it, and to give the patient concrete, action-oriented treatment. Perhaps this is a case of exorcism by action as opposed to exorcism by thought and insight.

We believe that it is necessary for professional mental health workers to alter their attitude towards their Puerto Rican patients. We must educate ourselves in an attempt to bridge the cultural gap that exists between these patients and ourselves. Clearly, the time has come, too, for us to redefine the existing criteria of pathology with regard to some of our Puerto Rican patients. We must be able to distinguish schizophrenic hallucinations from the experiences of mediums, mediums-in-training, and their patients. These may well be hysterical or hypnotic phenomena. Again, we must look more carefully at our treatment methods and goals.

In conclusion, we find that spiritism as practiced by our Puerto Rican patients provides many of them with a means of coping with adversities. Certainly, some people receive comfort and support from such rituals and absolutions. Unfortunately, however, many patients who suffer from mental disorders do not receive adequate, or, in some instances, any psychiatric treatment because of their involvement with spiritism. This is a problem that we as mental health professionals must face and, hopefully, explore.

It would seem that we must overcome our own natural resistance to spiritism and, like Freud, "bite" into this "sour apple":

> In matters of occultism I have become humble ever since the great lesson I received from Ferenczi's experience. I promise to believe everything that can be made to seem the least bit reasonable. As you know, I do not too gladly. But my hubris has been shattered. [Jung 1963, p. 364]

> The thought of that sour apple makes me shudder, but there is no way of avoiding biting into it. [Jones 1957, p. 391]

Bibliography

Bram, J. 1957. Spirits, mediums, and believers in contemporary Puerto Rico. *Transactions of the New York Academy of Sciences* 20:340-347.

Fisch, S. 1968. Botanicas and spiritualism in a metropolis. *Milbank Mem. Fund, Quart. Bulletin* 46:377-388.

Jones, E. 1957. *The life and work of Sigmund Freud. Vol. 3.* New York: Basic Books.

Jung, C. J. 1963. In *Memories, dreams, reflections,* ed. A. Jaffe. New York: Pantheon Books, Random.

Kardec, A. 1857. *The spirits book.* Anna Blackwell, trans. S. Paulo, Brazil: Lake.

Lewis, O. 1965. *La vida.* New York: Random.

Minuchin, S. et al. 1967. *Families of the slums.* New York: Basic Books.

Rogler, L. and Hollingshead, A. B. 1965. *Trapped: families and schizophrenia.* New York: D. Wiley.

Wakefield, D. 1960. *Island in the city.* New York: Citadel.

The Young American Expatriates in Canada: Alienated or Self-Defined?*

Carl L. Kline and Katherine Rider†

Kenneth Boulding has said, "A man may deny his parents, his wife and friends, his God, or his profession and get away with it, but he cannot deny his country unless he finds another one" (1969). Today, tens of thousands of young Americans are denying their country and they have indeed found another one—Canada. The Vietnam war has precipitated this mass emigration. It has made self-imposed exiles of young men who chose to leave their country rather than fight in a hated war.

Because this emigration of male youth from the United States into Canada is unprecedented, and because we were unable to find any reports on this subject in the literature, we became interested in the chance to study a representative group.

What were the processes by which such young men made the decision to leave their country permanently? What psychological mechanisms did they utilize in reaching their decisions? What happened to them in the process? Have these men been alienated by their experiences or enriched and integrated through an act of self-definition?

*This essay appeared in the *American Journal of Orthopsychiatry* 41:74-84 © 1971 in slightly revised form. Reprinted by permission.

†The authors wish to acknowledge the invaluable suggestions and assistance of Carolyn Kline in the preparation of this manuscript. Karen Berry and J. McRee Elrod offered valuable help in gathering data.

Statistics relating to the number of draft refusers and deserters now living in Canada are hard to find. According to the *New York Times*, there now are 250,000 deserters from the United States' military services. The Canadian Council of Churches, quoting Canadian government data, estimates that over 60,000 draft-age American males are now living in Canada. However, on the basis of Canadian immigration statistics, it would appear that no more than 18,000 of these men have achieved landed-immigrant status. The Committees to Aid American War Objectors say that 40 American expatriates arrive daily in both Montreal and Toronto, and approximately 12 war objectors a day are now coming into Vancouver.

To establish permanent residence and to be able to work requires landed-immigrant status, which is determined by a recently established point system developed to objectify decision-making by immigration officers. Under this system it is relatively easy for married college graduates to obtain the required 50 points, but more difficult for single men with a grade 12 education or less.

Research plan

We lay no claim to objectivity in this study. Reporting on the emotional experiences of others is full of pitfalls. The Vietnam war, even more than most wars, has created an atmosphere of emotionally determined anti-intellectualism among large numbers of Americans. We realize that the emotionalities and absurdities we see so clearly in others also are likely to be perceived by them in us. We were impressed by the attractiveness, the openness, the idealism, and the maturity of these young men and women, most of whom readily agreed to discuss their recent experiences and life histories with us.

This study includes 30 military refusers and the wives of

the 16 among them who are married; of this group, there were 10 men in each of the following categories—

1. draft refusers with landed-immigrant status who have been in Canada for more than 18 months;
2. draft refusers with landed-immigrant status who have been in Canada for less than six months;
3. deserters with landed-immigrant status.

By limiting our study to men with landed-immigrant status, we were able to stablize our sample by ruling out transients—those who come to look around but who return to the United States when they encounter unexpected hardships. The disadvantage of this limitation is that it excluded the men who could not garner the points to become landed immigrants, but who nevertheless stayed on illegally, and the men who chose to ignore the system and not become "landed." Both of these latter groups, in general, experience far greater adjustment difficulties in Canada; they tend to be angry and bitter with society in general. They are, by definition, truly alienated.

General facts about the sample

Typically, the subject was a white, Anglo-Saxon Protestant from a middle-class background, with high school or college education. His history was singularly free of evidence of psychiatric illness or characterological disturbance. Only one man had a history of a psychiatric problem and only one had been involved in an episode of delinquent behaviour. As nearly as we could determine through our interviews with these young men, family stability appeared to be characteristic. Although these men came from families averaging over 20 years of marriage, only 5 had ended in divorce.

The fathers of 75 percent of the men had served in

World War II; 2 fathers were conscientious objectors. In the 16 families where religion played a significant role, 6 were Roman Catholic, 6 Protestant and 4 Jewish. There were 17 families who still resided in the same locale where the young man was born. Four of the 30 were foreign born (from France, England, Cuba, and Canada). Geographically, half of the men were from the West Coast, one-fifth from the East Coast, and the remainder equally from the South and Midwest.

There were 18 who stated that their families were conservative Republicans, and 7, that their families were Democrats. Two of the families belonged to the Peace and Freedom party; the political affiliations of 3 were unknown.

As to education, 3 of the group were high school graduates, 15 had completed between one and three-and-a-half years of college, 9 had A.B. degrees, and 3 had advanced degrees. Three are attending university in Vancouver at the present time.

Response to draft registration

For many men, the legal requirement to register under the Selective Service Act eventually produced a life crisis. Those few who knew from the start that they would not cooperate in any way with the war left the United States without conflicting feelings. For the others, a variety of experiences caused them to move with varying speeds and styles through the processes that eventually led them to Canada. Decisions were catalyzed by such chance experiences as reading a book or magazine article, viewing a television program, or hearing of the induction of a friend. Military training, orders to Vietnam, or the sights and sounds of the war itself awakened these men so that, at the first opportunity, they deserted.

Jim is a good example of the latter group. Stationed

on a Navy research vessel in a noncombat area, he enjoyed and was interested in his work. He had not really associated his service with the Vietnam war. Then he was transferred to an oil supply ship in Vietnam waters. Once in the war zone, he perceived his position quite differently: "Living in the war zone where terrific tension was always present brought it all home to me. Grenades were always going off around the ship to protect us from swimmers bent on sabotage. Then there was the constant drone of planes and the bombs on the mainland. The war became very real to me. It became unbearable—I had to think of some way to keep my sanity. It was intolerable, unbearable living!" [Jim became very emotional while talking about this.] "The people—men on the ship—were really affected, but many of them didn't recognize it. They had a lot of defenses, like keeping the hi-fi on real loud to drown out the sounds. I felt stuck there. I felt no one could ever get off that ship. There were just two things: the war going on and just living that way. Just living war."

Of the 30, 21 were on university campuses when they became anxious about the war. Even on campuses where political activism was prevalent, it was difficult for these men to find people with whom they could discuss the war from a personal viewpoint. On more conservative campuses, Vietnam seldom was mentioned. As a substitute for dialog, many men researched the war in the libraries, reading about its history and studying articles by various experts.

Their reading led them to an awareness of the deep divisions in the country. Their suspicions that the Vietnam war was a big mistake were reinforced. They were further disillusioned by the proportions of the credibility gap, an expression which they rejected as a euphemism for government lies. Many whom we interviewed emphasized that they didn't leave just because of the war, but, rather, that they saw the war as one major symptom of a decaying American society, characterized by pollution, racism, violence, and exploitation of the underprivileged.

Often, men foundered in trying to choose among various alternatives. One young man who had first decided to go to jail, rather than to war, changed his mind and reported for his preinduction physical and was classified 4-F because of a hernia. For three months, he felt completely disoriented. "To continue with my draft resistance work, urging other men to go to jail, seemed very armchair, so I came to Canada."

The crisis these men faced created indecisiveness and emotional turmoil associated with feelings of being trapped. Loneliness and a sense of isolation were increased when efforts to engage parents in meaningful dialog were fruitless. Many men developed intense feelings of anxiety, doubt, bewilderment, and anger.

Only one of our subjects seriously considered suicide. However, another young man said he found comfort in occasional fantasies of ending his life. Assailed by doubts as to whether his rejection of the war might be based on cowardice rather than on principle, he entered the military service, got through basic training, and was permanently assigned to teach in a language school. He then felt that it took more courage to desert than to stay in such a plush assignment for the duration. As he put it, "On the day they locked up Captain Levy,* I hopped on the bus."

Men facing selective service alternatives felt that their lives were not their own; either they had to enter the military, subject themselves to being "channeled" by the government, or they had to leave "the system." The deferment game was seen by many as dishonest and

---

*Captain Levy was a young army doctor who refused to train troops in first aid measures to be applied in Vietnam; he felt that any preparation for Vietnam was evil. He was arrested, locked up, tried, found guilty of refusing to obey orders and imprisoned.

irrelevant to the issues involved. Accepting deferment as a college student created guilt for some, knowing that someone less privileged would have to take their place in Vietnam.

One young man who was an "A" student in a top-ranked university felt that he was hiding behind his 2-S classification. He withdrew from school and mailed his draft card with a "letter of resignation" to the selective service. For the next month, he toured the United States, riding the Greyhound lines on a 30-day pass. It was when he arrived in Washington, D.C., that he really said goodbye to his country. He described himself standing silently on the steps of the Justice Department in what he saw as a gesture of disdain for "its capacity for injustice."

The subjects gave the following reasons for refusing to participate in the war:

1. They view participation in the Vietnam war as immoral; they said that they would feel ashamed to have to admit to their children that they had participated.
2. Having been raised to cherish autonomy, self-direction, and individual responsibility, they reject authoritarianism and question the motives underlying the United States' use of power.
3. They see the Vietnamese, and other people, as human beings and don't buy the Madison Avenue techniques of dehumanizing them by calling them "the other side," "the V.C.," and "the Communists." They view much of this kind of terminology as racist propaganda.
4. They perceive war in the nuclear age as barbaric and stupid.
5. They condemn the United States' value system and argue that today's society is not worth saving.

Clearly, these men did not view military service as an opportunity for further maturation, achievement, and self-definition; to them, it is an irrational demand by an authoritarian and repressive government.

Edgar Z. Friedenberg says this generation feels it is locked in the back seat of a car that has been built to faulty specifications and is being driven at high speed by a middle-aged drunk, and it wants to get out of the car (1969). To this very apt metaphor, we would add that these young people believed the car to be bent on an illicit mission and that they had to get out of the car not only to survive but to preserve their self-respect.

A deserter we interviewed clearly illustrated this struggle for personal integrity. Sidney had entered the service with strongly conflicting feelings and had served with increasing conviction that it was wrong for him to have participated. When he realized that in just four months, he would be an "honorably discharged veteran of the Vietnam war," he decided he could not wear that label for the rest of his life. He mobilized himself, deserted, and made his way to Canada.

They rejected alternatives

All of the subjects in our study had been aware of the various manipulative modes of avoiding the draft. They knew about the phony medical problems, the psychiatric letter, the felony conviction, and the divinity school registration. Several engaged their draft boards in game-playing and put-ons. One man tried to convince his draft board that he was a dangerous anarchist, and even made two half-hearted attempts to get arrested. Several wrote complicated letters designed to confuse members of the draft board. These were ways of expressing disdain for the system, but most men saw the basic issues as too serious for game-playing. Instead, they turned attention to serious decision-making. In general, they expressed an unwillingness to sacrifice self-respect by dishonest maneuvering.

Conscientious objector status is a commonly considered alternative to military service. Today, there are about 34,255 conscientious objectors; in World War II, despite total mobilization, there were only 16,000 (Cornell 1969). These men are required to spend two years in an approved work assignment, termed "alternative duty." Some even serve in the military, but in noncombat roles. Those in our group who seriously considered seeking C.O. status often discovered that their own beliefs did not satisfy the official requirements, at least as interpreted by the decision-makers.

Men who applied often found themselves caught up in what was, to them, a cruel game. Following a draft board hearing on his C.O. application, one man said, "I was just naive enough to believe that they really wanted to consider my views, but when the hearing lasted five minutes and they clearly did not give a shit, I went to the consulate for information on Canada."

Another of our subjects applied for and obtained C.O. status. As his alternative duty, he was teaching in a ghetto school when a change in draft board personnel prompted a re-examination of his records. Abruptly, he was ordered to stop teaching and accept a hospital attendant's job. Instead, he left for Canada. Another man described how his older brother's C.O. request was refused after many months of costly hearings and appeals. Although he felt himself to be a conscientious objector, he chose coming to Canada over the humiliation and defeat endured by his brother.

Such experiences with draft boards were certainly ego-diminishing. The men resented the fact that a man's unwillingness to participate in war was weighed, measured, and microscopically examined against poorly defined standards and often by highly prejudiced and poorly qualified judges.

Going to prison as an alternative was variously viewed as "buckling under in another way," as pointless self-sacrifice, or as an act of self-destruction. Several said, "The United States today isn't worth it." One young man confessed that in view of the present political trend in the United States, he feared that he might never be released from prison if he went to jail. Many voiced objection to being placed in the role of "criminal," feeling that the label more appropriately fit the power figures responsible for the war. Some said, "If you go to jail you are forgotten. Going to Canada is a more significant protest." Wives often influenced their husbands against going to jail.

Unlike World War II, job deferments are uncommon, but they were considered and rejected by two of our subjects. Many thought of going underground and working in the resistance movement, and several did this for awhile before leaving the United States.

The mechanics of exile

The draft refuser, having made the decision to go to Canada, quietly proceeded with preparations to leave. As he saved money, he searched out information about Canada and planned his strategy. The planning phase for some lasted for several weeks; others prepared for as long as two years. In contrast, military deserters often made the decision to emigrate abruptly and had to act quickly. They often left without money, extra clothing, or even personal effects. Some came in uniforms, which they discarded as quickly as they could obtain other clothing.

Those who arrived without preparations had the most difficulty. Living in crowded hostels without furniture, they sat on the floor by day and slept on the floor at night. When they lacked even adequate clothes to wear for job-hunting, and were without money, they often became depressed. Some grew bitter and resentful.

They feel now that these hardships tested the strength of their determination to stay.

Our subjects had shared an uneasy curiosity upon emigration about other military refusers in Canada. Would they be the misfits and "freaks" sometimes represented by the news media? As they met their fellow exiles, they invariably were relieved and reassured. Friendships among them developed easily and proved stabilizing and supportive. Only a few isolated themselves from other Americans, doing so as part of their total rejection of everything American. One man expressed disdain for draft dodgers, and especially for deserters. Interestingly enough, he was an officer deserter who continued to feel superior to enlisted men.

Crossing the border was a major step in the whole process for most men. It was an emotionally charged experience, usually characterized by feelings of profound relief and joy.

Without exception, the men and women we talked with perceived Canadians as friendly, and felt life in Canada to be more relaxed. They appreciated the greater freedom of expression. The lack of military draft in Canada impressed them. Many of the men and their wives emphatically stated that they would never raise a child in a country with a military draft.

Despite Canada's official policy of accepting military refusers who meet immigration requirements, some of the subjects in our study encountered unexpected problems in obtaining legal status. One young couple, a deserter and his wife, was turned down by the Vancouver immigration office. They were ordered by letter to leave the country within two weeks, and were required to turn the letter over to Canadian immigration on their way out of Canada. The despair and fear they felt has been experienced by other frightened, unhappy exiles in similar positions. However, within a few days, this particular couple was able, with the help of an anonymous "Quaker lady," to recross the border as landed immigrants. One young deserter we talked with made thirteen hazardous border crossings before he was finally landed.

Parental attitudes

Perhaps the most striking finding of our study relates to parental reactions to military refusers. Overt disapproval was common, and, often, the parents appeared oblivious to what their sons were attempting to say to them. Parents commonly dismissed the subject abruptly. Effective door-closers were used: "Oh you will go when the time comes." "Don't be immature." "I served in World War II." In a sense, such parental reactions were similar to those of a father who ignores his son's refusal to enter the family business. Frequently, these parents were deaf to their son's refusal to enter the business of war.

Among the psychological mechanisms used by parents confronted with the fact that their son was refusing war and leaving America forever, complete denial was the most common.

Jimmy and his new bride spent a few days with his parents before leaving for Canada. Unable to accept the fact that his son was deserting the navy and becoming an exile, the father took them to his furniture store, where, as though he had not heard their plans, he told them to pick out furniture for their apartment in Los Angeles. He was even denying the existence of the war and certainly he was denying the crisis that his son and daughter-in-law were facing.

Another couple made several unsuccessful attempts to talk with their parents. When the young man received his induction notice, he announced their plans to leave the country. Farewell parties were given for them, but no one acknowledged that their decision to leave the country was related to the draft.

Another example of obliviousness to a son's plight is reflected in Ed's experience. Ed was sensitive to his father's feelings and carefully planned how best to prepare his father for his planned desertion from the navy. From the ship, he wrote letters in which he described his deep disaffection with what he was experiencing, emphasizing his horror of the war and all that it implied. He was quite open in sharing these feelings with his parents. When home on leave, he talked to his father about his plans, but his father responded with an analogy, comparing Ed's service in the navy to a business contract—something that must be honored. Ed commented, "He saw it through a businessman's eyes. These were his values and he looked at my situation in those terms. It was really difficult to let him know, and then he really closed himself off, didn't say a word and then he did some strange things, acting like it was't going to happen, like we never had that talk." Many parents did not believe their sons were really leaving until they received a phone call from them in Canada.

The men did not expect agreement from their parents, but they hoped for the support inherent in dialog. One man whose own father was remote had many long talks with his father-in-law, a career military man who disagreed with him but respected his opinions. When support was absent from parents, teachers, ministers, or family friends, other sources were looked for; some searched their family histories for ancestors who had shown independent spirit in immigrating to the United States, perhaps to avoid military service; most turned to books written by such authors as Sartre, A. J. Muste, Malcolm X, Schweitzer, Bertrand Russell, Camus, Martin Luther King, and Gandhi.

As would be expected, anger was sometimes direct and open. Frank, who received no understanding from his family, said, "I am opposing my whole background. My father just doesn't understand; he feels he has failed in bringing me up properly. He is very hurt, which makes me sorry. When I phoned my father to say I was leaving, he said, 'Frank I don't want to talk to a coward,' and he hung up."

Although mothers generally tended to be more understanding than fathers, outright approval was a common reaction of mothers-in-law. Mary had known Jim for a year before they decided on marriage, to be followed by Jim's desertion. Her parents, who lived in the eastern United States, had never met Jim. When Mary called home and said to her mother, "Jim has leave and we are getting married," her mother's response was, "Did you say Jim has leave or is *leaving*?" Mary admitted the truth of the matter, to which her mother said, "Good, I've been collecting information about going to Canada and I'll bring it along when I fly out for the wedding." Mary's father was not so understanding, and he did not come to the wedding.

While our subjects spoke matter-of-factly about their parents' inability to talk openly, their hurt and disappointment were clearly visible. They tried to explain the older generation's reactions in varying ways: "They live in a different world." "America is their religion." "When you get in a rut you don't think any more." "My father is pretty wrapped up in putting the kids through college." "They said when you can't fight the machine, go with it." "They're old and the fight has gone out of them." "It's not that they're against thinking, they just have never done it." "I suppose it is hard when your son has just received a lucrative appointment to a good brokerage firm and you see all you invested in raising him about to pay off—to have it all melt away." "Let's face it. We are the products of affluence—we have had more opportunities for intellectual pursuit and travel and our horizons are wider." "It's part of a group phenomenon—my parents became opposed to the war too when it was appropriate for the middle class to oppose it. What is needed is a change in consciousness in the American people."

Perhaps the young people were simply reacting to the explosion of the family myth. Having been brought up to believe that "you can always turn to your parents in time of trouble," they were dismayed to discover that this wasn't true. In the face of major crises in which their sense of security is threatened, many parents behave unpredictably. This is something known by every psychiatrist who has seen the reactions of parents to a daughter's illegitimate pregnancy, to a son's unapproved marriage, or to a child who drops out of college to join the hippie community.

Some parents were supportive of their son's plans. One family moved to Canada so that their son could have his family and home available to him.

Generally, our subjects expressed concern for their parents and an understanding of their reactions to the crisis. Even when the parents were openly hostile, the young people expressed hope for eventual re-establishment of a relationship on a more mature footing.

Role of wives

Nearly thirty years ago, Dr. Karl Menninger wrote, "War probably injures women even more than it does men, everything considered. . . . Fundamentally a woman is more predominately than a man the embodiment of the erotic power which is arrayed against self-destruction" (1942).

The wives of the men we talked with in this study supported and encouraged their husbands in their resistance to the war. Joe and Carol had known each other for over a year, and were married just three days before driving to Canada in a rented car. They had met while working in the VISTA program. Both were university graduates with a deep interest in helping minority groups.

"VISTA taught us many practical things—how to organize and get things done." Obviously, they had learned their lessons well, as evidenced by the efficient way they worked together to establish themselves in Canada. Within a week of their arrival, they had purchased a used Volkswagen, rented an inexpensive apartment, purchased second-hand furniture, and Jim, despite the unemployment problem, had located two part-time academic jobs. They applied for landed-immigrant status and were promptly accepted.

Another wife, Elizabeth, had been raised in a military family. She had never thought of opposing war until she began work in the amputee ward of a military hospital on the West Coast. In telling of her reaction, she said, "I was shocked and horrified by what I saw and heard." About this time, she married Harold. "I remember thinking," she said, "that I would rather shoot him in love than have his leg blown off in hate." She admitted that she planned to shoot him in the foot if necessary to prevent him from going to Vietnam. He applied for a conscientious objector discharge, and was refused. After lengthy and expensive legal proceedings and with orders for Vietnam in his pocket, they made the decision to desert to Canada. Escape was difficult because the military police were hounding Elizabeth, while looking for Harold. The story of their separation and reunion across the border was recited by Elizabeth with tears in her eyes. In summary, she said, "I had a hard time accepting that my country would treat people that way."

Fortunate is the young man who, when he loses his illusions about his parents, finds a girl to believe in him. In talking with these young women, one could not help but think of the story of *Lysistrata*. Perhaps by standing at the side of their men who refuse to fight, these modern young women have a potentially more effective weapon against war than Lysistrata and her friends had with their method of sexual abstention.

Adjustment in Canada

Among the three groups we studied, we found few basic differences in adjustment patterns. The majority were becoming absorbed into the Canadian culture. Only one of the 30 men expressed a desire to return to the United States to live. In fact, only those with meaningful parental ties mentioned a desire even to visit the United States.

Characteristically, they expressed continued social concerns and strong feelings against the Vietnam war. Although many declared themselves against war, some said they would fight for Canada if attacked, even by the United States. The majority of these Americans have chosen to be politically inactive since coming to Canada, but they expect to become more involved later. They express a feeling of responsibility to participate in the affairs of their new country. None regretted the decision to reject military service and come to Canada.

Summary

This study has focussed on the processes by which 30 young Americans rejected military service and separated themselves from their society through self-exile to Canada.

Coming from seemingly stable, rather conservative middle-class families, these men and women were raised to be autonomous, self-directed, and independent. Faced with a major life-crisis brought on by confrontation with the selective service system and the Vietnam war, they entered into the lonely process of decision-making with a feeling of isolation. They had to assess their own values and make decisions affecting their very existence.

Often, mentors in the older generation had erected psychological barriers which made them inaccessible to dialog; they often were totally oblivious to the needs of these young men. They sought what help they could find in books and in the relationships with their wives. Being unable to find an alternative to military service that did not bear the price tag of diminished self-respect, they came to Canada. In all instances, their emigration resulted in increased self-respect, greater confidence in problem-solving ability, and restored belief that their lives were again in their hands.

Erikson has emphasized the importance of fidelity in the development of maturity in young people (1968). The subjects in this study perceived the selective service and the Vietnam war as incongruous with their beliefs and thus contrary to the whole concept of fidelity. In fact, they appeared to share a kind of conviction that they had just narrowly escaped serving as solicitors in a sordid contract. They don't want to be used for war; they want to be useful for peace.

Fromm defines alienation as "a mode of experience in which the person experiences himself as an alien" (1955). He emphasizes that the alienated person is out of touch with himself. These young people appeared to believe that they had to come to Canada to avoid experiencing themselves as alien. They equated emigration with ego-preservation. To them, cooperation with the selective service meant dehumanization and sacrifice of selfhood.

Since our contact with young men making other decisions about the draft is limited, we cannot comment on how the men in our study differ. They are certainly young men who trust their own decisions and are guided by them much more than by decisions of the culture or the group. They saw the parental generation as trapped, rigid, and unresponsive; they rejected these models as they sought to maintain personal integrity without self-alienation by seeking more acceptable models. Although they were not conquered and subdued by their society, neither were they able to influence its attitudes significantly. In this very literal sense, they were alienated from their society, but not from themselves.

Fromm has said that major social catastrophes like economic depression and war drastically emphasize our sense of helplessness (1955). The young people in this study refused to succumb to such outside forces. Decision-making and emigration often altered their personal relationships and family life styles. However, facing the issues as they perceived them and acting positively upon them, they apparently discovered new boundaries of self-definition.

Recognizing that the psychological-developmental continuum extends into and throughout adult life, we have attempted to view the experiences of these young men and women as important development milestones, as significant phases in their psychological separation crises with their parents, as an opportunity to exercise autonomy in the face of a mammoth authoritarian system, and as a chance to open up opportunities for identification with a new country and people. The effective way in which these young people have handled major life crises appears to us to indicate a level of mature emotional functioning that is often aspired to, but seldom attained.

Bibliography

Boulding, K. E. 1969. The impact of the draft on the legitimacy of the national state. *Fellowship Magazine* July.

Cornell, T. 1969. The war and the draft: an overview. *Christianity and Crisis* Dec. 22.

Erikson, E. 1968. *Identity and the life cycle.* New York: Norton.

Friedenberg, E. Z. 1969. Current patterns of generational conflict. *J. soc. Issues* 25:21-38.

Fromm, E. 1955. *The sane society.* New York: Holt.

Menninger, K. 1942. *Love against hate.* New York: Harcourt.

Institutional Racism in the Modern Metropolis
Harold M. Baron

Among Ralph Bunche's field notes for his work on the preparation of Myrdal's *An American Dilemma* is the record of an interview that he had with the chief clerk of an Alabama court. The chief clerk went to great lengths detailing to Bunche his liberality towards blacks and explaining how he had no personal animus toward them. He went so far as to declare that he would not do anything to keep Negroes in their place—but the chief clerk did allow that he sure liked to find them there. The court official could well have been speaking for modern urban America, except that less candor is employed today, now it is called "benign neglect."

Social science has described the behavior of the racially dominant whites in terms of vicious circles of causation and a seamless web of personal discriminations, prejudices and anxieties. Often the reality of the systematic subjugation of black people has been hidden under neutral abstractions like "minority-group relations." The dominated blacks have been labeled deviants and deficients. The stranglehold of such categories is so great that Frank Riessman, a man who was struggling to break with them, still came up with a book entitled *The Culturally Deprived Child* (1962). Within this prevailing analytic framework, there is little implication that there are the controllers and the controlled. Instead one is asked to believe that the racial confrontations in the metropolises are grounded in the defensive ignorance of

99

whites and the unfortunate problems of the blacks. The claim for the modern ghetto seems to be like the one made for the British Empire—that it came about in the fit of absent-mindedness.

Even when recognition is given to the need for a new vocabulary in order to catch up symbolically with the growing disenchantment of black youth, the substantive results are largely the same. The National Advisory Commission on Civil Disorders (the Kerner Commission) did feel impelled to strike out in one direction, that of dealing boldly with some of the cultural symbols of racial oppression. Jarringly they stated: "Our nation is moving toward two societies, one black, one white— separate and unequal" (1968). Their pronouncement that white racism "is essentially responsible for the explosive mixture which has been accumulating in our cities since the end of World War II" (1968) has legitimized the usage of that term.

Nevertheless, after a careful analysis of the entire Kerner Commission Report, one is led to the conclusion that its conceptual innovation is basically limited to a refashioning of symbols. While "white society" and "white institutions" are singled out in the introduction as the main causative factors for contemporary urban racism, they are not given primacy in the body of the text. Far from being a penetrating analysis of white society and white institutions, the report, essentially, ends up being one more dreary litany of the characteristics of the black community as deprived, depressed and discriminated against. White society, the source of these conditions, is treated as an undifferentiated blur. Little or nothing is said about the institutional structures, both corporate and bureaucratic, that control this society or the elites that dominate these institutions. Evidently it was deemed safe to delve into the frustrations of the powerless blacks, while a critical investigation of the prerogatives of the empowered whites was forbidden turf.

The redeeming grace of the Kerner Commission Report is a certain humility in its claims as to the effectiveness of current programs or the progress that is at hand. But its failure to analyze the structures of control within white society is a failure to confront the fundamentals of white racism as a well-institutionalized system of subjugation. Instead the report still tends to limit the definition of racism to terms of individual attitudes and blanket features of white culture. This basic theme was confirmed when Senator Fred Harris, one of the commission's staunchest liberals, later wrote that "the unwillingness of white Americans to accept Negroes as fellow human beings is precisely what we meant by racism" (Grier and Cobbs 1968).

This kind of conceptual framework, which deflects attention away from institutions and institutional controls, makes it very easy to rationalize modes of analysis and acting that ameliorate certain conditions, but still leave the basic control structures intact. Such reasoning reflects the underlying assumptions that have guided most social science work on race relations for the past generation. This work must be judged egregiously irrelevant, if not in many cases wrong. Twenty-five years ago Gunnar Myrdal in his book, *An American Dilemma*, which became the classic in the field, laid out these assumptions in his generalizations about race relations in the North:

> The social paradox in the North is exactly this, that almost everybody is against discrimination in general but, at the same time, almost everybody practices discrimination in his own personal affairs. It is the culmination of all these personal discriminations which creates the color bar in the North and for the Negro causes unusually severe unemployment, crowded housing conditions, crime and vice. About

> this social process the ordinary white Northerner keeps sublimely ignorant and unconcerned. This aloofness is, of course, partly opportunistic but it can be fought by education. [1944, 1966, Vol. II, pp. 1010-1011]

Myrdal predicted that racial subordination would be broken down as "the white Northerner is gradually waking up and seeing what he is doing to the Negro" (1944, 1966). It should be noted that he did not predict anything like the social and political turmoil—even mass violence—that have been necessary to achieve the minimal changes that we have today. The wrongness of his predictions is most deeply grounded in Myrdal's overarching assumption that America's racial dilemma was one of conflicting values in the minds of whites. Through neglecting the historical processes of social institutions, he ignored the more basic truth that the conflict over racism in America is one between an oppressed black people, determined to throw off the shackles of control, and the controllers of that society.

It is incumbent upon us now to proceed to a definition of racism that will overcome the criticisms just raised. American racism has primarily been an affair in black and white, characterized throughout history by the systematic subjugation and exploitation of persons of African ancestry. The origins of this system basically lay in the international trade in African slaves and the extensive plantations that were run by their labor. This trade in human commodities and the material commodities they produced was a crucial element in the protracted historical processes through the world. Throughout this history, racism has sustained a number of institutional metamorphoses down into our era of the modern metropolis and neo-colonialism. Specifically, in the United States direct controls over black people have undergone major transformations from slavery to peonage and jim crow, to the web of urban racism. While we must note that other groups have been subjected to racial derogation and exploitation in this nation, the basic institutionalization of racism evolved for the control of black people.

Racial regulations have been embodied in every major sphere of American life from the family to the Constitution. These institutional controls have been bolstered in the abstract by ideological and normative justifications, and individually by adjustment to roles of superordination for whites and subordination for blacks. The racial differentiation in values, roles and styles has become so great that today we note the emergence of distinctive black and white variations of American culture.

We find that in each historical epoch there has been a clear and specifiable set of institutional arrangements by which black people have been dominated. The relationship has been one of active control rather than one of a hierarchical ranking according to the degree to which certain culturally preferred characteristics are possessed by individuals in the group. In addition to these institutional structures, there have been more abstract and diffused ideological and cultural expressions of racism, such as the doctrine of racial inferiority, that prescribe the dominance of all whites and the degradation of all blacks in terms more general than those of the particular social mechanisms of control.

Therefore, in a manner somewhat analogous to the Marxian distinction between base and superstructure, we can look for two distinguishable elements in the overall structure of racism—first, an institutional elaboration in economic, social and political formations; second, an ideological elaboration in conceptual systems, myths, values and norms. These distinctive components are mutually related and mutually supportive in forming a functional whole. Differentiation between the specifiable institutional basis of racism and the more abstract diffused ideology of racism provides us with an analytic tool that can cut through the indefiniteness of explanations based on doctrines of vicious circles and shapeless multiple causation. We can also avoid a mechanical kind of reductionism. In order to comprehend historical transformations, we should concentrate on the basic dynamics of change which tend to arise out of conflict and tension within the institutional base. Meanwhile, we can still recognize that the ideological elements have a certain independence of their own in any causative development. By grasping the simultaneous distinctiveness and mutual reinforcement of the social structure and the rationale, we can also comprehend how changes in the one do not mean automatic changes in the other. And we can explain away many seeming anomalies when the obligations and motivations of both individuals and groups become understandable in terms of varying relationships between these two sub-frames of reference.

Let us illustrate this relationship briefly from the history of chattel slavery. In that era, the control of blacks was direct and their economic exploitation was open. However, slave-holding families were only a fairly small minority among whites in the ante-bellum South. The large plantation owners, who set the social and political tone of the South, were very few in number. While the plantocracy's control of the society was based on this minuscule group's ownership of black chattel slaves, they were able to generalize their system of control to all whites through an elaborate ideology of the master race, a generalization so complete that the southern-born historian Ulrich B. Philips could describe the main theme of southern history as "it shall be and remain a white man's country" (1928, 1949). All whites, regardless of their social or economic conditions, were to perceive themselves as elevated through the debasement of the black man. The direct controls of slavery became justified by theories of racial inferiority that branded the man of color, be he slave or free, with the mark of the pariah. Aristotelian theories of politics, the will of God, the Biblical tale of the casting out of Noah's son Ham, doctrines of biological inferiority—all were propounded as defenses of the institution of Afro-American slavery. *The net of these theories of racism was cast wider than the institutional base.* Generalization of the slaves' disabilities into a doctrine of racial right provided the poor non-slaveholding white with a stake in the system. He was encouraged to value himself and his culture in terms of his distance from, and his privileges over, blacks. The smallholders and propertyless among the whites, even though they were subordinated to the planter class themselves, came to define their personal worth in terms of their superior racial status. Denied an economic stake in the exploitation of the black man, the poor white gained a social stake in the black man's degradation. As John Hope Franklin has summarized:

> While uniting the various economically divergent groups of whites, the concept of race also strengthened the ardor of most Southerners to fight for the preservation of slavery. All slaves belonged to a degraded, "inferior" race, and by the same token, all whites however wretched some of them might be, were superior. In a race-conscious society, whites at the lowest rung could identify themselves with the most privileged and efficient of the community. [1956, p. 85]

In the last sixty years, great technological changes and massive population shifts within American society have created a transformation in both the location and the institutional forms of racial interaction. On the eve of World War I, direct contact between the races took place in a milieu that was rural and southern. Nine-tenths of the black people in the United States lived in the South. Three-fourths of the blacks, compared to one-half the whites, lived in rural areas. Cotton was king, ruling the life of the South and black Americans. Even in the towns, the ethos and style of the planters' world set the cultural tone.

An astounding demographic revolution has taken place in the intervening period, as, under the pressures of wartime tight labor markets, the black peasantry was discovered to be a valuable labor reserve for northern industry. Today, almost half the black population lives outside the South. Over three-fourths live in urban areas—a larger proportion of blacks to whites. Concentration in the large metropolitan areas has become the most unique feature of the demography of black people in America. During this decade, the black metropolitan population has been growing at a rate twice that of the white metropolitan population. Currently, 68 percent of all black people in the nation live in metropolitan areas compared to 64 percent of the white population. Fifty-four percent of all blacks live in the central cities of the metropolitan areas, while only 27 percent of the whites live in the central city. Within the metropolitan areas, the increase of the black population is basically limited to the core cities while the growth of the white population takes place in the suburbs (U.S. Dept. of Commerce 1968). Racism, in both its institutional and ideological forms, has now become urban and national.

Accounting for the origins of a social formation is not sufficient to explain the perpetuation of racism. Its persistence within our society can no longer be explained in terms of a base within the southern plantation system. Racial oppression today is rooted in the institutional life of the great metropolitan centers—North and South.

From their colonial beginnings as coastal trading centers, American cities were part and parcel of the subjugation of black people that was involved in the worldwide expansion of European power. However, when the northern settlements became stabilized to a yeoman-oriented society, the proportion of blacks in the population declined and there was a dilution of the direct controls over them. Slavery was abolished and some of the civil disabilities were moderated. It should, nevertheless, be noted that legal systems of segregation and jim crow were first elaborated in the pre-Civil War, northern cities, not in the South. As far as the few blacks who lived in the North were concerned, the ideology and ethos of racism were always prevalent, and they were constantly reinforced by important political and economic alliances between dominant groups in the North and the South, except during the Civil War. (Today, the most important form of this *entente* is perhaps the symbiotic relationship between the military-industrial complex and the southern congressional committee chairmen.)

The eve of the great population shifts of this century was the period that Rayford Logan has characterized as the nadir of the black man in American life and thought (1965). His abandonment by his erstwhile allies through the betrayal of Reconstruction had caused a deterioration in his conditions both in the North and in the South. On the ideological level, the rise of modern imperialism with its doctrines of Anglo-American superiority gave racist formulations a new significance. Clearly, the womb of the urban North was ready to nurture its own racist institutions.

Without an institutional base developing in the metropolitan setting, the ideological aspects of racism would have become greatly attenuated, especially under the attacks of social protest and the political action movements. Such an ideological transformation has been very evident in the major cities of the South during the past 20 years. Originally, these cities had a jim crow racial ethos that was compatible with their position as the *entrepots* for a plantation hinterland. Today, they are becoming characterized by an impersonal kind of racial ethos that is increasingly similar to that of the northern metropolises—the southern city, too, has become economically dependent upon national corporations.

The generation of the distinctively modern forms of urban racism operated in conformity with the traditionally debased position of the black man in American society, but it took place within the existing major metropolitan institutional networks—such as the labor market, the housing market, the political system and the educational system. As the black population grew in the urban centers, distinctive, new formations developed in each of the institutional areas. A black ghetto and housing market, a black labor market, a black school system and a black welfare system came into being—not as parts of a self-determining community, but as institutions to be controlled, manipulated and exploited. When the black population did not serve the needs of the dominant institutions by providing a wartime labor reserve, it was isolated so that it could be regulated and incapacitated (Baron 1969, 1971).

Therefore, our model of urban racism has three major components regarding institutional structures:

> 1. Within the major institutional networks that operate in the city, there have developed definable black subsectors that function on a subordinated basis, subject to the advantage, control and priorities of the dominate systems.
> 2. A pattern of mutual reinforcement takes place between the barriers that define the various black subsectors.
> 3. The controls are so pervasive over the lives of black men that they form a system that is analogous to neo-colonial forms of rule.

Procedures and rules necessary for the origination of the black subsectors had to be openly and formally discriminatory. Restrictive residential covenants, systematic violence, and blanket exclusion from better paying jobs were among the instruments used in bringing into being the racial duality of the major institutional systems. Once a black subsector was well established, the formality of the racial barriers could be lowered and, yet, the system could still retain most of its functional efficiency. Maintenance of the basic racial controls is now less dependent upon specific discriminatory decisions. Such behavior has become so well institutionalized that the individual generally does not have to exercise a choice to operate in a racist manner. The rules and procedures of the large organizations have already prestructured the choice. The individual only has to conform to the operating norms of the organization, and the institution will do the discriminating for him.

The fact that the black subsectors exist on a subordinated basis is necessary to make the mutual reinforcement among sectors effective. These subsectors have become the primary basis upon which the racial distinctions are institutionally structured. The second-class outcomes for blacks from any one sector are so strong and enduring because the subordinated subsectors provide concrete organizational forms and procedures that can be bolstered. It is not just attitudes and individually controlled behavior that are reinforced.

Mutual reinforcement among subsectors, criteria, rules, and procedures within any single organization may now be much less based on race in order to have a discriminatory effect. The racial distinctions and differentiations in any one institutional area operate as instruments supporting the segregation and unequal treatment that take place in the other institutions. A particular organization's racist procedures can be hidden under seemingly neutral rules that are based upon the outcomes of some other institutional operation. These outcomes might not have a racial label but nonetheless they have a high racial correlation. A few examples: the school system using the neighborhood-school policy, which, combined with residential segregation, operates as a surrogate for direct segregation; suburbs, in creating very restrictive zoning regulations, or urban-renewal developments, in setting universally high rents, can eliminate all but a very few black families on the basis of income; given the racial differentials produced by the school system, an employer, by using his regular personnel tests and criteria, can screen out most blacks from desirable jobs.

Taken as whole, these racial controls form a pervasive system of subjugation of one social order by another; the nearest analogy is to neo-colonial types of dominance over nations of the third world. Yet, on a day-to-day basis, these institutional formations are characterized by the general kinds of social relations that prevail in a metropolitan setting. The social interaction between the races is no longer defined by clear-cut status. It tends to be impersonal, based on secondary relationships, and often regulated by the mediation of market-type conditions or seemingly neutral administrative regulations. Blacks have often been in competition with other low prestige groups. In fact, competition was encouraged in the use of black workers as strikebreakers in industries where they were generally excluded from regular employment.

Therefore, under the new institutional arrangements of metropolitan racial controls, we find a shift in the ideology of racism and its symbols. Bastide (1957) and van den Berghe (1967) have both pointed to the distinctions between the way dominant groups label blacks in a paternalistic rural order and in a competitive urban order. Under the former conditions, the black person is symbolized as something apart, dependent and child-like, or, in harsher terms, as bestial; he is viewed as being subject to a different set of norms. Under modern, urban conditions, he is now symbolized as deprived, depraved or delinquent. In other words, in the metropolitan social order there is an assumption of a uniform normative system to which the black man inadequately conforms. John Horton has critically summarized this approach:

> whatever is different or distinctive in his life style represents a kind of negative reaction to exclusion from the white society. The Negro is the creation of the white. Like the criminal he is a pathology, a reaction-formation to the problem of inadequate opportunities to achieve and compete in the American system. [1966, p. 711]

Regarding the program implications of this ideology, Sherri Arnstein in her excellent article, "The Ladder of Citizenship Participation," has noted that the pathological definitions of racial problems have often encouraged the substitution of therapy for political contention. Powerlessness is made synonymous with mental illness and

> under a masquerade of involving citizens in planning, the experts subject the citizens to clinical group therapy. . . . Citizens are engaged in extensive activity, but the focus of it is on curing them of their "pathology" rather than changing the racism and victimization that created their "pathologies." [1969, p. 218]

"The liberal administrators' solution to the Negro question entails the expansion of opportunities for mobility within the society and socialization of the deviant (the Negro and anti-Negro) to expanding opportunities." (Horton 1966) Definitions of deviation, pathology and social problems all imply a prior definition of normality, social health and the good society. By defining away the thoroughly institutionalized structure of racial controls, the racial strategies of sophisticated managers (which are similar, be they liberal or conservative) tend to perpetuate that system of subjugation. They assume that there is a united society that can consensually achieve a unified normative order. Their definition of normality is that of modern American white men, who are the unreconstructed product of a 350-year history as a master race. Their definition of the black man is that he is an inadequate white man who only needs to overcome his deprivation. In this process, the validity of black people deciding their own goals is denied.

Ralph Ellison, in his critique of Myrdal's *An American Dilemma*, wrote:

> But can a people live and develop for three hundred years simply by *reacting*? Are American Negroes simply the creation of white men, or have they at least helped to create themselves out of what they found around them? Men have made a way of life in caves and upon cliffs, why cannot Negroes have made a life upon the horns of the white man's dilemma? [1966, p. 301]

The black man has fashioned his own community. Present day articulation of the black experience, black power and black nationhood indicate the growing thrust for an autonomous definition of what is normal and what is healthy. This thrust, rather than the liberal reactions to it, constitutes the dynamic element in the restructuring of race relations in America. The basic mental health of the black community depends upon its ability to define and enforce its own standards of a good society, rather than its members adopting the standards of their oppressors. Therefore, those activities that strengthen the political and quasi-political movement for black liberation (or, conversely, weaken the system of white oppression) are the most significant contributions to mental well being.

The strategy of sophisticated whites, furthermore, overestimates the strength and viability of the established order into which it would increase the opportunities for the inclusion of blacks. Since the doctrines of racism are so widely diffused through urban society, and racial structures are so well entrenched, major changes in racial institutions are upsetting to the overall power relations and balance of the society. The systems of prestige, concession, and accommodation of interests through which the exercise of basic power is mediated in our society have become so intertwined with modes of racial evaluation and subjugation that a fundamental reordering of the position of blacks as a group implies a restructuring of the whole society. In effect, what is at stake is not only the domination of white over black, but also the continuation of the present institutional forms of control within the white community.

Bibliography

Arnstein, S. 1969. A ladder of citizenship participation. *Journal of American Institute of Planners* 35:216-224.

Baron, H. M. 1969. The web of urban racism. In *Institutional racism in America,* eds. L. Knowles and K. Prewitt, pp. 134-176. Englewood Cliffs, N.J.: Prentice-Hall.

——————. 1971. The demand for black labor: historical notes on the political economy of racism. *Radical America* 5:1-46.

Bastide, R. 1957. Race relations in Brazil. *International Social Science Bulletin* 9:495-512.

Ellison, R. 1966. *Shadow and act.* New York: Signet.

Franklin, J. H. 1956. *The militant South.* Boston: Beacon Press.

Grier, W. H. and Cobbs, P. 1968. *Black rage.* New York: Basic Books.

Horton, J. 1966. Order and conflict theories of social problems as competing ideologies. *Amer. J. Soc.* 71:701-713.

Logan, R. W. 1965. *The betrayal of the Negro.* New York: Collier Books.

Myrdal, G. 1944, 1966. *An American dilemma.* 2 vols. New York: McGraw-Hill.

National Advisory Committee on Civil Disorders. 1968. *Report of the National Advisory Committee on Civil Disorders.* New York: Bantam.

Philips, U. B. 1928. The central theme of southern history. *American Historical Review*. 34:30-43.

Riessman, F. 1962. *The culturally deprived child.* New York: Harper §.

U.S. Dept. of Commerce, Bureau of Census. 1968. *Recent Trends in Social and Economic Conditions of Negroes in the United States.* Current Population Reports, Series P-23, No. 26.

van den Berghe, P. 1967. *Race and racism, a comparative perspective.* New York: Wiley.

Who Should Be Studied?*
Elizabeth Herzog

The time has come for some shifts of focus in studying problems of race and poverty. Contrary to custom, this call for change carries no overtones of guilt or blame. Since current demands for change are usually associated with one or both of these emotions, it is in order to explain the unorthodox absence of either, before discussing why some shifts are needed and what they should be.

Why no guilt or blame

A sketchy review of the recent history of research focus with regard to race relations and poverty reveals a respectable record. The forties saw considerable study of prejudice—its nature, its manifestations, its causes, and some possible clues to its cure. One thinks immediately of such names as Gunnar Myrdal and his collaborators, of Gordon Allport, Marie Johoda, Stuart Cook and the Commission for Community Inter-relations, Klineberg, Hartley, Frenkel-Brunswik, and many others. Much of this work was analyzed and synthesized in Allport's book on *The Nature of Prejudice,* first published in 1954. The prime target groups for such studies were the dominant whites in various walks of life—the people who felt, and acted on, prejudice against minorities. The main effort was to document the existence and functioning of

*The essay appeared in the *American Journal of Orthopsychiatry* 41:4-12 © 1971 in slightly revised form. Reprinted by permission.

prejudice and to describe its manifestations. Such documentation would seem to be a necessary first step toward conquering the effects of prejudice and attacking its roots.

Of course, there is always a good deal of overlap between the main focus of one phase and the next. Phases don't end neatly at a single point in time. At any one time, someone is likely to be studying what most people are not studying. However, the late fifties and the sixties did see a considerable shift of emphasis away from those who are in a position to make others suffer because of their prejudices and to enact discriminatory regulations, and toward a focus upon those who suffer from prejudice and discrimination.

This shift was functional. The existence and nature of prejudice had been established—and those explorations did far more than document the obvious. To cite only one example, the whole concept of the authoritarian personality grew out of this phase of research.

The next phase performed an equally useful function: to document the effects of prejudice and discrimination on those against whom they were directed. The Supreme Court decision of 1954 rested partly on the results of research showing that there could be no such thing as separate but equal, because the kind of separation involved precluded equality. By now we have documented and re-documented the harm it does children to grow up as members of a group subject to prejudice and discrimination, and the harm it does adults, and the harm it does those who wittingly or unwittingly inflict such injury—though this last has been less documented. Some generalizations drawn from the evidence are oversimplified or distorted, but the basic and appalling harm is beyond dispute (U.S. Department of Labor 1966; Clark 1965; Coles 1966; Commission on Civil Rights 1967; National Advisory Commission on Civil Disorders 1968; Pettigrew 1964).

The concept of self-hate, which was one product of this focus, was something of an illumination before it became popularized and stereotyped into something of a bane. Another product was emphasis on the concept of what has been called "fate control"—the need of a person to feel that he is, at least to some degree, master of his own fate, rather than a helpless pawn controlled by forces and individuals wholly beyond his influence.

Meanwhile, the war against poverty was declared, and the poor as well as the black came under the research spotlight. The existence and effects of poverty came to be recognized and admitted. We even began to recognize that some effects attributed to being black were to a large extent the effects of being poor (Herzog and Sudia 1967). We still have to recognize that point more fully, but at least it has been brought out into the open.

This phase too was necessary and useful, even though some of the studies that comprised it may have been neither necessary nor useful in themselves. But now it is time for a change of focus and a change of target groups.

Candidates for study

Among those who are demanding a change of focus, either explicitly or by implication, are the black and the poor. They are beginning to rebel against being studied. "We're under the microscope twenty-four hours a day," declares the president of a Negro student council. And an inner-city Negro girl who is one of a select few being bussed to a white suburban high school says, "Now the Negro is on stage, performing before an all-white audience, trying to sway and correct their opinion of blacks."

AFDC mothers, white or black, along with low-income mothers not in the Aid to Families of Dependent Children program, are also beginning to resist the high-minded probings of social scientists. "If you've come to study us," one of them told a research interviewer, "we've been studied enough!" Such a reaction is neither uncommon nor hard to understand. Recently, I reviewed a proposal to send research teams of four or five people, singly or in pairs, into inner-city homes, to observe mother-child interactions and train mothers to develop patterns presumably more conducive to the development in their children of skills basic to school achievement than those observed. (That word "train"—so reminiscent of performing seals—appears with uncomfortable frequency in proposals for improving the lot of the poor and the black.) Other investigators, armed with pencils, questionnaires, and beneficent zeal, are attempting, through carefully structured interviews, to find out how poor families tick and discover ways of helping them tick faster and more melodiously.

It must be recognized that an enormous amount of earlier research involved similar invasion of the homes and privacy of prosperous middle-class whites. Still, it is interesting to fantasy analogous investigations of the nonpoor by welfare mothers and their neighbors. If, for example, welfare mothers proposed to interview and observe the nonpoor in order to help them correct their over-permissive child-rearing practices, would the doors of middle-class homes and the psyches of middle-class mothers be opened wide to their researches?

Leaving that question unanswered, the fact remains that the poor and the black are growing less and less hospitable to proliferating questionnaires and swarming investigators. We may be moving into a rat-bites-maze situation. Resistance of research subjects is an important consideration, but not the only one. Perhaps the most important reason for advocating a shift of research focus is that in order to learn what we need to know in the present phase, we must look at different people and situations, and pose different questions.

The present moment demands answers to such

questions as: how can the nonpoor and the nonblack be induced to share affluence and influence? How can those who profit by the status quo be persuaded to permit change? What gains, manifest and latent, do the nonpoor and the majority groups reap from the very existence of the poor and the minority groups? How can the psychological needs that are satisfied by a position of power and advantage be satisfied in ways that do not demand disadvantage and powerlessness on the part of others?

To say that it is time to study the nonblack and nonpoor is to include a number of groups. It includes diverse segments of the white and the prosperous. It also includes those Echols has described as less prosperous now but having aspirations and expectations toward prosperity (1969). It includes the amazingly vocal "silent majority," and those who give momentum to what has been called the white backlash. It includes blue collars and red-necks as well as purse-keepers and gate-keepers.

It also includes the various categories of researchers and trainers who gain rewards of money and prestige by serving the poor and documenting progress or lack of progress toward our avowed goals. Some of these technicians combine sincerity in wanting to abolish poverty and prejudice with a blind commitment to techniques they have acquired through long, hard years of study and practice, and with a need to foster their own self-image as the model of the technical virtuoso. Such considerations can be as powerful as the enhanced status, influence, and fees produced by our war against poverty. Prominent among candidates for study is the fraternity of social scientists in which I claim membership. The fact that we are members of the culture—and the subculture—to be investigated, subject to its institutions and permeated by its values, suggests that the proposed self-study would require a phenomenal display of intellect, dispassion, and brute courage.

Study of the "haves" would, of course, include study

of their values, manifest and latent. We have been very busy inquiring into the values and motivations of the "have-nots": how to motivate them to earn and to learn, and to learn so that they can earn. If we could really document among the "haves" the full extent to which the money-prestige-status complex dominates our society, it might be as shocking as the documentation we have witnessed of racism, poverty, hunger, and pollution. This is one message that the dissident young are trying to shout into our ears.

A number of voices have been demanding a shift of research focus from the poor and black to the nonpoor and the nonblack, and perhaps they are beginning to be heard. A main theme of the *Kerner Report* was the need to study the white population and effect changes in its attitudes and practices if belated justice is to come to those we are learning to call "black" (National Advisory Commission on Civil Disorders 1968). A parallel theme is equally timely, with regard to those we are now being told not to call "poor." (One agency has recently instructed its staff to shun that four-letter word in favor of less abrupt adjectives—just about seven years after they began priding themselves on summoning the courage to use basic English.)

James Baldwin, in an interview in December of 1969, said, "How violent the situation becomes, how extreme the situation becomes, isn't up to the blacks in America, it is up to the whites in America." (Ludington 1969) John Leonard asks:

> Isn't it time that [social scientists] . . . stop arguing about whether ghetto-specific culture is a pathological distortion of mainstream culture . . . and face up to the fact that unless white America provides black America with adequate housing, education, employment, health services, and access to the "mainstream," our cities are going to burn down? [1969]

A VISTA volunteer writes:

> If changes are going to come, which they are, they are going to be made in one of two ways. The first is if those in power realize it is to their interest to change, and the second is revolution. Perhaps, then, the real role for VISTA is to work with the "haves" rather than the "have-nots." [Kaplan 1968]

Acceptance of change

These voices, along with others that are urging us to shift our focus of attention, speak from an assumption that substantial change is, and should be, under way, but that it must move much more quickly. That the more vocal and active members of a society advocate more and more speedy change is not news. But I think the extent to which this view currently commands acceptance is news, even though the acceptance may be more in word than in deed.

Perhaps one of the biggest changes in recent years concerns our attitudes toward change itself. Through the ages, the older generation has always exclaimed about how much change has occurred and how different things are today. And, in large measure—at least for the industrialized world—their exclamations have had a solid basis in fact.

Nevertheless, we wear our change with a difference. It seems a fair guess, so far as this country is concerned, that not since the revolution of 1776 has so large a proportion of citizens agreed that no matter how much change has occurred in our social, economic, and political institutions—the ones that affect our own lives and outlooks—a great deal more change must happen very soon. Some would define "must happen" as "should happen," and some would define it as "is unfortunately bound to happen." Not all would accept in either sense the statement that a great deal more change must happen very soon. Yet I would still cling to the thesis that—in one sense or the other—more would accept it today than fifty or twenty or even ten years ago.

During the Civil War and in the years preceding it, many people did accept the need for change in the institution of slavery. But, by and large, those who believed that change should or would happen were not the ones who accepted slavery as their own institution. The North was advocating abolition of a Southern institution. The South, in wanting to secede, did desire to change its own political situation, but it was by no means proposing a change in its own institutional system —in fact, quite the contrary.

We, on the other hand, are saying with varying degrees of enthusiasm or dismay that, one way or another, our own lifeways are undergoing drastic change. It behooves us, therefore, to learn more about those who will determine the extent to which changes will be tolerated and tolerable.

The people we need to understand are the ones who must change and must permit change, if we are really to win the two closely linked wars: against poverty and against prejudice. To share means to let someone else have some of what you have. This may or may not mean that the haves would have less of everything; but even if they would have no less material goods or advantages, they would have less of a monopoly on what the have-nots now lack. If we are talking about money, the haves might need to accept less of it—either through taxes or through controlled profits—in order that the have-nots get more than they now do. If we are talking about privilege, they might not need to resign the prerogatives involved, but they would have to give up any exclusiveness to those prerogatives. And this, for some, means giving up part of an ego crutch.

Accordingly, we need to learn what will induce the haves to share with the have-nots. Some say it can only be done through fear. Some say it can be done through demonstrating that the haves also would profit by sharing their prerogatives. And some say it can be done through love, if the love is wise and powerful enough.

The first two motives—fear and self-interest—are by no means mutually exclusive. On the contrary, the fear bred by violent protest in Watts and elsewhere convinced some people that their own self-interest demanded concessions, if only in self-defense. Some of us believe there are more constructive ways to promote change. The optimists today are those who believe that self-interest can promote acceptance of drastic change, even in the absence of immediate perceived threat.

The hope of promoting substantial basic change without destructive revolution draws some encouragement from game theory. For one who is no expert in game theory, it is still possible to perceive a difference between what are called zero-sum games and non-zero-sum games. In a zero-sum game, what one side loses the other side gains. Poker, for example, is a zero-sum game, and so is horse racing. The gain of the winner is equivalent to the loss of the loser. There are games, however, in which both sides can win or both can lose. Some business ventures are of this type, and so are some marriages. The famous "prisoners' dilemma," described by Anatol Rapoport and others, is an example of a game in which both sides win or both sides lose (1960).

Many discussions of low-income Negro families assume a zero-sum situation in which the wife gains the authority and dominance that the husband loses. Closer acquaintance with inner-city family life, however, suggests that when the self-respect and economic competence of the husband are undermined, both spouses lose (Liebow 1967). If his psychological and economic status are enhanced, both can gain. The non-zero-sum situation is also the avenue to success in international negotiations.

Some current collaborations between private enterprise and the federal government have been undertaken in the hope of developing a non-zero-sum game situation. The objective deserves support, although some current efforts to approach it are appropriate targets for study under the proposed shift of focus.

One potential direction for theory and research would be the development of social and economic situations that avoid the zero-sum imperative and cultivate a situation in which all parties can gain, even though not all gain the same amount and not all gains are measured in dollars.

Institutional changes

Such comments lead into the obvious fact that learning what we need to know requires studies that go beyond the behavior, attitudes, and opinions of individuals. It will require, among other things, study of change itself. History and anthropology are the social disciplines that have been most concerned with the processes by which change occurs in a culture. We have not drawn on their potential contribution as heavily as we could and must.

Probably most social scientists would agree that, to a large extent, culture change is likely to be gradual. As Murdock (1967) puts it, much cultural innovation involves merely developing, modifying, or recombining "elements of habit already in existence." But he also points out that some innovations "give rise to elements that show little or no continuity with the past," and that "crises are particularly conducive" to this kind of innovation. As one example in the history of the United States, he cites the social and legislative innovations of the New Deal. Today, some of these innovations are viewed as encumbrances of the past that must be sloughed off. But in the thirties, they represented a daring step forward, away from the hallowed doctrine of *laissez-faire* and toward a recognition that the state is responsible for the welfare of its citizens.

The revolt of the poor and the black—and also of the young—against the role of psychosocial guinea pig may be a blessing in disguise, for it gives new cogency and urgency to the sometimes neglected recognition that social wisdom is not to be sought solely through exploring the psychology and interactions of individuals or even of groups. Granted that we need to study the nonblacks and the nonpoor in order to discover how they can be induced to permit institutional change, we also need to study the institutions and organizations in which, or through which, change must be effected. To some extent, this means studying the individuals who comprise and influence the institutions; and to some extent, it means studying the institutions themselves. Edward Sapir, whose name and memory are magic among anthropologists old enough and lucky enough to have come under his spell, used to say that an institution, once established, has a life of its own, and cannot be studied merely as an expression of the culture and the historical moment in which it occurs.

John Gardner has said more than once that our institutions must have a built-in capacity for change. However, he has not, to my knowledge, explained how this can be achieved. Some of our young activists (and some not so young) think they have found the answer. Just bulldoze away all the institutions, they say, and then we can decide what we want in their place. Such doctrine is a luxury reserved for those who regard anything earlier than 1960 as irrelevant and are therefore unhampered by history. When that ardent innovator, Mussolini, first marched at the head of his forces, he too expected to replace the evil order of the moment with an instant utopia. Yet the system he substituted was neither utopian nor long-lived. Greater familiarity with other efforts to make way for utopia before designing it might mute enthusiasm for the bulldozing approach to reform.

If we are to introduce deliberate change, we need to learn more about the lifeways of institutions and organizations. The subject, of course, is far from new. However, to a large extent, institutions and organizations have been studied more with a view to learning how they work and to improving their *status quo* operations than to effecting change in them. Now change is being demanded, from inside as well as from outside some institutions that would repay a shift of study focus. Offhand, one thinks of determined groups in the Senate and the House, of local governments and federal departments, of social agencies—public and voluntary—of labor unions, universities, school systems.

The proposed shift of focus would include the processes and components of decision-making and of benefits: Who makes decisions? How and why are those individuals in positions to make decisions? What is the basis on which decisions are made and action taken? Who benefits in what ways by what actions and decisions? What are the currencies—including, but by no means limited to pecuniary gains—in which benefits accrue? It would also include review of past changes for whatever light they can shed on ways to bring about needed change with minimum trauma for individuals and groups.

Conclusion

I have tried to indicate the need for a shift of focus from the poor and the black to the nonpoor and the nonblack, and have noted that, by various voices and for various reasons, such changes are being proposed. I have suggested further that the shifted focus must include not only individuals and groups but also the structures and processes of institutions and organizations, and the process of change itself.

The time has come to focus attention and study on those who have it in their power to determine whether change will be constructive or destructive, and on discovering ways to make both the fact and the perception of change tolerable, if not welcome, to the "haves" as well as the "have-nots."

Gordon Allport once applied to social research Bohr's principle of complementarity, drawing from it a comforting thought: although each investigator cannot consider all aspects of a problem, we can overcome this limitation by complementarity of investigators and theorists—that is, investigation of many facets of a problem by many individuals, and pooling of their results. I would add that we can also profit by complementarity through time, shifting the main focus of study and attention to suit the needs of the historical moment.

If the next phase, marked by focus on the nonpoor and the nonblack, has not quite begun, at least it is being demanded. A reasonable hope is that it's waiting in the wings, ready to be ushered on stage.

Yet in hoping for its successful debut, one must also hope that our addiction to fashions in focus—as in everything else—will not immediately convert our currently overworked study targets—the poor and the black—into forgotten populations. There is a fertile intermediate area between total concentration and total neglect. It is stultifying to assume that only stylish subjects and populations should be studied, and that fruitful study can be accomplished only by stylish techniques, so that each phase breeds its own herd of sacred cows. On the contrary, there must also be within each phase some degree of complementarity in subject matter and in method. Here, too, a comment of Allport's is relevant:

> Among our students, I trust, there will be many adventurers. Shall we not teach them that in the pastures of science it is not only the sacred cows that yield good . . . milk? [1960]

Bibliography

Allport, G. 1954. *The nature of prejudice.* Reading, Pa.: Addison-Wesley.
——————. 1960. The open system in personality theory. *J. Abnorm. Soc. Psychol.* 61:301-311.

Bureau of Labor Statistics. 1966. *The Negroes in the United States—their economic and social situation.* Washington, D.C.: U.S. Department of Labor, U.S. Government Printing Office, Bulletin No. 1511.

Clark, K. 1965. *Dark ghetto.* New York: Harper §.

Coles, R. 1966. It's the same, but it's different. In *The Negro American,* eds. T. Parsons and K. Clark, pp. 254-279. Boston: Houghton §.

Commission on Civil Rights. 1967. *Racial isolation in the public schools, Vol. 1.* Washington, D.C.: U.S. Government Printing Office.

Echols, A. 1969. Illusion, deception, pacification; white traps for black leadership. Speech presented at Citizens' Conference on Community Planning, at Richmond, Va.

Herzog, E. and Sudia, C. 1967. Family structure and composition: research considerations. In *Race, research and reason: social work perspectives,* ed. R. Miller, pp. 145-164. New York: National Association of Social Workers.

Kaplan, J. 1968. The experiences of a VISTA volunteer in New Mexico. *Social Work* 13:12-14.

Leonard, J. 1969. *Burn culture, burn.* New York: Columbia.

Liebow, E. 1967. *Tally's corner.* Boston, and Toronto, Canada: Little.

Ludington, N. 1969. Interview with James Baldwin. *Washington Post* Dec. 14:E-8.

Murdock, G. 1967. How culture changes. In *Current perspectives in social psychology,* eds. E. Hollander and R. Hunt, pp. 90-99. London, England and Toronto, Canada: Oxford U. Pr.

National Advisory Commission on Civil Disorders. 1968. Report. Washington, D.C.: U.S. Government Printing Office.

Pettigrew, T. 1964. *A profile of the Negro American.* Princeton: Van Nostrand.

Rapoport, A. 1960. *Fights, games and debates.* Ann Arbor: U. of Mich.

II. the community

Community Mental Health as a Pacification Program*
James M. Statman

> There is no necessity for working social scientists to allow
> the political meaning of their work to be shaped by the
> "accidents" of its setting, or its use to be determined by
> the purposes of other men. It is quite within their powers
> to discuss its meaning and decide upon its uses as a
> matter of their own policy.
>
> C. Wright Mills 1961, p. 177

To be professionally concerned with problems of
social and mental health in America is to take a political
stance. No longer can we remain professionally detached
from the political and social upheavals that surround us.
The rush of events of the last decade has made this quite
clear. No longer can we self-righteously proclaim an "end
to ideology," assert that ideology has no place in the
counseling professions, or maintain the myth of a value-
free social and behavioral science, for such declarations
of neutrality suggest a less-than-critical acceptance of
prevailing social and political values. In a society in which
health, education, and welfare are largely matters of
government policy, and low priority matters at that, it
becomes especially important for those concerned with
the planning, administration, and execution of such
services to critically examine their roles. The omnibus
community mental health programs established in the

---

*This essay appeared in the *Radical Therapist* © 1971 by Ballantine Books,
in slightly revised form, under the title "Community Psychology as a
Pacification Program."

urban ghettos serve real political and social functions both in these neighborhoods and in the society as a whole. In this paper, we will attempt to examine some of these functions so that we may, as Mills suggests, come to understand and control the political meaning of our work.

It has long been recognized that individual mental health is related to the quality of the social and economic milieu in which the person exists (e.g., Hollingshead and Redlich 1958; Srole et al. 1962; Langner and Michael 1963; Peck, Kaplan, and Roman 1966). The problems of individual survival posed by life in the urban ghetto, as well as the tensions generated by intergroup social conflict and rapid social change, surely must take their toll (Klein and Statman 1969). Thus, the comprehensive community mental health approach aims not simply at bringing services closer to the person, or at coordinating and oiling the bureaucratic wheels of existing health services, but also at confronting oppressive institutions within the community. The approach then, is to provide community as well as group and individual therapy; to include what is termed "social action" as well as "mental health" aspects (Peck et al. 1966). Peck, Kaplan, and Roman, in 1966, for example, were among the first to decry the "failure to recognize the potential mental health implications of social action programs or conversely the need to build certain social action components into community mental health programs." While we would agree with this concern, we would add that with the birth of comprehensive community mental health programs, such as the Albert Einstein-Lincoln Hospital project in New York, the time has come to begin to evaluate the social action implications of community mental health.

Such an evaluation obviously cannot be drawn in a vacuum. Indeed, the most general defining characteristic of such programs is that they self-consciously and purposely exist, functionally as well as geographically, within a community. Thus, it is only within the context of the community in process—more likely than not, a community undergoing rapid social change—that they can be judged.

Any evaluation of community mental health programs, then, must begin by looking at the community itself. While there are obviously many intercommunity variations, we would suggest that it is not unreasonable to characterize the urban ghetto today as being in a state of active transformation and rebellion. The movement of black and other minority peoples for liberation has been the most explosive and far-reaching event of recent times. Every ghetto neighborhood has been affected; every block, housing project, and high school has been reached; few have remained unchanged. Within every urban ghetto, indigenous, militant social action has been planned and often executed, changing the social and economic reality of the ghetto as well as the psychological reality of the ghetto resident.

White society has responded to the black liberation movement with both the carrot and the stick. Blacks and other minority people in America have always known the face of white oppression, and the police still patrol the ghetto like members of an army of occupation. Yet along with repression and "backlash," we have also seen "wars on poverty" and "great societies." Indeed, it has become something of a cliché to note that ghetto uprisings, though first met with armed might, are later buried under a deluge of benevolent social welfare programs.

The comprehensive community mental health approach is clearly a part of this white response. As the black movement has escalated in militancy, so too have both faces of the white power structure. (Only recently, as the black movement pushes still further, has the carrot been withdrawn, leaving only the stick.) Federally sponsored community mental health programs are one manifestation of this escalation. Such programs are created in the heart of the ghetto. They influence all the service agencies that affect the community. They seek out neighborhood leaders, open storefronts, and hire community people. Their presence is quickly noted; they cannot be ignored.

The oppression and exploitation of colonial people, whether in Asia, Africa, and Latin America or in the black and brown ghettos of the United States, has, under varying social and historical conditions, operated at many levels and taken a variety of forms. Most obvious, of course, is that oppression is enforced by the occupying police or army, through the club, the dog, and the gun. Here, the message is clear: one must obey or be destroyed by the sheer brutality of the oppressor. However, the use of massive force represents only one means of inducing obedience; it is not necessarily the most effective approach. Indeed, there is much in the literature of social psychology (cognitive dissonance theory, for example), as well as in the history of oppressed peoples in general, to suggest that it is often by employing only enough force to insure compliance that the greatest efficiency—and greatest harm—is achieved. This may be especially true if such force is presented in a form that is not readily perceived as coercive, or that in fact is seen as helpful in intent by both the agents of oppression and the oppressed. The confusion and doubt generated by such covert forms of control make effective opposition difficult and thereby create a form of oppression far more total than that of the armed occupier.* Thus, in the urban ghetto of America today, it is the social worker, the psychologist,

---

*An interesting analysis of the oppressive functions of seemingly beneficial health and social service programs, within the French colonial system, has been provided by Fanon (1965).

and the educator who by playing the key oppressive roles have become the "soft police."

Our paper will focus upon such repressive functions, inherent in the community mental health movement. Regardless of the altruistic intent of the staff, federally funded community mental health programs aimed at the ghetto serve to pacify the neighborhood—to mystify and mollify justifiable outrage and, thereby, to prevent action for meaningful change. Our analysis suggests that by diverting neighborhood concern towards problems of "mental health" and away from efforts to confront the oppressive economic and political institutions in our society, such programs function to maintain the status quo rather than to advance the interests of the community.

Our analysis will focus upon a brief consideration of three interrelated questions:

1. Do urban ghettos need "mental health" or does the professional clinical approach serve to divert community resources from more meaningful efforts?
2. Does the employment of neighborhood leaders as mental health aides or in other paraprofessional job slots serve as a form of cooptation, alienating these leaders from their community and thereby weakening the neighborhood power base?
3. Is it naïve to believe that federally funded social action programs are free to confront the oppressive institutions in our society?

Let us first consider the question of social action. Such programs are usually envisioned in terms of grassroots organizing aimed at modifying oppressive institutions within the community. Yet, the changes in the community's social and economic conditions engendered by such concerted actions are not their sole value, for within the process of organizing, of rising up through struggle, and, of course, in winning, lies a potent form of therapy—a rekindling of hope and of personal efficacy in those long suffering the weight of oppression.

Yet, social action obviously means more than developing civic pride or conducting a neighborhood pep rally. In attempting to change those institutions which oppress the community, one soon discovers that they do not yield to the application of mild pressures or the force of moral indignation, and that such institutions are in fact interrelated in a complex web that imprisons the community. The experiences of the peace and civil rights movements of the last decade, as well as that of the labor movement, are quite clear; social action, if it is to succeed, requires militancy, and whether it is at first directed at private institutions, such as slum housing, or whether municipal institutions, such as the school, sanitation, public housing, or welfare systems, are attacked, the issue must inevitably find the community and the ruling power structure at odds. Why should we doubt this? Obviously, the oppression of the ghetto is more than an accident of history, a bad habit, or a product of malign neglect. Such oppression exists as an integral part of our political and economic system, and will be defended by those ruling elements in the system that profit from this practice. Thus, only militant organizing and action can lead to liberation.

Can we really expect social action projects that owe their continued existence to governmental support to be free to challenge governmental and corporate institutions that oppress the ghetto? How long would local power structures permit their influence to be threatened by a government-sponsored militant opposition? Thus, despite the honest intent of the staff, such programs have, built into their structure, a brake upon their effectiveness, for as social action increases in militancy, pressures will arise within the organization to go slow, to compromise, and to tone down the program in order to save it. Well-meaning staff members will gradually face a conflict between their program, which they have created, nurtured, fought and worked hard for, their jobs, and the pressure for that degree of militancy required for successful social action. To expect that such social action programs will opt for militancy is like expecting an Army-sponsored college peace group to storm the Pentagon.

Our concern, however, is not due simply to the built-in lack of efficacy characteristic of these programs. Rather, their pacificatory function lies in their ability to involve militant and potentially militant individuals and groups in their futile programs. Such involvement leads to a situation in which a federally funded agency is able to locate and, to some degree, give direction to, and control, ghetto opposition. Because the community mental health social action projects will undoubtedly be better funded and equipped than grassroots social action groups, there will be pressure on indigenous organizations to cooperate with these projects. In order to secure needed resources here, leaflets can be typed and printed or sound equipment borrowed. Increasingly, local groups will come to depend on and have a stake in the program. Even if militant neighborhood organizations ignore or oppose the community mental health project, the conflict between groups can serve only to split and confuse the community, and to wastefully engage the energies of the militant group.

The social action aspect of community mental health programs serves as a good example of cooptation. As William Gamson (1969) has noted, cooptation is an important, though subtle, form of social control. This mechanism, which "involves yielding access to the most difficult and threatening potential partisans," (Ibid.) attempts to defuse potentially explosive opponents by incorporating them into the structure of the organization, of the system which they oppose, and inducing them to identify with, and subject themselves to, the rewards and punishments that the organization bestows. Perhaps the clearest example of the cooptive function of community mental health programs can be seen in their emphasis upon the cooptation of neighborhood leaders through the creation of what has been condescendingly termed—paraprofessional positions.

The employment of indigenous personnel in social action and mental health service programs functions not simply to teach and train, but also to alienate these leaders and potential leaders from their community, to turn their energies away from militant social action for the community and towards personal success. Let me cite a rather striking example of such cooptation. During the 1969 American Orthopsychiatric Association convention in New York, a community control dispute erupted at the Lincoln Hospital community mental health program. As the convention opened, several staff members were arrested in a sit-in at Lincoln Hospital, and others were suspended. This dispute spilled over into the convention, and soon became a volatile issue. At the invitation of the dissidents and with the cooperation of the hospital administration, almost 30 convention participants were given a tour of the Lincoln Hospital project and encouraged to discuss the controversy with both clients and staff. On this tour, several delegates noticed a young black neighborhood worker, a militant who had spent time in the South as a civil rights worker, sitting in his office, reading, surrounded by posters of Malcolm X and other revolutionary leaders, seemingly oblivious to the conflict boiling all around him. The delegates expressed surprise at finding him so curiously uninvolved in the dispute. His somewhat annoyed explanation was quite simple. As part of his training program, this young man had been given the opportunity to enroll in a local community college. It was midterm time and so, regardless of the issues, he had to study for his examinations.

Who were we, he added, with our advanced degrees, to criticize him for seizing his chance for success? Although one could only agree with him, it seemed clear that the community had lost one of its potential leaders.

While cooptation can be employed by incorporating neighborhood leaders into many types of organizations, community mental health programs present an especially effective form of mystification and cooptation—what we may term the "psychologicalization of discontent." No one will deny that ghetto communities are in need of improved mental health services, or that neighborhood people will find some value in seeking out and participating in such programs. However, in an environment of extreme poverty and oppression, to focus upon individual problems of mental health is to divert community energies from their primary task—their own liberation. The problem of the ghetto is not one of psychopathology. To convince an individual in an oppressed community that the root of his problem is intrapsychic is to mystify him, pacify his legitimate and healthy anger, and, surely, to oppress him.

Bibliography

Fanon, F. 1965. *A dying colonialism.* New York: Grove.

Gamson, W. A. 1969. *Simsoc.* New York: Free Press.

Hollingshead, A. B. and Redlich, F. C. 1958. *Social class and mental illness: a community study.* New York: Wiley.

Klein, R. A. and Statman, J. M. 1969. Community crisis and inter-group tension: a progress report. Paper read at the annual convention of the American Psychological Association, Sept. 1969, at Washington, D.C.

Langner, T. And Michael, S. 1963. Life stress and mental health. *The Midtown Manhattan Study.* New York: McGraw-Hill.

Mills, C. W. 1961. *The sociological imagination.* New York: Grove.

Peck, H. B., Kaplan, S. R. and Roman, M. 1966. Prevention, treatment and social action: a strategy of intervention in a disadvantaged urban area. *Amer. J. Orthopsychiat.* 36:57-69.

Srole, L. et al. 1962. Mental health in the metropolis: *The Midtown Manhattan Study,* Vol. I. New York: McGraw-Hill.

Community Regulation: Process and Problems*
Gary L. Tischler and Sheila Wellington

Currently, there is a health rights movement astir in this country. Founded upon the belief that health is a right of the many and not a privilege of the few, the movement has gained impetus from the growing anger of a citizenry overwhelmed by the enormous cost of health care and frustrated by the medical profession's seemingly infinite capacity to sustain an archaic, overburdened delivery system.

In the area of mental health, the health rights movement has been supported by both legislative and executive action. The initial thrust came from the Mental Health Study Act of 1955, which established a Joint Commission on Mental Illness and Health to study and evaluate the human and economic problems associated with mental illness and to develop:

> comprehensive and realistic recommendations . . . as give promise of resulting in a marked reduction in the incidence or duration of mental illness, and, in consequence, a lessening of the appalling emotional and financial drain on the families of those afflicted or on the economic resources of the States and of the Nation. [Joint Commission on Mental Illness and Health 1961]

*This essay appeared in the *American Journal of Orthopsychiatry* 41:501-505 ©1971 in slightly revised form under the title "The Effects of Consumer Control on the Delivery of Services." Reprinted by permission.

In the early sixties, President Kennedy, taking into consideration the report of the joint commission, went before Congress and stated:

> Mental illness and mental retardation are among our most critical health problems. . . . I propose a national mental health program to assist in the inauguration of a wholly new emphasis and approach to care for the mentally ill. . . . Merely pouring Federal Funds into a continuation of the outmoded type of institutional care which now prevails would make little difference. We need a new type of health facility. [Kennedy 1963]

Congress responded with the passage of the Community Mental Health Centers Act of 1963. Framed around the principle of responsibility for a total community, geographically defined, this statute called for the organization of programs comprehensive in scope and coordinated in such a way as to assure that the diverse mental health needs of all community residents would be met, regardless of whether they were young or old, rich or poor, resident or transient, chronically ill or acutely disturbed, and irrespective of race, color, or class.

By defining responsibility in terms of the mental health needs of a population rather than those of individual patients, by structuring a program within geo-political boundaries, and by insisting upon the inclusion of citizen groups representing consumer interests in planning, the Community Mental Health Centers Act served as a catalyst which brought the health rights movement into apposition with the political quest for decentralization of authority. In urban areas the coalescence of the quest for decentralized authority with the health rights movement was almost invariably accompanied by increased citizen pressure for community control over human services. Recent crises at the New Jersey College of Medicine (Duhl 1969) and Lincoln

Hospital (Roman 1969) not only testify to the affinity between the issues of health rights and community power, but also underline the need to develop workable and effective models for creative collaboration between the provider and consumer of services. For the past five years, the Hill-West Haven Division of the Connecticut Mental Health Center has been striving to elaborate such a model.

The Hill-West Haven Division

The Hill-West Haven Division is an integral part of the Connecticut Mental Health Center. The center was conceived and planned as a university-affiliated state facility that would be engaged simultaneously in the provision of exemplary patient care, in the training of mental health workers, and in the conducting of research. Believing that a mental health center, which is also an academic institution, has the responsibility for developing new models of health care, the center was organized as a unit system. The autonomy of the units provides an administrative and service grouping which permits flexibility, continuity of service, and the opportunity to test diverse models of care. One of the original units of the center was the Hill-West Haven Division. Supported by a Community Mental Health Center Staffing Grant, the division is the only component of the Connecticut Mental Health Center which provides comprehensive mental health services to the population of a geographically defined area.

The area consists of approximately 75,000 people and includes the Hill neighborhood of New Haven and the city of West Haven. The Hill is the last major inner city area of New Haven to undergo urban redevelopment. Currently, it is in the throes of marked social transition. Families dislocated from other areas of the city have resettled in the Hill, which has also become the major locus for the settlement of immigrants from the rural

South and from Puerto Rico. During the past decade, the percentage of blacks has increased from 12 percent to 32 percent of the total population. Approximately one-half of the Spanish-speaking inhabitants of New Haven now reside in this community. Poor income, unemployment, low educational level, substandard housing, and over-crowding are characteristic of the neighborhood.

West Haven, geographically continguous to the Hill, is a predominantly lower-middle-class working town of approximately 50,000 inhabitants. The city is the largest of New Haven's suburbs and has experienced moderate population growth during the past decade. Its non-white population, some 4 percent of the total, is concentrated in census tracts which lie just beyond the New Haven city limits. West Haven will shortly experience a rapid development of new housing and urban redevelopment. While the city government has begun to plan for physical and social renewal, a dearth of social and health programs currently exists. The community therefore remains heavily dependent upon New Haven based agencies for social and health care services.

From its inception, the Hill-West Haven Division was charged with the responsibility of providing comprehensive mental health services both to the Hill and to West Haven. In meeting that charge, a service model evolved which not only accommodated the essential elements of comprehensive care defined in the Community Mental Health Centers Act, but also facilitated the development of preventive focus aimed at modifying features of the social, economic, and institutional environment which tend to breed alienation, apathy, regression, and power-lessness.

The model holds that service to a community represents a *working alliance between provider and consumer* to—

1. seek out and modify, through research, indirect clinical service, and social action, those vectors

within a community that are harmful to mental health;

2. support individuals in their efforts to deal with life stresses, whether these stresses are internal or external, through the provision of a full complement of direct clinical services which assure ease of access and continuity of care to area residents;

3. develop an effective manpower base within the community with the essential skills to carry out the above tasks through a training program for community residents.

Consumer participation, social action, direct and indirect clinical care, research, and training are each viewed as critical dimensions of service to a community.

Forging an alliance

The working alliance between provider and consumer represents the cornerstone of the Hill-West Haven Division's model of service to a community. However, even if one starts with the premise that the broad policy and mission of a service institution ought to be determined jointly by provider and consumer, there is still an enormous gulf between the two which must be bridged. The gulf is not only a function of disparate backgrounds and attitudes, but also of the prerogatives hitherto assigned the clinician-healer. Surrounded by the aura of omniscience with which societies tend to endow their healers and bulwarked by a special competence gained through professional training and validated by licensure, the clinician-healer has been cast in the mold of a beneficient authority. The authority, couched in terms of expertise and authoritativeness, is frequently used to justify total control over the boundaries of a health care system.

The mental health profession's suzerainty over the domain of the emotionally disturbed has not been challenged seriously until recently. Mental illness is rarely considered a dominant social issue; the mentally ill themselves are unable to organize for political and community action. Therefore, pressure groups involved in protecting the interests of the mentally ill rely heavily upon a membership drawn from the formerly ill and families and friends of individuals who are or have been emotionally disturbed. Membership in such groups, however, is limited because of apathy and the stigma associated with mental illness, thus blunting the impact of interest group pressure which generally applies in the public policy arena. Therefore, the group is forced to turn to the mental health profession for leadership. As a result and, almost by default, the clinician-healer becomes the spokesman for the consumer, a position which magnifies his authority and almost insures that the prerogatives of the mental health profession will be maintained intact.

The health professions have traditionally claimed for themselves the prerogative of defining service priorities and reviewing ongoing programs. The rationale given is that:

1. System overload is prevented through keeping service commitments within reasonable bounds;
2. Personnel are buffered from extraneous outside interference as they work at their allocated tasks;
3. Adequate quality control over ongoing service is assured.

Institutional self-definition, however, is an unfortunate corollary of internal control and accountability and, in the mental health field, has allowed health care systems to limit their psycho-social problem-solving to those areas deemed of primary import. As a result, service gaps were created which led to massive discrimination against the more disadvantaged sectors of the population (Duff and

Hollingshead 1968; Hollingshead and Redlich 1958; Kosa and Zola 1969) and contributed materially to widening the gulf between provider and consumer (Klerman 1969; Ryan 1969).

At this point in time, it is not possible to bridge the gulf with statements of good intentions. Action must be taken. First, the provider must recognize that the consumer—wise in the ways of his own world, aware of the problems inherent in negotiating the institutional service maze, and knowledgeable about the impact of that maze upon both his life space and survival capacity —has the experience, right, and obligation to participate in ordering the service patterns for his community. Recognition must be accompanied by an act which verifies the consumer's role as a collaborator-in-service rather than just as a recipient of service. This can be done through building regulatory mechanisms into the system which guarantee the sharing of responsibility and authority between provider and consumer. These mechanisms not only confirm the alliance between consumer and provider, but also create a set of checks and balances within the system which help control the subsequent emergence of major gaps in service.

From participation to regulation

Initially, citizen involvement with the Hill-West Haven Division was informal. While counsel was sought from community members and numerous grass roots groups about program goals and priorities, neither the authority of the community in relation to the division, nor the accountability of the division and its staff to the community were made explicit. A large part of this was due to the absence of appropriate structures or groups within the catchment. No mechanisms through which social and health care programs could be coordinated or regulated were then in existence. Much of the division's initial energies, therefore, were devoted to the task of community development. Its strategic goals were to develop mechanisms which enhanced the participation of consumers and potential consumers in all aspects of programming and which facilitated the integration of all health and social services in the community. The division, in collaboration with other agencies and various community groups, served as a catalyst for developing an organized community through the evolution of organizational structures which could represent the health and social service interests of both the Hill and West Haven

In the Hill, the first effort was to bring together representatives from the forty health and social service agencies serving community residents. From this gathering emerged the Hill-Interagency Council (HIC), which consisted of middle management and line workers. HIC, in concert with the Hill Executive Coordinating Board, then stimulated the formation of a citizen group, the Hill Health Committee, which served as a forum for dealing with issue-oriented problems related to health and social services. When the Hill was designated as a Model Cities Neighborhood, the Hill Health Committee became the health task force of the Model Cities Program with responsibility for health planning under model cities funding. The committee was reconstituted as the Hill Health Board. Its membership consisted of community residents and agency directors so that priorities for health planning and the delivery of services would represent a collaborative effort. In West Haven, staff participated with other agencies in the formation of a community services committee, which was needed to develop comprehensive plans for all health services—not only for mental health services—and for educational improvement and community organization.

Thus, by the spring of 1969, organized structures existed in both communities which allowed the consumer's role in the regulation of the Hill-West Haven Division to be formalized. The Community Services Committee of West Haven and the Hill Health Board were designated as the consumer groups to which the division would be accountable. They had wide responsibility in the areas of program development, personnel practices, and the establishment of service and research priorities. All subsequent changes in the basic structure and direction of the division were to be approved by these groups, which could also act as initiators of change.

Forging the alliance between provider and consumer was not a conflict-free process. At times it strained the division's relations with the community and with parent organizations. To understand this strain, one must recall the enthusiasm and optimism which characterized the Kennedy era and the social programs instituted at that time. Anthony Lewis (1971) has described the period as representing "a last glow of liberal optimism, a societal confidence since overwhelmed by the appalling problems of war and race and poverty and pollution."

President Kennedy himself (1963) spoke of the mental health movement as "a bold, new approach," and envisioned the centers as "a new type of health facility, one which will return mental health care to the main-stream of American medicine and at the same time upgrade mental health devices."

In taking the preventive and curative mission of the Hill-West Haven Division to the consumer, the staff shared in this sense of optimism and purpose. They also shared in an overestimation of the ability of even the most committed professionals and their community allies to solve ancient, complicated problems. A staff of scarcely over fifty, divided between two communities, was described as being able to contribute meaningfully to virtually every aspect of community life. Despite their exuberance and tirelessness, however, this did not take place. While understandable in retrospect, the failure created a "credibility gap" which subsequently gave the community cause to question both the intent and ability of the division to "deliver." At almost every major interchange between the community and the division—discussing a proposed grant, altering the staffing pattern of a component, instituting a new training program for area residents—a neighborhood person stood up and recalled the unfulfilled promises and dashed hopes of the past.

Upon occasion, the staff's commitment to consumer participation and to social change had worked at cross purposes and resulted in friction within the community. For instance, in the fall of 1967, the division was asked to conduct a series of seminars on sex education by a racially integrated neighborhood group consisting of parents of children attending the one predominantly black public school in the community. Postulating that anxiety over interracial sexuality might have been motivating the request, considerable effort went into the program, which was well received. Two years later, the division was again asked to present the series. By this time, however, *de facto* segregation had become a public issue. The parent group with whom the division was working consisted of several leaders pressing for an integrated school system. As articles on racial imbalance appeared in the press and a racial fight occurred at one of the city schools, the parent group requested several staff members to speak out (which they did) on the deleterious effects of *de facto* segregation on the student population. At the same time, the issue was brought before the consumer board to which the division related. The board, which consisted primarily of representatives of community welfare and health agencies, civic and religious organizations, public and parochial school administrators, the chamber of commerce, the police department, and representatives of major employers, took a position in favor of integration. Before that position was made public, however, the board's chairman, a highly placed executive in one of the town's largest industries, resigned. Some staff members were accused of being "Ivy League puppets" and ruffling the calm waters of the community. Consumer board members were accused of being "hard hats" and of "whitewashing" the real problems of the community. As a result of this friction, other resignations from the board followed. Association with the division's board came. to be considered "radical" by a small segment of the community. This outcome modified the base of support which the board itself could generate.

The parent organization was aware of the staff's zeal and ideological commitment and was willing to tolerate, but not ascribe to, the model of service to a community which Hill-West Haven Division advocated. Its tolerance was severely tested during the "summer disturbance" in 1967 when the division's facilities were converted into a refuge for people burnt out of their homes, frightened of remaining in them, or caught in the curfew. The division was also used as a meeting place for neighborhood groups that were attempting in a variety of ways to be helpful to community residents. As increasing fears of further trouble developed in the neighborhood, community representatives approached staff with the request that they intercede and arrange for residents to be bussed out of the area. The request was accepted. Staff negotiated the donation of two buses from the local bus company to evacuate people into the suburbs. This action was not well received by the city government who charged staff with injecting "terrorism" into the community. Ironically, at the same time that the division was engaged in these activities, another part of the center was being used temporarily as a communication center and staging area for state police—a symbolic testimony to the schism within the institution. In the aftermath of the "disturbance," the parent organization sharpened the lines of cleavage by making it quite explicit that it viewed the stance of the division too partisan, too involved, and far beyond the limits of the staff's professional competence.

The impact upon the division

The impact upon the Hill-West Haven Division of the shift from informal community participation to more formal consumer regulation can be measured in both structural and functional terms. The former involves questions of organization and program, the latter, questions of task performance.

Structurally, the effect of the transition was minimal. That is to say, the division is still organized as it was and still offers essentially the same services today as it did at the time of transition. In the Hill, the major emphasis to date has been upon personnel and personnel practices with the intent of facilitating the selection of employees who seem to have a great capacity to appreciate the needs of the community and to communicate effectively with residents. Additionally, staffing patterns have been modified to include more residents of both communities among the work force. A training program geared to sensitizing all staff to the life style and needs of the poor has also been advocated. Programmatically, concern has been expressed about the current allocation of resources for dealing with the problem of drug addiction.

Functionally, the transition was accompanied by modifications in staff task performance. Since the staff members act as mediators between a health care system and its consumers, the manner in which they respond to an organizational shift cannot help but affect the delivery of service. At the time of transition, four basic response patterns were noted. These included—

1. *Fear and disorganization.* This response pattern

was characterized by a belief in consumer ir-
rationality and the certainty that the care-giving
agent would be turned upon and struck down in
some act of retribution. For these staff members,
consumer regulation was the equivalent of mass
anarchy. They reacted as though things were out of
control and felt that the institutional support upon
which they had previously relied would no longer
be available. Rumors proliferated about rape and
theft in the parking lot. Concern with such behavior
preoccupied the inpatient staff. Sexual and racial
imagery permeated conversations.

2. *Retrenchment and denial.* This response pattern
was typified by an attitude of provider-power and
the certainty that the "tried and true" would be
vindicated. For these people, consumer regulation
was an inconvenience. They firmly believed that no
change in the status quo was possible. On the
inpatient service, control and orderliness were the
topics of the day. Disaffection with leadership was
expressed for having failed sufficiently to educate
the community as to "how things really were" in
the field of mental health. It was generally felt that
had the community known, they would never have
wanted to get involved.

3. *Romance and surrender.* This response pattern
was characterized by reverence and awe of consumer expertise. For these staff members, consumer
regulation was seen as an opportunity, but an
opportunity which could only be seized if they
surrendered all of what they had been. *Black Rage,
The Autobiography of Malcolm X,* and *Soul on Ice,*
were discussed with an enchantment that had
previously been reserved for Hildegard Peplau,
Sigmund Freud, Carl Rogers, and Gerald Caplan.
After all the years of sailing in uncharted seas
with captains who knew little of navigation, the

opportunity was at hand to achieve knowledge and relevance suddenly and swiftly.

4. *Collaborative engagement.* This response pattern was the most common one. It was characterized by an acceptance of the consumer as a legitimate collaborator tempered by anticipatory anxiety. The anxiety stemmed from the uncertainty of whether the consumer boards, in the process of ordering service patterns and establishing priorities, might not also begin to prescribe treatment for individuals. For these people, community regulation was seen as a vehicle for facilitating creative innovation following community dialog. Some concern was expressed that a reordering of priorities might order some of them out of jobs. Overall, however, the group's reaction was positive, although tentative. They reserved the right to judge the outcome on the basis of their own experience.

All of the response patterns noted, except the last, tend to compromise a staff member's functioning and, therefore, have an adverse effect on the delivery of service. In the first instance, the resultant anxiety was so great that it led to a functional paralysis and an abrogation of responsibility which was catastrophic; in the second, retrenchment was followed by a constriction and rigidity which not only diminished spontaneity and flexibility, but also affected an individual's capacity to listen or to hear; and, in the third instance, a dilettantism developed characterized by the absence of a conceptual focus around which work could be oriented and an inconsistent, tentative approach to problem solving with clients.

The first three response patterns described above proved either to be transient or so discomforting as to force the staff member to leave. Periodically, during times of stress within the division or strain between division and community, these response patterns recur, but they involve fewer people and are less intense. Of those whose leaving can be traced to greater involvement with community control, interestingly, the majority held jobs removed from any direct contact with board members, community leaders, or militants.

Conclusion

These are troubled times for mental health professionals. A confluence of social, political, and historical forces has stripped the mystique away from the clinician-healer. In the process, the exact limits of responsibility which he had accepted for dealing with the mental health problems of society were laid bare. These limits proved unacceptable. Change was demanded. The gauntlet of comprehensive care was cast down. As the clinician-healer stooped to pick it up, the armor with which he had chosen to cover himself creaked, thus confirming the need for change. But change has been difficult—particularly since it is perceived as being imposed; particularly since the resolution requires the individual to enter into the realms where he had never dreamt to tread.

In the preceding pages, the attempts of one health care system to come to terms with the call for change were outlined, the rationale for a shift from institutional control to shared authority was set forth, and the impact of the shift was assessed. The regulatory mechanisms governing the operation of a health care system merely provide the foundation upon which the system rests. It is a foundation which requires time to build and its construction is neither easy nor painless. Its strength and capacity to sustain the demands of society in the area of health care have yet to be fully tested. However, the lessons to be learned hold promises for the people we serve and rewards for those of us who can learn to serve better.

Bibliography

Duff, R. S. and Hollingshead, A. B. 1968. *Sickness and society.* New York: Harper §.

Duhl, L. J. 1969. Newark: community or chaos. *Journal of Applied Behavioral Science* 5:537-572.

Hollingshead, A. B. and Redlich, F. C. 1958. *Social class and mental illness.* New York: Wiley.

Kennedy, J. F. 1963. *Message from the President of the United States Relative to Mental Illness and Mental Retardation.* House of Representatives Document No. 58, 88th Congress, 1st Session, February 5, 1963. Washington, D.C.: United States Government Printing Office.

Klerman, G. L. 1969. Mental health and the urban crisis. *Amer. J. Orthopsychiat.* 39:818-826.

Kosa, J., Antonovsky, A. and Zola, I. K. 1969. *Poverty and health.* Cambridge: Harvard.

Lewis, A. 1971. *New York Times* Jan. 18:39.

Roman, M. 1969. Community control and the community mental health center. Paper presented at NIMH staff meeting on metropolitan topics, 21 November 1969, at Washington, D.C.

Ryan, W. 1969. *Distress in the city.* Cleveland: The Press of Case Western Reserve University.

Joint Commission on Mental Illness and Health. 1961. *Action for Mental Health* Appendix 1:301-305. New York: Basic Books.

Advocacy and Democracy: Towards a Research Program*
Robert Ross and Alan Guskin

Introduction

The last few years of urban crisis have generated a new concern about the citizen's role in the planning process. Given the complexity of the issues and the growing sophistication of techniques in urban and social planning, many observers have argued that community groups, especially in low-income neighborhoods, need the expertise of professionals to defend their interests in the policy process. From this perspective, the idea of planners who are advocates for low-income communities has generated a great deal of interest, especially within the planning, legal and health professions, and a great deal of commentary on the part of social scientists, policy makers, and others interested in the inner city. The phrase "advocate planner" is commonly used to designate the role of a professional city planner or architect who is acting as advisor and sometimes spokesman for organizations of poor people or minority groups in the inner-city policy process.

Background: the structural context

The most common justification and argument for advocacy can be gleaned from a document of one of the most experienced and dedicated advocate groups in the

*This is a much revised version of a paper published in the *American Journal of Orthopsychiatry* 41:43-57 © 1971. Reprinted by permission.

country—Urban Planning Aid of Boston. In one of their fund-raising documents, they state:

> Government planning without community participation helps to destroy democratic values. It can produce feelings of impotence and fierce struggles for power and self-determination by those at the bottom of the urban system.
>
> The groups with power and those able to present their case forcefully are the ones reckoned with, while the needs of the poor and the black community are rather easily neglected.
>
> One way to correct this is through the processes which planners are beginning to talk about as *advocacy planning*. The advocate planner tries to make public planning less one-sided by providing special help to the groups which tend to get passed over. [Urban Planning Aid 1968, p. 1]

These assertions were made in a setting of a contemporary urbanism and urban government that is notable for the extreme complexity of factors, layers of organizations, and specialized knowledge needed to make the system operate. The scale and scope of government responsibility alone is huge. From air pollution to rat control, the policy-making apparatus is a maze of bureaucracy and very few specialists are able to make their way through this maze—the demand for those who can is high.

The scope of the problems facing municipal (and other) governments create, in turn, an objective necessity for advance planning. Correspondingly, a decision-making process emerges that takes into account as much of the relevant data as possible. Dependence on computers and various other kinds of social data collection, and the ability to project into the near future (when the policy or program under consideration actually becomes operative), generates very esoteric specialties. Also, the length of lead-times stretches further and further into the future (Michael 1968).

In the face of these developments, the ordinary citizen frequently finds the details of the city planning processes beyond his ken. Passive acquiescence serves as consent for many whose basic interests are more or less served; apathy or frustrated rage (its near relative) is the response of those who do not comprehend the processes or who feel their interests are excluded from the process of tacit representation.

The advocate's role, then, appears to respond to two major themes in contemporary community development and reform. On the one hand, advocacy in planning seems to accept the idea of a pluralism of contesting interest groups in American society as a flawed, but more or less adequate, way of understanding the political process in America. However, it asserts that the poor, black and minority ethnic groups are left out of the process by which other groups contend, reasonably successfully, in order to advance or defend their vital interests. The title of the key document in the discussion of advocacy, for example, is Paul Davidoff's article, "Advocacy and Pluralism in Planning" (1965).

On the other hand, addressed as it is to planning and the provision of services in the inner city, the movement for advocacy suggests another aspect of American political life besides that of interest group contests—namely, the increasing importance of technical expertise in the management of the policy-making apparatus of an advanced industrial society.

In this context, the demands for community participation in black communities and elsewhere and the rise of the notion of advocacy take on important historical meaning. The black community is attempting to gain, from the relatively affluent society that surrounds it, fundamental changes—especially in areas of land development, housing and, of course, education. The demand for participation in planning—for whatever service or project is underway—reflects the black community's view that only it or its direct agents can be trusted with its representation. It was thought that by decentralizing power and authority to the neighborhood level, citizens' interests would, in some cases, be weighed in the decision-making process. A number of obstacles have made it clear that, by itself, this is an inadequate strategy for reallocating power alignments and the representation of interests. Two such obstacles are relevant here:

> 1. When they began attending meetings of various committees or boards, the residents of low-income communities were often manipulable, for the issues were presented to them by experts or political professionals in technical terms which obscured their ability to differentiate between possible alternatives (Arstein 1969, p. 219);
> 2. Community control is a relatively undifferentiated concept, especially in the black community where, because of residential segregation, class interests internal to the black community as a whole frequently conflict.

Moreover, citizens of inner-city areas, like all of us, confront some key problems. For example, until recently, the average time for the development of one type of nonprofit subsidized housing was 44 months. In order to complete such a project in that time, countless layers of governmental and financial negotiations must be undertaken. Full-time work by sophisticated corporate managers is required (Goldston 1969; Alexander 1969). The estimation of traffic potential on newly routed streets, to take another example, is not likely to be in the repertoire of skills possessed by most community activists—especially in areas where schools do not generate high numbers of trained personnel in residence. So the need to put technical ability at the service of what are called "client" populations has emerged from the social and technological trends of the sixties.

Emerging from these insights into the inherent inadequacies of the community control and community action ideas, then, is the notion of advocacy *for* the community on the part of professionals who are responsible to the community, rather than to an agency of the city government or another group. But in order to respond fully to the need to redistribute power, the advocate must address himself to the nontechnical as well as technical problems faced by his community clients, for example, community organization, and education about what he, the advocate, can actually offer. We shall return later to problems that arise in the course of meeting these needs. At this point, it is necessary to indicate what the implications of the advocate planning concept are for American democracy.

The perspective of political pluralism

In the fifties, the most widely accepted view of American power and political processes was that of "pluralism" (Dahl 1967). Briefly, its argument may be summarized thus: since town-meeting democracy was both mythic and inadequate to the tasks of governing a highly complex society, by a process of virtual representation through a variety of interest groups, a system developed by which the individual citizen's interest were nonetheless fairly adequately advanced by the interplay of more or less equally powerful groups. Such groups were, at least, able to veto each other and governmental actions that would be deeply threatening to the individual's ability to survive or prosper.

Of course, this view of American politics came under attack from a variety of sources. C. W. Mills, for example, argued that this horse-trading of interest-lobbyists took place only at the "middle levels" of

(Congressional) power, whereas real priorities, such as the cold war or monopoly expansion, took place among a "power elite" (Mills 1956). E. E. Schattschneider, a political scientist, argued that the process of lobbying in Washington was very much a process of settling disputes between the already affluent and established—leaving out, basically, the working class and the strata below it in wealth and power. (See Gamson 1968 for a review of some of these perspectives.) And Gabriel Kolko (1962) has shown the persistence over time of inequalities in wealth and power, despite various reforms.

In the sixties, it became clear that political processes were not inclusive in their pluralism. For example, groups like the poor, black, and other ethnic minorities did not have the resources to compete successfully in the influence process. Further, it also became clear that as a regulator of other basic processes of an advanced technological state, the quasi-welfare state of the postwar era did not protect the white middle-class consumer of drugs, food, mass media, or, for that matter, air. Advocacy, seen in this light, is a way to compensate for an imperfect pluralism.

As the theories of pluralism were blooming, another generation of political theory appeared that justified the emerging bases of power. This family of perspectives had as its institutional and intellectual base the reform-minded liberalism of the late fifties and early sixties. It was in these years that the theory of the democratic Chief Executive, who should be unencumbered by a stalemated or conservative Congress, was elaborated and celebrated. Building on the traditions of the New Deal and the charismatic residues of FDR, reforming liberalism associated itself with a political style best understood as "deference to the executive." (See, e.g., Burns 1963). The Bricker Amendment, Congressional opposition to trade with Communist nations, and even the controversial Gulf of Tonkin Resolution were all defeated or passed respectively in the name of giving the President "freedom of action."

The development of this deference to society's executives seems to emerge as the social order in which we live becomes more highly technological, and the sophistication—technical, scientific, and political—needed to run it becomes an ever more demanding prerequisite for those who would guide the destiny of cities, states, regions, and nations. This is a commonplace truism but it implies a series of ideological and political developments that seem to form the guiding precepts of the managers of the society and their academic colleagues.

Commanding the height of the public and private organs that make social policy are men who are trained or talented in management. Peter Drucker wrote:

> The professional manager has emerged as a new focus of social order, or social mores, and of individual aspirations. The manager is the agent of economic and social development. . . . For the manager is the carrier of our new capacity to organize. [1959, p. 57]

Among the key skills held by these managers is the judicious use of technical, scientific, and professional advice bearing upon the problems that the political leadership must act or decide upon. The managerial perspective may be seen as another way to "patch up" pluralism. By manipulation of groups from the top of executive hierarchies, groups or interests not served or defended by "normal" political processes may be linked to power. "Experts" within the hierarchy come to stand as surrogates for the contending groups themselves. (See Moynihan 1969, for his account of this process in the War on Poverty.)

The War on Poverty, and even before that, urban renewal, seem to have created a sense that these professionals—sometimes planners, sometimes advisors or researchers—are the key factors in what is called "innovation." Given the complexity of the task of simply maintaining livable conditions in the cities, the expert's perspective becomes increasingly visible and valued.

Recent reforms

A new generation of social programs succeeded the urban renewal and public housing reforms of the first wave of postwar concern with the slums of the inner city. Spurred by the militant civil rights movement and the black liberation radicalism that succeeded it, "community action" of various forms, followed by Model Cities, and briefly by black capitalism, have been the reforming vehicles of the last few years. These programs were generated by professionals and social scientist-engineers who dwell in the middle layers of formal and informal government. Of course, these plans are delivered into the hands of the publicly celebrated executives upon whom the media focus political attention; but their genesis indicates to us the nature of the transformation occurring in fundamental political processes (Moynihan 1969).

Basically, these developments presume that solutions to social problems can be engineered through the application of management techniques—which may be participatory—for objectives that social scientists have identified as "strategic" (that is, objectives that have some decisive impact over a broader range of what is defined by various policy elites as deviant behavior).

As Marris and Rein (1967) and Moynihan (1969) have demonstrated, such programs would probably fail to create the consensus between community and political and business leadership envisioned by the Ford Foundation social scientists in its "gray area" programs; rather, poor people, once in control of some organizational resources, have tended to oppose what they saw as an establishment, despite its protestations of benevolence. Similarly, it is seen to be the case that many of the Model Cities programs will result in little more than the creation of model plans with little commitment to them on the part of the community residents, and almost no hope at all of implementation through a public sector that is financially committed to subsidizing other apparently deserving public needs—like highways, airports, and, through the ABM, defense electronics firms.

And here we have the crux of the matter. Pluralism cannot be considered outside of the context of class inequality. Over time, some will compete more successfully, more powerfully, than others. A combination of wealth and access to bureaucratic bases of power appears to be the chief component of successs in the competition for the resources of the public sector. The same holds true in competition for the scarce resources of technical skills and planning capacity in the society: if knowledge is power, than it tends to flow to the already powerful, defined and utilized in the ways most expeditious to their purposes. This is the political conclusion of processes that have as their base an oligopolistic economy; it is the reality facing all reform effort.

What we have been pointing to is that the movements towards advocacy in a number of professions concern not merely the delivery of more or better service to disadvantaged populations in an unequal society. Rather, the *need* that calls forth the phenomenon reflects deeply seated trends in the development of the social system—trends that some conceive of as post-democratic. These general trends in our social system potentially place great restrictions on the efficacy of advocacy and community action programs. We have felt compelled to raise these matters in the context of advocacy programs, for too often such projects are seen as subjects for the so-called "nitty-gritty" practical problems of the practicing professional. As we turn now to some of these problems—of role conflict, of professional identity, of relations with community clients, and so forth—these trends should be kept in mind.

Roles of advocate planners

A review of the articles and conference material on advocacy yields a series of descriptions of the roles and beliefs they hold. These are presumptive hypotheses, not conclusions, for though they are "informed" observations, they are not based on systematic research.

From the point of view of the advocate planners their actions reflect the realization that it is mainly by means of political and technical advocacy that past and present abuses can be attacked. Also evident to these planners has been the lack of success of past planning efforts to effect equitable change on either a city-wide or specific community basis (Hatch 1968).

Advocate planning can best be defined in terms of the work or role(s) the advocate planners perform:

1. While much of what he does differs in many respects from the work of the traditional planners and professionals, the advocate planner or advocate professional still utilizes his skills as a physical planner or architect, or health planner or psychologist. Along with community members, the advocate planner attempts to develop programs alternative to those being pursued by the city planners or politicians, and attempts to assess the differential costs and benefits of each of these programs for the poor and the residents of the ghetto. This might involve developing plans for alternative highway routes, or advocating the type of rehabilitation program that can be an alternative to building demolition. Given the nature of the city-wide policy

process, this frequently means that the advocate is not merely creating "alternatives," but also is *oppositional* to the existing municipal administration or its agencies (Piven-Rosen Exchange 1970).

2. But one of the basic problems for a planner who attempts to advocate ghetto community interests through alternative plans is that in many communities, the poor are unorganized and often unable to articulate issues in ways amenable to the formulation of actual proposals. As a result, some advocate planners have seen their major task as creating organizations of the poor that could articulate and support the community's concern. These advocates raise such questions as—How do you get people to be involved as model-city program representatives? How do you effectively involve poor people on decision-making boards for planning urban renewal sites? (See Edelston and Kolodner 1968). The result of this community organization frequently involves a confrontation strategy where the community attempts to fight the plans laid down by the city agencies. The oppositional tone of this activity reflects both the substantive inequities perceived by the organizations, and a sense of formal impotence. Also, it is symptomatic of the defensive nature of much of this work: "they" initiate a proposal, for example, a school location and "the community" and its advocates "oppose" it.

The problems which attend the community organization role of the advocate planner are similar to those experienced generally by organizers: the uncertain boundaries of the community, the lack of participation of certain community groups, and the fact that frequently the community's experience has taught it to reject the plans of others, rather than to develop alternatives.

3. Related to the advocate planner's role as community organizer is his function as a liaison-spokesman for his client with city planners or political-bureaucratic decision makers. This role may naturally develop as the next step after political protest and after communities are better able to present a somewhat unified voice. Often, such a role brings the advocate planner into direct confrontation with conventional planning concerned with city-wide issues.

The liaison role may be seen by the orthodox city planners as "constructive" when there is some concern by the city government for developing the ghetto areas. In such situations, the liaison-spokesman role of the advocate planner becomes an important middleman function between the poor and the city's planning department. Provided the advocate is a trained planner, he may be able to talk the "language" of the city planner while being committed to the interests of the poor. This role may be particularly difficult for the advocate planner who may be viewed by the poor as an undercover agent of the city agencies. This problem may be acute when the advocate himself is from a different ethnic background, or when the community is not well organized. A great difficulty related to his being suspect is that in non-homogeneous black communities there may not be a consensus of community interest to represent.

Moreover, the problem of the role of advocate as liaison-contact person is not merely one of perception or trust by the community with which he is working. The process of negotiation, the discussion of "feasibility," the exchange of notes and memos, all these may, in fact, result in *a pacification of discontent* that is grounded not merely in perception but in objective conditions of life. Thus, the advocate may find himself torn between two realities: that of bureaucratic and technical detail, which is necessary, and that of anger and anguish, which is just. A planner who worked with a New York City community for 10 years with little result has commented: "Protest without planning could have done as much."[Piven 1970]

4. Another role that has been performed by some advocate planners is that of the social scientist who collects data to support protests (e.g., abusive policies and actions of government agencies or private groups, census information, surveys of facilities, conditions, and opinions). The particular effectiveness of this role is that it deals with city agencies on their own terms. Thus, respectable social scientists become advocates for the poor (i.e., their clients) with the agencies that are effecting them, and use their data for purposes of changing proposed plans. A peculiar problem for the social scientist in this role is that he may believe he is representing the poor by his collection of data about and from the poor (this is especially true when he is working for an agency that is a nominal advocate for the poor—e.g., OEO, Model Cities), but in actuality, he may be viewed by the poor as not advocating for them and surely not part of them. (See Kaplan, 1969.) This problem bears some similarity to the more general advocate planner problem of being perceived by the poor as establishment agents or manipulators.

Here too, the advocate as researcher faces two realities. Officialdom requires (or sometimes merely wants) certain data for the sake of budgets, proposals to Washington, etc. But the poor and black communities have had little experience with these studies: they say they want action, not questionnaires. The result is frequently quite mechanical: a survey is done that, predictably enough, indicates "the people" want good housing, better transportation, protection from criminal violence, and always, decent schools and jobs. Occasionally, of course, such work will be an important guide to policy that is beneficial to a community: problems unrecognized may be found (for example, infant lead poisoning from peeling paint); population densities may be found to be higher than realized because of undetected illegal subdivisions and conversions; or surface quiescence may be found to obscure deep anger. Nevertheless, even the sincere advocate researcher has most typically had to face the quandary of giving trivial information to policy-makers about the poor, rather than, for example, getting significant "intelligence" back to the community. This latter function has most often been performed by activist students, who have occasionally done tactically valuable investigation of land-holding, political corruption, etc. (The flow of information is thus usually *upward*, enabling elites to plan for *their* objectives with more accurate data than otherwise available. Communities thus served are planned *for*. The opposite of this "surrogate pluralism" would be for detailed data and reconnaissance about the elites and their plans to flow *down,* enabling communities to plan for themselves.)

So far, the advocate planner role has been viewed as that of a physical planner or architect, a community organizer, a liaison-advocate (spokesman) for the poor with government agencies, and a social scientist. Because of the necessity for performing more than one of these roles, advocacy planning seems amenable to team practice, combining people who have all, or most, of the skills needed to carry out these functions. One example of this team effort is the Urban Planning Aid (UPA) group of Boston. The group included at one time faculty members in architecture, city planning, and sociology, and an urban anthropologist, as well as such practicing professionals as a civil engineer-architect, a community organizer-sociologist, a lawyer, and a transportation planner.

Potentially, however, these roles do create some shared problems for the advocate planner. Probably the single most important problem is that of trust by the client group. This relationship probably reaches its greatest test when the planner begins negotiating with the target agency. Since the client usually is a minority group and the advocate usually a white upper-middle-class professional, the suspicion can be considerable—especially if any compromise is proposed. (See Kaplan 1969.)

The client's fears of being manipulated by the advocate planners are further stimulated by existing funding arrangements. If the focus of action is a city agency (e.g., redevelopment) and the advocate planner's salary is paid by another city/federal agency (e.g., OEO, or Model Cities), the clients may feel their interests will be compromised in favor of the "establishment." This role ambiguity may require some advocate planners to prove themselves through a heightened *verbal militancy* in an attempt to prove commitment to the client. The implications of this for relationships between advocate planners and conventional planners, or citywide or regionwide planners, may be considerable. The need to be militant on an issue could lead advocates to reject, for the moment, longer-range issues in order to fulfill the long-range organizational requisites of immediate action and success, even if such desires do not adequately resolve the structural problems facing the community (Michael and Guskin 1969).

Generally, we would anticipate that this need to continually prove oneself may take a large psychological toll on those, if any, who choose to be full-time advocate planners. Along with financial problems, it may also lead planners who are interested in such work to do it on a part-time or even voluntary basis, thereby enabling them to maintain their professional integrity in the eyes of other planners without compromising what they see as the dictates of their conscience. On the other hand, this might lead the less thick-skinned and more professionally oriented planner to not follow these dictates directly but to work on longer-range issues less directly related to the immediate demands of poor communities. Our sense of these factors gives us the impression that the advocate planners tend to be the more risk-oriented, less professionally integrated, younger, and less technically oriented planners. There is some indication that this is currently the case (*AIP Newsletter*, September, 1968).

Ideology of advocate planners

The key factor that may determine a professional's decision to be an advocate planner, instead of another type of planner, probably is his ideological orientation and commitment. In a role (or roles) that is so highly politicized, the planner's values are critical. This is especially so from the point of view of the poor—the main client group of advocate planners.

The most salient value-orientation that seems to be common to advocate planners and the communities they serve is a strong belief in the participation of the poor and citizens generally in decisions (i.e., plans) directly affecting their lives. This participation is seen by some as a right, an end in itself, and only secondarily as an instrumental act for the purpose of making plans more effective. It reflects a commitment to perfect pluralism. Much of the activities of the advocate planner are based on the implementation of his value. Hatch, the founder of the Architect's Renewal Committee for Harlem

(ARCH), states this "participation ethic" most strongly when he says that:

> We must recognize that the salvation of the ghetto and of the nation lies not so much in the provision of a little more goods and services ... but in the new sense of manhood which comes out of controlling the institutions which now make decisions on behalf of black people. ... A respect for these special psychological needs and a sense of guilt at the disservice which the architectural and planning professions have done to the poor underlie the new profession of advocacy—and *it* must be sensitive to the need for black leadership. [1968, p. 73]

The priority placed on "participation ethic" by advocate planners separates them from other types of planners, though nowadays, it seems, many use the participation rhetoric. It thus has important implications for the type of people who will become advocate planners and the type of plans around which advocate planners will attempt to organize the poor: that is, if the poor are to be involved as key decision-makers, then all plans must deal with what the poor consider most important. Given the defensive and oppositional setting of the inner-city communities, their desires for immediate payoffs will be primary. They have critical needs that must be filled if they are to think about broader community-wide issues. Those who, like James Q. Wilson (1963), identify the citywide elite as the bearers of progressive change will see this as "obstructionist."

A second major value-orientation of many advocate planners is their belief in the necessity of some short-range payoffs. While some advocate planners have long-range perspectives, the nature of the overwhelming needs and conditions of the poor lead the communities they serve and themselves to seek as many immediate victories as possible. These victories, in turn, strengthen the cohesiveness of the community. Rather than representing a faulty analysis of the ultimate needs of the society, this belief seems to reflect a major concern for an immediate reorientation of the present urban decision-making processes, which fail to take into account the poor. (It also reflects a need of the advocate planner to prove his worth to his client.)

A third critical value-orientation that most advocate planners seem to hold is a distrust of the established decision-makers in public and private bureaucracies (Peattie 1968). This distrust is probably most evident in matters relating to urban renewal. It is also very prominent in their clients' targets of protest. Most advocates seem to spend a good deal of their time in controversy with such agencies. If they were not distrustful before they began their work, they quickly become so, from an identification with their clients' problems or from their perception of the reality of establishment "oppression." The egalitarian ideological underpinning of these planners' attitudes is, of course, an implicit base for this distrust.

Advocate planners also seem to distrust government bureaucracies because they have been, and are, relatively resistant to change, because they often place major emphasis on organization efficiency rather than on analysis of the clients' problems, and because of the irrelevancy of traditional planning, embedded in these bureaucracies, in dealing with the present social crises. Finally, the high saliency of the participation ethic makes the advocate planner suspicious of decisions emanating from the top.

Finally, advocate planners seem to strongly believe that there is no separation between planning and politics or planning and values. They perceive planning decisions as being made within a context of competing vested interests and value orientation, albeit among only certain sectors of society. The prominent recognition of this distinguishes advocate planners from other types of planners.

Thus, the primary goals of the advocate planners' clients, and therefore their own commitments, are to improve the quality of their clients' community and individual life. This presumably leads the advocate planner to propose, organize, plan and act for the interests of a particular community, as against those of other interests or communities in the city. This is based on a belief by the clients and the advocate planner that there are limited resources in the city that are being denied them and that they need.

The strategies of change that the advocate planner and his clients utilize revolve around the inherent conflict in the interests of different community groups in the city and the need to organize in their own community to attain their own interests. There is also the implicit assumption that the resources they need can be attained in the particular community through the assertion of their power. Hence, there is a strong behavioral commitment to the belief that democratic strategies inherent in the advocate planner/community relationship can achieve the resources that the community needs. The problem with this commitment to a democratic strategy at the community level is that many of the most critical needs of the poor are not related to their immediate community but reflect citywide, regional, and national power centers. Hence, the advocate planners are attempting to perfect a political pluralism in a political system that is increasingly centralized and that has limited its pluralism to only certain sectors of society.

The limits of community reform

An unequal pluralism, technocratic trends, and certain inherent strains in the role and training of planners are the problems delineated thus far. But the concept of professional advocacy for the poor, or any other group seeking redress, must address itself to still other structural realities of contemporary society. Chief among these is that the strategic levers of power for many service-oriented objectives are not located at the neighborhood level. This should not need lengthy explication after a generation of big government, but brief illustration of some key variables will indicate the nature of the problem faced by community planners.

Resource availability in the public sector under present taxation and fiscal policies does not directly depend on the direct actions of an affected neighborhood. Obviously, this applies to the budgetary and legislative process in Washington. The size and scope of the corporate economy entails the proposition that though government will grow, the kinds of public allocations, or the kinds of programs so subsidized, are subject to a political process in which national elites, rather than locally mobilized citizens, are the most important actors. An illustration using one key regulatory agency is the Federal Reserve Board. Its action in raising or lowering prime interest rates, for example, is more decisive on employment and unemployment than almost any Model Cities proposal could be. (See e.g., Delaney 1970.) Similarly, welfare service and urban renewal programs compete with one another in the budgeting process, and they compete as well with health programs, farm subsidies, etc.; that is, they compete within roughly one-half of the federal budget that is "left over" from defense allocations. In turn, defense allocations are the least amenable to public reaction and debate of all the contestants in the federal arena. Community planners have come up against the symptoms of this problem again and again; they design programs that cannot compete successfully in the bidding for federal funds.

Of course, the relevant arena is not only federal: the citywide fiscal situation is bleak. A basically regressive real property tax base is being eroded rapidly, and the bonded indebtedness alternatives are limited and lead to further regressive budgetary practices. Thus, the practical alternatives that are open to even the most progressive city administration are relatively limited. The two pincers—policy set nationally, and limited resource locally—are illuminated and exacerbated by the suburbanization of industry and the way the governments involved have sought to deal with this basic trend.

As industry and middle-class whites have moved out of the inner city, the basic governmental response of the last fifteen years had been to build high speed highways to give commuters access to their downtown jobs, and to give industry needed transport facilities. But the poor family without a car, or the working-class family with more than one wage earner and only one car, have not been serviced with the public transport to take them to jobs or to other sections of the city in a cheap, attractive, efficient mass transit system. In the course of building these highways, housing for the poor has been eliminated, the objective impact of the outlay of public money has been redistributive, favoring the affluent, and industry has been further encouraged to move out of reach of inner-city job seekers. Meanwhile, federal housing programs encouraged segregated suburbs, and public housing intensified inner-city segregation. In this complex mix of policy and basic social trends, it would seem that any given community could have little leverage—even if mobilized and adequately equipped with technical advice.

Maris and Rein summarized the failure of community organizations they studied in this way:

> Since the promotion of a national policy to reallocate services and jobs to benefit the poor lay beyond their scope, the projects naturally emphasized other aspects of poverty that lay more within their means. Any approach to reform must accept some practical limit to its aims, and work within a setting that partly frustrates its ideals. But by

ignoring the wider issue, the projects risked deceiving both themselves and others as to what they could achieve, and provoking a corresponding disillusionment. The difficulties of younger people from the ghetto in mastering the demands of employment, or the insensitivity of schools and social agencies, only became crucial as the resources to provide decent jobs, and training were assured. Forced to apply their remedies without the backing of complementary national reforms of which any wide-spread success depended, the projects could only act as pioneers, exploring the means to implement a policy that had to be undertaken. And even as pioneers, they were handicapped by lack of any forseeable funds adequate to the need. The competition for scarce resources accentuated institutional rivalries; unemployment and the impoverishment of social services embittered relations between poor neighborhoods and any official source of help. Thus, the search for an enlightened, rational plan to promote change, endorsed by the whole community, set out to confront problems aggravated by a vacuum of national policy it could do nothing to fill. [1967, pp. 91-92]

Thus, the role of advocacy planning or any community-oriented strategy must face the reality of its limited resources to change policies and decision-making structures at state, regional and national levels. One of the objectives of the proposed research is to explore the way such constraints have affected and/or been perceived by practicing advocates.

One prediction which emerges from this review is that more and more professionals who identify as advocates will move toward identifying themselves as partisans in an ideological sense. The categories of thought which create such self-identification are likely to be diverse. Some will think in system terms of capitalism and socialism; others will think in terms of national welfare rights organizations and the mobilization of clients on a national, not just city or state level. The struggles for equality and social justice as seen by both the participants and their advocates seem to be shifting from the intense neighborhood preoccupation which has been the case until recently.

What does this portend? The professionals so engaged may very well find that in order to do work in the *general* interests which motivate them, the *particular* neighborhood focus of their work will be deserted, modified or transformed into the notion of national policy focus. Besides the indications mentioned earlier, Paul Davidoff's latest contribution to the discussion of advocacy in planning is a symptom of this shift (1970). From the beginning, he asserts, ideological advocacy was seen as part of the conception of the advocate: the general interest in the client, the planner's idea of what serves it, the program, and the theaters of operations are the relevant legislative, community or media arenas. Ronald Caines, until recently Director of Advocacy Programs of the American Institute of Planners, has written an article putting "national" programs at the "top of a ladder of advocacy" (1970). Recent conversations held with officials of the organization Planners for Equal Opportunity indicate less direct neighborhood work is being done now than they had expected a few years ago.

Summary

Advocate planners are representative of new groups of professionals who seek to redress the imbalance of power and benefit which seems to exclude the poor and powerless from successful competition for public goods. Committed as they are to a strategy of neighborhood reform, this review has observed that there seems to be grounds for anticipating that the constraints of such a strategy will lead them to seek ways to broaden the scope of their work.

Advocacy planning, and the community action programs from which it grows, should be seen in a context which accounts for the reasons they have become the preferred strategies of significant numbers of urban activists and analysts. This entails an analysis of the social and technological trends of recent years which puts a premium on access to technical knowledge, while locating political initiative in the executive managerial structures of government and the private sector.

The roles, values and dilemmas facing practitioners of advocacy were discussed. Tentative generalizations about the relationships between planner and client community, about the kinds of people attracted to advocacy work, and about the political and value orientations they hold (and about the kinds of social scientific information they may use or generate) were formed. The choices which confront the planners concerning research, relationships with administrative agencies and clients, and career choices were discussed. In this review we have focussed on issues which seem researchable by interviewing planners themselves but they do not exhaust the discussion of advocacy planning.

The importance of research on advocacy

The process of social reform and invention is confounded by several factors. The organization and mobilization of interests in contemporary American society systematically favors some kinds of solutions to social problems over others (e.g., attempts to "use" private business to meet social need). Compounding such political or structural factors are cultural and communication elements. Ideas and programs which seem to hold promise for the urban area attract broad strata of academics, liberals, activists, professionals, and government officials who engage in discussion and justification of the new strategies or tactics. Community organization, development and advocacy are one set of these inventions which attract immense attention and generate large controversy, even while little data is available. The proposed research would provide some quantitative and systematic data about an area for which there is no such material available. Beyond the pressing topical importance of such work lie the broader questions of theoretical import about our society:

1. Knowledge about advocacy planning touches upon some of the most fundamental processes of this period in social history. The availability of expertise is of fundamental importance for access to power in an advanced industrial society. This research is concerned with experiments which make such expertise available to relatively impotent groups in the society; such empirical material will permit strategies which are aimed at democratization and reform to be based upon more than rhetorical propositions.

2. Beyond this, the process of professionalization is an obvious concommitant to increasing technical complexity in all spheres of life. Research in this area would explore, in effect, a phenomenon stemming from a revival (or creation) of a service ethic among one group of professionals. We presume it is not different in kind from developments in other service professions. Thus, by exploring the outlook of advocates as professionals and their discontents (if any) with orthodox work, we will be illuminating developments which are very general (Dumont 1969). As young adults who have experienced the ferment of the sixties move into professional and other careers, their participation in social change-oriented work becomes part of the political life of the society. If advocates are disillusioned with prospects for change, or if their experience leads them to different strategies than that implicit in community action, then we will be learning about an important input to the political process of the next decade.

3. With regard to the practice of advocate planning, such research would provide insight into the type of training the advocates have received and, therefore, the kinds of training needs that such new forms of professionalism might require. An example would stem from the organizer role the planner is called upon to take and therefore the kinds of preparation for such roles which could be built into the training of planners.

4. Similarly, the research would reveal what the advocates feel they need in the way of collateral fields of knowledge, other specialities, etc., in order to be more effective. The utilization of expert knowledge quite frequently requires prior preparation. An example might be the need for the development of a manual for the use of community groups on the nature of the city-planning process, city politics, and what the services of a planner actually are. (This example stems from the writers' observation of an advocacy situation in Chicago mentioned earlier. The community organization which hired a planning firm found that at its public meetings, residents interpreted the *firm's proposals* as the city's policies.) Paralleling the significance of how communities use experts are the potential findings about the kinds and sources of scientific information of which the planners make use.

5. Another example of possible practice-relevant findings stemming from research on advocacy relates to the problems of cross-cultural communication. If planners identify this as an important barrier to effective practice, in case follow-up, research could explore with planners the viability of various solutions: training in observation, the use of community people as communication links, etc.

6. Advocacy research will reveal the basic patterns of funding and tenure in advocate situations. By

doing so, it may provide information for important policy and analytical tasks. It would tell us, for example, whether taking on advocate roles is significantly discouraged by the need for it to be volunteer work. When funding is available, one could discover the kinds of constraints implied by different sources: private donations, Model Cities, etc. This latter material leads to another important aspect of probable duties—namely, the political tone and style of the work.

7. A critical aspect of such research would be the kind of political context in which community planning is done. Do the advocates find that most of their work is oppositional and/or unsuccessful? If so, then the strategy of community-level reform must be carefully rethought. Either resources and political pressures must insure the adequacy of the advocate-community participation in city decisions —an unlikely prospect, given the history of the War on Poverty—or alternatives or new combinations of local and national strategies will be necessary. As part of a review of a particular social invention, research would illuminate some of the limitations of that strategy and context in which new beginnings might be made.

8. Returning finally to the advocates themselves, research would give a new, professionally specific set of data about the characteristics of a group of new professionals. Findings which relate, for example, age, experience of the social movements of the sixties, type of training and social background to the exercise of a new role in the society cannot but help to give us new insights into urban development and the people who will be doing it.

Bibliography

Alexander, R. 1969. The marketer in the ghetto. *Industrial Marketing* 10:57-72.

American Institute of Planners. 1968. *AIP Newsletter* Sept.

Arnstein, S. R. 1969. A ladder of citizen participation. *Journal of the American Institute of Planners* 4:216-224.

Burns, J. 1963. *The deadlock of democracy.* Englewood Cliffs, N.J.: Prentice-Hall.

Caines, R. 1970. Advocacy for the seventies will aim at public policies. *AIP Newsletter* Jan.

Dahl, R. 1967. *Pluralist democracy in the United States: conflict and consent.* Chicago: Rand McNally.

Davidoff, P. 1965. Advocacy and pluralism in planning. *Journal of the American Institute of Planners* 4:331-337.

Davidoff, P., Davidoff L., and Gold, N. W. 1970. Suburban action: advocate planning for an open society. *Journal of the American Institute of Planners* 35:12-21.

Delaney, P. 1970. Economic slowdown hampers programs to aid poor in cities. *New York Times* May 21:1.

Drucker, P. 1959. *The landmarks of tomorrow.* New York: Harper §.

Dumont, M. n.d. Remarks. In *Proceedings of the National Conference on Advocacy and Pluralistic Planning,* pp. 23-28. New York: Hunter College Urban Research Center.

Edelston, H. C. and Kolodner, F. K. 1969. Are the poor capable of planning for themselves? In *Citizen participation in urban development,* ed. H. Spiegel. Washington, D.C.: National Training Laboratories Institute for Applied Behavioral Science.

Gamson, W. 1968. Stable unrepresentation in American society. *American Behavioral Scientist* 2:15-21.

Goldston, E. 1969. BURP and make money. *Harvard Business Review* 5:84-99.

Hatch, C. R. 1968. Some thoughts on advocacy planning. *Architectural Forum* 5:72-73, 103, 109.

Kaplan, M. 1969. The role of the planner in urban areas. In *Citizen participation in urban development,* ed. H. Spiegel. Washington, D.C.: National Training Laboratories Institute for Applied Behavioral Science.

Kolko, G. 1962. *Wealth and power in America.* New York: Praeger.

Maris, P. and Rein, M. 1967. *Dilemmas of social reform.* New York: Atherton.

Michael, D. 1968. *The unprepared society.* New York: Basic Books.

Michael, D. and Guskin, A. 1969. The implications for the change-over to long-range planning of the rise of advocate planning. Working paper #2. Second work group meeting on psychological aspects of the change-over to urban long-range planning. (From work supported by a special research grant from NIMH Center for Metropolitan Studies.) Ann Arbor: Center for Research on Utilization of Scientific Knowledge, Institute for Social Research.

Mills, C. W. 1956. *The power elite.* New York: Galaxy Books, Oxford U. P.

Moynihan, D. P. 1969. *Maximum feasible misunderstanding.* New York: Free Press.

Peattie, L. R. 1968. Reflections on advocacy planning. *Journal of the American Institute of Planners* 34:80-88.

Piven, F. F. 1970. Whom does the advocate planner serve. Comment by Sumner Rosen. *Social Policy* 1:32-34.

Urban Planning Aid. 1968. Fund-raising proposal: development of advocacy planning, July 30.

Wilson, J. 1963. Planning and politics: citizen participation in urban renewal. *Journal of the American Institute of Planners* 29:242-249.

The Emergence of Community Development Corporations in Urban Neighborhoods*
Michael Brower

The most exciting political invention in recent years is the Community Development Corporation, or CDC. In the last few years several dozen CDCs have been created in nonwhite urban ghetto neighborhoods. There are also a few in rural poverty areas, and more recently, a few have been started in poor white urban areas. Part of the broader movement towards decentralization and local neighborhood control of social and governmental services, the urban CDC is a multi-purpose organization incorporated, usually on a nonprofit basis, and managed and controlled by neighborhood people independently of any municipal or other existing level of government. This paper examines the economic, psychological, and political climate of the urban nonwhite ghettos, concludes that a lack of power in such areas is a fundamental underlying problem and argues that the CDCs are an important and healthy means of creating social and economic benefits and of developing more power in the hands of ghetto residents. A brief account is given of

*This essay appeared in the *American Journal of Orthopsychiatry* 41:646-658 © 1971 in slightly revised form. Reprinted by permission. The research was conducted while the author was on the faculty of the M.I.T. Sloan School of Management, part of it with support from the M.I.T. Urban Systems Lab, using funds provided by the Ford Foundation. The author has also benefited greatly from association as a consultant with the staff of the Center for Community Economic Development in Cambridge, which is supported by a grant from the U.S. Office of Economic Opportunity.

some of the early CDCs, and some conclusions are drawn from their experiences.

The complex web of problems in low income nonwhite ghettos

The economic problems of low-income ghettos have received a great deal of study and attention, perhaps because they are the most easily quantified. Unemployment runs twice or three times the national average, and underemployment is much higher; together, these problems affect one-quarter to one-half of the ghetto labor force. Thirty-five to 40 percent of nonwhite inner city families had incomes below the poverty level in 1966. Only 3 to 8 percent of Negro males were professional and managerial workers, compared with 30 percent of all employed males in the United States (U.S. Department of Labor 1967, 1968a, 1968b, 1968c, 1969b). Only a small minority of businesses are owned by nonwhites, even in the heart of the ghettos, and these are the smallest and least profitable ones. Capital flows out of the ghettos through white-owned businesses and banks and white-controlled prostitution, numbers, drugs, and other rackets. (Clark 1965; Fusfeld 1968, 1969). Human capital also flows out if the brightest, healthiest, best educated, most energetic young men leave the ghettos.

Similarly, overcrowded and deteriorating housing has been well documented, as have the low quality and scarcity of health, education, and other social services in ghetto areas. (Clark 1965; Report of the National Advisory Commission on Civil Disorders 1968).

Recently social scientists have analyzed the devastating psychological impacts of the pressures and conditions of the ghetto, and the compounding, multiplying effects of prejudice and racism. Kenneth Clark wrote:

> It is now generally understood that chronic and remediable social injustices corrode and damage the human personality,

thereby robbing it of its effectiveness, of its creativity, if not its actual humanity. . . . Since every human being depends upon his cumulative experience with others for clues as to how he should view and value himself, children who are consistently rejected understandably begin to question and doubt whether they, their family, and their group really deserve no more respect from the larger society than they receive. These doubts become the seeds of a pernicious self- and group-hatred, the Negro's complex and debilitating prejudice against himself. [1965, p. 63]

Clark went on to relate the then widespread use of hair straighteners, bleachers, and other ways of trying to make oneself look "whiter," the high rates of homicide, suicide, delinquency, drug addiction, crime, and family instability to these results of injustice, rejection, and enforced segregation.

Black psychiatrists (Grier and Cobbs 1968; Pinderhughes 1966, 1968a, 1968b; Poussaint 1966, 1967) have analyzed the psychological impacts of slavery, racism, prejudice, segregation, and the ghetto environment. Alvin Poussaint in 1966 summed up the then current results:

The most tragic, yet predictable, part of all this is that the Negro has come to form his self-image and self-concept on the basis of what white racists have prescribed. Therefore, black men and women learn quickly to hate themselves and each other because they are Negroes. [1966, p. 420]

Poussaint goes on to point out, as do other students of poverty (U.S. Department of Labor 1969a), that low social class and income levels alone have important negative psychological effects, independent of race. But:

being a Negro has many implications for the ego development of black people that are not inherent in lower-class membership. The black child develops in a color caste system and inevitably acquires the negative self-esteem that is the natural outcome of membership in the lowest stratum of such a system. Through contacts with institutionalized symbols of caste inferiority such as segregated schools, neighborhoods, etc., and more indirect negative indicators such as the reactions of his own family, he gradually becomes aware of the social and psychological implications of racial membership. He may see himself as an object of scorn and disparagement, unwanted by the white high caste society, and as a being unworthy of love and affection. Since there are few counter-forces to this negative evaluation of himself, he develops conscious or unconscious feelings of inferiority, self-doubt, and self-hatred.

From that point in early life when the Negro child learns self-hatred, it molds and shapes his entire personality and interaction with his environment. In the earliest drawings, stories, and dreams of Negro children there appear many wishes to be white and a rejection of their own color. They usually prefer white dolls and white friends, frequently identify themselves as white, and show a reluctance to admit that they are Negro. Studies have shown that Negro youngsters assign less desirable roles and human traits to Negro dolls. One study reported that Negro children in their drawings tend to show Negroes as small, incomplete people and whites as strong and powerful. [Ibid., p. 420]

And Oscar Lewis, after lengthy studies in Mexican, Puerto Rican, and Puerto Rican-American slums, reported:

there is a hostility to the basic institutions of what are regarded as the dominant classes. There is hatred of the police, mistrust of government and of those in high positions and a cynicism that extends to the church . . . a strong feeling of fatalism, helplessness, dependence and inferiority. [1966]

These problems are all related to the fundamental underlying fact that these ghetto residents lack not only income but also status and power. To be a complete, healthy man in our society has traditionally meant being powerful and productive, exercising power, and being respected for one's power. But black men, unemployed or underemployed, unable to provide adequately for their women and children, or to protect them from the violence of criminals or the racism and brutality of police and other authorities of white society, feel impotent and powerless, and this penetrates to the core of masculine self-esteem, identity, ambition, and hope. Ghetto residents who have no savings and own no property have no reserve power for emergencies, no potential for becoming wealthy, or even feeling some degree of financial security. They lack the basic currency of respect and authority determined and measured by a capitalistic society. As one black ghetto resident said:

> A lot of times, when I'm working, I become despondent as hell and I feel like crying. I'm not a man, none of us are men! I don't own anything. I'm not a man enough to own a store; none of us are. [Clark 1965, p. 1]

In the words of Lord Acton's famous warning, "power tends to corrupt and absolute power corrupts absolutely." White middle- and upper-class Americans have been preoccupied with these dangers for centuries, blindly and blissfully unaware that it can be equally valid that a *lack of power* tends to corrupt. The psychological effects described above are the form of corruption that overtakes human beings and communities when they suffer from lack of power over the basic forces and decisions that shape their lives. They develop, in the words of Poussaint, "conscious or unconscious feelings of inferiority, self-doubt, and self-hatred," and feel, as Lewis reported, "hostility," "hatred," "mistrust," "fatalism, helplessness, dependence, and inferiority."

And if a lack of power is corrupting, then total lack of power is *absolutely* corrupting. The person totally lacking in power escapes into a world of complete apathy or fantasy, or he may erupt into violence.

unlimited by any fear of consequences. Writing of the 1964 Harlem riot, Clark wrote:

> The Negro seemed to feel nothing could happen to him that had not happened already; he behaved as if he had nothing to lose. His was an oddly controlled rage that seemed to say, during those days of social despair, "We have had enough. The only weapon you have is bullets. The only thing you can do is to kill us." [Ibid., p. 16]

Collectively, as well as individually, the ghetto residents lack power. They have, or had until recently, no control or even influence over the schools that provide "death at an early age" (Kozol 1967) for their children. Police protection is often nonexistent or blatantly (and sometimes violently) discriminatory against them. Murders go uninvestigated. Dope pushers operate openly, as do numbers runners and pimps. Nonwhite ghettos are unable to procure their fair share of other basic city services, including trash and garbage removal, and street repairs and cleaning. Fire insurance was, until recently, impossible to obtain for many ghetto-owned businesses; theft insurance still is. Playgrounds are scarce and littered with broken glass, their equipment broken and unrepaired.

White middle-class society has traditionally blamed all of these problems more on the black morals, or lack thereof, than on their true causes—poverty, discrimination, prejudice, and the lack of black power. This sentiment is sometimes shared by middle-class blacks, such as the woman who urged Harlem mothers to organize a community group to buy brooms and sweep the filthy streets. Kenneth Clark correctly wrote about this woman:

> She did not understand that it is not the job of the people to sweep the streets; it is the job of the Department of Sanitation. It had not occurred to her to advise these women

to organize to gain these services to which they were entitled. In a middle-class neighborhood, the people see to it that government does provide services. To lecture the miserable inhabitants of the ghetto to sweep their own streets is to urge them to accept the fact that the government is not expected to serve them. But to force the government to provide sanitation and care is an effort beyond their capacity for, in such ghettos, people are so defeated that their sense of powerlessness becomes a reality. They are immobilized against action even in their own behalf. [1965, p. 56]

The creation of community development corporations

Over the past decade or so local leaders in dozens of ghettos have become increasingly aware of these complex interrelated causes, and have arrived at some or all of the following conclusions about cures for their problems, although they would not necessarily phrase them in these terms or this order:

1. A solution to the problems of ghettos and the underlying white racism cannot be found through the escape of a small proportion of the most successful blacks into integrated middle-class communities, leaving behind the vast majority of ghetto residents.

2. The treatment of the economic needs and psychological problems of individual ghetto residents, important though it is, can never bring about a cure for the basic underlying social problems. When the vast majority of residents of an area suffer similar problems, the pathology is social, not individual, and it must be treated as such.

3. Ghetto residents need to wield power, both for what that power will secure in rights and services and for the enhancement in pride, stature, dignity, and self-confidence that comes with wielding power. These changes among blacks and

the wielding of power by blacks will in turn confront, contradict, undermine, and reduce white prejudice.

4. Individuals acting alone cannot obtain or wield much power unless they have great wealth or great charisma. Organizations are needed in the ghettos to develop, consolidate, wield, and enhance power.

For these reasons, during the early years of the 1960s (and in some cases ten or twenty years before that), ghetto leaders built organizations to attack a variety of the social needs and problems of their neighbors. But usually these organizations sought a single objective or a very few objectives, such as blocking urban renewal, fighting gouging landlords, boycotting selected stores or businesses, or seeking jobs. Sometimes these organizations survived and added new purposes, but often they folded after winning or losing their original objectives.

Then in the latter years of the 1960s two other ideas began to achieve widespread support:

5. To attack successfully the many interrelated problems of ghetto poverty it is necessary to make coordinated attacks on several basic parts of the problem at once. This requires multi-purpose development organizations controlled by ghetto residents.

6. Outside funding for ghetto organizations, whether from government or foundation sources, is temporary and uncretain at best, always subject to outside influences and pressures from donor agencies, and likely to be cut off whenever the organization begins to challenge traditional power relationships. Consequently, these ghetto organizations need to develop some permanent sources of income under their own control.

So it was that evolving out of earlier, simpler forms of organizations, because of ideas and understanding such as these, there was born the Community Development Corporation, or CDC. Under a variety of names and organizational forms, the CDCs usually, although not always—

1. are organized by leaders in a neighborhood with a specific geographical area and a specific ethnic (sometimes white) community as a base;
2. are set up as nonprofit corporations;
3. have a variety of economic and social objectives, with the underlying more controversial goal of building power implicit, less openly expressed, and perhaps at times unrecognized;
4. have provisions for considerable local participation in the management and ultimate control;
5. develop and maintain a number of economic enterprises in which the CDC starts with 100 percent ownership and maintains at least a strong minority position, in part to promote development of the community and in part to provide funds for the CDC when profits develop sufficiently.

Structures and activities of community development corporations*

East Central Citizens Organization (ECCO), Columbus, Ohio (Kotler 1968, 1969; Miller 1969).

ECCO, perhaps the first of the neighborhood CDCs, was set up in 1965 as a nonprofit tax-exempt corpora-

*This section is based primarily on extensive field trips and personal interviews. Other sources were newspaper articles, annual reports and other unpublished materials from the CDCs, as well as the published sources cited. Especially useful is the descriptive CDC directory published by the Center for Community Economic Development (1971), 1878 Massachusetts Ave., Cambridge 02140. Since this paper was written the Twentieth Century Fund has published a book by Geoffrey Faux (1971) which is now the best single source of information available about CDCs.

tion to serve an area of about one square mile with over 6,500 residents, about 70 percent of whom are black. It received a donation of a settlement house from a local (formerly white) church, assistance from the National Council of Churches and the Stern Family Fund, and, beginning in 1966, federal Office of Economic Opportunity (OEO) grants that to date have totalled about $750,000.

ECCO's membership is open to anyone in the area over 16, of whom there are about 4,200. Total membership is said to be about 1,500, of whom 100 to 200 turn out for the annual assembly. ECCO is governed by a council of 30 community people, 14 elected by the annual assembly (of whom 4 must be teenagers), and 4 elected from each of the 4 neighborhood clubs that founded ECCO.

The early activities of ECCO dealt with social services and mild pressures on the municipal government: day care, equipment for a tot lot, reprimanding a policeman, better sanitation services, legal services, more foot patrolmen, family planning information, and a Youth Civic Center (YCC) for teenagers. Besides offering recreation facilities, YCC runs job training and placement and remedial education programs. Then, in 1968, the ECCO Development Corporation was set up to promote housing and business development programs, which are now getting under way.

The Bedford-Stuyvesant Corporations (Bedford-Stuyvesant Restoration Corporation and Bedford-Stuyvesant D & S Corporation 1969; Inner City Development Corporation 1969; Kennedy 1967; Tobier 1968).

The biggest of the CDCs, and among the most successful, Bedford-Stuyvesant is also one of the most conservative. Set up by Robert Kennedy in the spring of 1967, it has two side-by-side nonprofit corporations that operate out of the same set of offices in the nation's second largest black ghetto. The white organization, D & S Corporation, has a blue chip Wall Street board and is run by former Assistant Attorney General John Doar. The black organization, Bedford-Stuyvesant Restoration Corporation, has a chairman, State Supreme Court Justice Thomas Jones, and a President, Former Deputy Police Commissioner of New York Franklin Thomas, generally considered to be solid citizens of the establishment.

Financed by a variety of foundation grants and by the largest of the OEO Title I–D Special Impact grants totalling nearly $20 million by 1970, the Bedford-Stuyvesant corporations have an impressive list of accomplishments to their credit:

1. An economic development program had assisted 43 individual Bedford-Stuyvesant businesses in obtaining $4.3 million in financing, with job creation of 1,160 by the end of 1969.
2. IBM set up a new computer cable factory in an old warehouse, which employs over 200 people. According to one news account, many of these employees were formerly employed and were not hard-core unemployed.
3. The exteriors of 1,466 row houses on 35 blocks have been renovated at an average cost equivalent (if done by outside contractors) of $450 per house, with property value increases as high as $1,000 per house, but with a charge to the homeowner of only $25. Previously unemployed residents, 2,235 of them, were trained in painting, carpentry, masonry, and landscaping for this work, and about 70 percent have gone on to other permanent employment. Homeowners, to qualify for renovation, had to organize a block association, in which 50 percent of the residents on the block agreed to participate. A

total of 275 blocks did so and applied for renovation—about one-half of all the blocks in Bedford-Stuyvesant. The lucky 35 blocks were chosen by lottery from among the 275 applicants.
4. Eighty Manhattan banks and financial institutions have been persuaded to set up a mortgage pool of $100 million for home mortgages in Bedford-Stuyvesant. By the end of 1969, 578 people had applied and 286 loans had been approved for a total of $4,468,000—an average of $15,600 per loan. An additional 102 loans were in process for a total of $1.6 million more.
5. Four run-down homes have been purchased for rehabilitation and sale to area residents, and there are plans for rehabbing as many as 200 more.
6. Two "Superblocks" have been created—one completed and dedicated—by closing off a street and putting in terraces, benches, and playgrounds where formerly cars ruled supreme.
7. The corporation has purchased 25,000 square feet of land and secured financing to put up a 52-unit six-story apartment building.
8. An abandoned dairy plant was purchased and converted into an attractive modern community center, office building, and headquarters for the Bedford-Stuyvesant corporations. A shopping center-village will be developed around it.
9. The corporations have run a sizeable Opportunities Industrialization Center (OIC) for training of the formerly unemployed.

Other activities have included training Community Planners, running a TV series for half a year, and planning for a community college, which plan has apparently fizzled for lack of funds.

Despite all of this, and more in the planning stage, questions are still raised about this CDC. The results are impressive, but very small compared to the size of the task. Bedford-Stuyvesant has 450,000 people in 635 blocks, with unemployment of 6.2 percent and underemployment of 28 percent in 1969; both are surely much higher today. Forty-three percent of the families had incomes under $4,000 per year (U.S. Department of Labor 1968b). The scale and clout of what is needed to cope with such a massive ghetto boggle the imagination, and the twin corporations have certainly not yet turned the area around. And most of the tangible benefits so far have fallen to the middle-class home owners of the area, with very little benefits except for some training and jobs going to the vast lower class. Then, too, the organizational structure of these corporations is anything but democratic. Senator Kennedy himself chose and named the men to serve on both boards—not just the board of white financial bigwigs but also the board of the black corporation, which supposedly represents the community. New board members are not elected by the community; they are named by the present board or its chairman. There is thus built-in little direct community participation and absolutely *no* accountability to anyone—except to government grant donors and individual consciences.

The West Side Community Development Corporation (Ellis 1969; Miller 1969b).
Out on the west side of Chicago, in a ghetto including the infamous Ward One, base of both the mafia and Daley's machine, five grass roots organizations banded together in 1968 to form the West Side Community Development Corporation, or WSCDC. In contrast to Bedford-Stuyvesant, neither the WSCDC nor its member organizations were set up by any white establishment figures. Nor have they any white parallel corporation helping to raise funds or provide services. Barely tolerated originally, they are now under fire from

the Daley machine. But they do have one terribly important and impressive thing going for them: they are run by men who represent people of the streets, the poorest, and perhaps the angriest, people of the community.

The WSCDC was formed by five constituent community organizations, several of which are, or operate as, CDCs themselves. There is the Conservative Vice Lords, the outgrowth of a once greatly feared youth gang, which now owns two frozen custard franchises, an ice cream parlor, a pool hall, and the African Lion fashion shop, which promotes a police-community relations program and a black culture and history program. There is the Cobras, 2000 strong in 1967 as a tough street gang but, by late 1968, also oriented towards business development. The West Side Organization (WSO) started in 1964 and since then has placed over 1000 constituents in jobs, organized a militant welfare union and claims to have successfully processed 1,300 welfare grievances. The WSO publishes a regular newspaper, runs a Christmas food program, a drug addict program, a community mental health center, and very successful filling station and McDonald's hamburger franchises. The WSO has a four-man paid staff, large numbers of volunteer workers, and appears to command broad support from the people of the area. The other two constituent organizations in WSCDC, both born in 1967, are the Student Afro American Group and the Garfield Organization, which includes neighborhood block groups, high school student groups, and church organizations. The Garfield Organization owns a holding company named Go Forth, Inc., which operates a Midas Muffler franchise, a supermarket, and a couple of restaurants.

With a loan of $250,000 from the Chicago First National Bank, the combined WSCDC has bought an old truck terminal and some new trucks and equipment. WSCDC has a long-term guaranteed price contract for the supply of baled waste paper to the Container Corporation, which is also providing management, technical and moral support. Half the truck terminal will be used for collecting and baling paper; the other half will be used for promoting distribution of black products. If WSCDC can get the contracts, despite Daley's efforts to block it, WSCDC would like to run a newspaper distribution agency. Other projects are being planned; all depend on raising investment capital.

In an area where a direct effort to wrest political power from the machine may be worth a man's life, these tough people of the streets are trying instead to build a base of economic and organizational power with which to better the lives of their people. They are working in an area of 20 square miles, with a population of 400,000 people. This is almost as large as Bedford-Stuyvesant, and the WSCDC leadership appears to be more directly representative of the vast mass of the people in their ghetto than is the management of the Bedford-Stuyvesant Corporations. Yet, so far, they have received little or no government support and only occasional sprinklings of church and corporate aid, except for that of Container Corporation. So, survival and growth are constantly jeopardized by a lack of adequate funding.

The Hough Area Development Corporation (HDC) of Cleveland.
HDC operates in one of the poorest ghettos in the nation. Its area is about 2.5 square miles with a population of about 60,000. Open unemployment in Hough and other Cleveland black slums went up from 13.7 percent in 1960 to 15.5 percent in 1965, while it was dropping in the rest of the country. At 15.5 percent, it was 6½ times the rate for Cleveland as a whole, and it is surely higher today. Beyond that, as many as one-half of

the people in Hough are sub-employed, according to the Labor Department survey (U.S. Department of Labor 1968a). Median family income dropped 16 percent from 1960 to 1965, while it was rising in Cleveland and the nation as a whole (U.S. Department of Labor 1967).

HDC was set up in 1968 and received the first Title I–D Special Impact grant from the OEO; it later received a second grant for a total of over $3 million.

HDC created Community Products, Inc. (CPI), a wholly owned injection rubber molding plant, that sells to the big auto companies, IBM, and other corporate giants. CPI was not expected to start turning a profit until late 1970 or early 1971 during its second year of operation, at the earliest. But the product is of high quality, the market potential is good, the contracts are coming in, and the outlook seems promising. Half the employees are former welfare mothers. When the operation is profitable, HDC plans to sell part of the stock to its employees and part to local community residents.

HDC's biggest project will be the Martin Luther King, Jr. Plaza, combining a street-level shopping center containing a supermarket, a branch bank to be sold eventually to blacks, and a variety of other black-owned stores, with a project of rental town houses for low-income families above the center. Other HDC programs include the Handyman's Maintenance Services (HMS), which trains hard-core unemployed men and sends them out on maintenance and landscaping jobs, a credit union soon to open, and two McDonald's hamburger franchises. When it becomes profitable shares in HMS will be distributed to its workers.

HDC was started by a black preacher-community leader, DeForest Brown, and the head of Cleveland CORE, Franklyn Anderson, together with forty other outstanding local leaders. On its large board sit representatives of most major community organizations in the area. HDC's achievements to date are real, but still partial, with the full promise yet to be realized. Its experience shows that it takes a long time to put projects together, get them underway, and see them begin to show a profit. Nevertheless, HDC had earned enough support and power by 1970 to weather a storm of nasty criticism launched by one Cleveland newspaper and to come out with strong backing from diverse elements in Cleveland and a renewal of their federal government grant, after passing through a whole series of searching investigations.

Other community development corporations.

For lack of space, I will only mention here a number of the most exciting and promising of the other CDCs. There is the empire of organizations and activities constructed by Reverend Leon Sullivan in Philadelphia (Llorens 1967; Sullivan 1967), which grew out of the contributions of $10 per week over 36 weeks by 7,000 parishioners in his and related churches. Sullivan's projects now include a magnificent shopping center plaza, an apartment house, a garment manufacturing company, an electronics and metals working factory, a nationwide chain of Opportunities Industrialization Centers for training hard-core unemployed, a program of part-time courses for local businessmen, a training school for black economic development organizers from around the country, and an organization for promoting shopping center development in other cities. There is FIGHT, in Rochester (Northwestern University School of Business 1967; Ridgeway 1967), with its subsidiary manufacturing organization and other economic projects. FIGHT was founded with help from organizer Saul Alinsky, and it is militant and grass roots controlled—it has had a series of tough political campaigns in which leadership passed to younger hands in fiercely fought open community elections. The Woodlawn organization in Chicago (Brazier

1969; Silberman 1964), also organized with Alinsky's help, once militant in fighting the University of Chicago, urban renewal, and slum merchants and in pursuing employment for residents of the area, is now turning towards capital ownership and economic development as goals. Operation Breadbasket in Chicago, led by Jesse Jackson (Ewen 1968; *Playboy* Interview 1969), perhaps not, strictly speaking, a CDC, is a nonprofit organization with many similar objectives to the CDCs and enjoying tremendous local participation and support for a wide range of economic and social activities. The Real Great Society in Spanish East Harlem is combining community organizing, housing rehabilitation, street schools for high school drop-outs, and the development of a new clothing business. Operation Bootstrap in Los Angeles (*Business Week* 1967) is run by former Civil Rights activists who will have no part of federal funds and strings, and who are rapidly building up, besides their other projects, Shindana Toys, with considerable help from Mattel Inc., the giant toy makers. Shindana proudly announces that its goal is to overcome Mattel's million to one lead and put it out of business. And there are many, many more of these CDCs and CDC-like organizations, in Chicago and Boston, St. Louis and Baltimore, Washington and Roanoke, Seattle and Detroit, and a dozen other cities at least.

Lessons from experiences with the community development corporation

Some important lessons from this brief experience are:

> 1. The CDC is a workable, viable form of organizing in the ghetto to promote economic and social development and to some extent to develop political power.

2. These organizations can and do vary tremendously in size and in the area of their constituency. At their largest, in Bedford-Stuyvesant, for example, they could hardly be said to be operating in a single neighborhood. The neighborhood impacts of the Bedford-Stuyvesant Corporations, however, can be seen in their Superblock developments and in their promotion of block organizations in one-half of all the blocks in Bedford-Stuyvesant. For such a large area, perhaps it would be better, as proposed by Rosenbloom (1969), to have a single large Urban Development Corporation for the area of the city or even the state, and much smaller Local Development Corporations for neighborhoods.

3. It takes a long time to build up a staff of competent people, let them gain experience, study projects, secure financing, find or construct facilities, hire and train employees, find markets, and begin to operate a new ghetto manufacturing operation. From the beginning date of production, it takes two or three years before a solid profit can be expected (Brower 1972, Brower and Little 1970). Simpler projects and services can get underway in only a year or two; shopping centers on the other hand take longer. On the whole, the CDC will probably not generate a significant flow of its own income during its early years.

4. Most CDCs will need sizeable amounts of outside, probably largely governmental, financing for at least five to ten years and perhaps even longer in some cases. So far, only a fraction of the support necessary for significant success has been made available, and this to only a minority of all the CDCs.

5. Success must be measured by a wide range of criteria, difficult though this is, and not just by some simple economic numbers such as amount

invested, or number of projects generated, or numbers of employees hired or placed, or profits generated. All of these are important. But since the goals are to promote the general economic, social and human development, and, ultimately, the total power available in a ghetto, the methods and attacks must be multiple to accomplish this, and so too must be the criteria for measuring success or failure (Brower 1972).

6. There are very real problems involved in obtaining a high degree of local participation in planning, organizing, managing, staffing and controlling a CDC. The existing CDCs range from being very strongly involved with the grass roots to being practically isolated from them. And there is probably considerable conflict between emphasizing sophisticated economic and management analysis and leadership on the one hand, and emphasizing continuing participation and involvement of uneducated poor people of the area on the other hand. The former is obviously vital, yet as Roasbeth Kantor (1968) has warned, without meaningful participation, part of the basic purpose of the CDC will be lost and there is a risk that the CDC will become just another big bureaucratic business out of touch with the alienated people. She has suggested that all employees of the CDC should be members of it, that broad-scale community participation perhaps should be valued above financial profitability, that common community activities involving a great many people should be sought and carried out, and that in larger areas decentralized sub-CDCs might be used. It seems to me important that these and other ideas be tried out, because meaningful, continuing, widespread community participation in the activities and control of the CDC is one of the most important needs and

difficult challenges the CDCs (and, on a larger scale, all of our institutions) face today.

7. The CDCs alone cannot provide more than a tiny fraction of the employment and the funds for public purposes needed in the ghettos. The ghettos need, as does the rest of the country, a national full-employment policy, and adequate national funding for housing, education, health, and an income floor for every family in the country. Without these programs, no CDC can turn a ghetto around and make it soar and ghetto development is doomed to failure.

8. Even with highly successful federal programs of full employment, family income support, and funding for social needs, ghetto development will *still* fail unless these and other public and private programs provide adequate support for, plan and carry out programs together with, and channel resources and operations through, indigenous locally controlled neighborhood organizations whose underlying fundamental purpose is to increase the power exercised by the ghetto residents themselves.

Bibliography

Bedford-Stuyvesant Restoration Corporation and Bedford-Stuyvesant D & S Corporation. 1969. *Annual Report 1968.* Brooklyn: Bedford-Stuyvesant Restoration and D & S Corporations.

Brazier, A. M. 1969. *Black self-determination: the story of the Woodlawn Organization.* Grand Rapids, Mich.: Eerdmans.

Brower, M. 1972. The criteria for measuring the success of a community development corporation in the ghetto. In *Minority economic development: a revolution in the seventies,* eds. S. Doctors and S. Lockwood. New York: Holt. (In Press).

Brower, M. and Little, D. 1970. White help for black business. *Harvard Business Review* 48:4-16, 163-164.

Business Week. 1967. A self help program stirs a Negro slum. March 25.

Center for Community Economic Development. 1971. *Profiles in community based economic development.* Cambridge: Center for Community Economic Development.

Clark, K. B. 1965. *Dark ghetto.* New York: Harper §.

Desiderio, R. J. and Sanchez, R. G. 1969. The community development corporation. *Boston College Industrial and Commercial Law Review* 10:218-264.

Ellis, W. W. 1969. *White ethics and black power: the emergence of the West Side Organization.* Chicago: Aldine.

Ewen, G. 1968. The 'green power' of operation breadbasket. *Commerce, Chicagoland Voice of Business and Industry* April.

Faux, G. 1971. *CDCs: new hope for the inner city.* New York: Twentieth Century.

Fusfeld, D. R. 1969. Anatomy of the ghetto economy. *New Generation* 51:2-6.

——————. 1968. The basic economics of the urban and racial crisis. Department of Economics, Working Paper No. 2, Research Seminar on the Economics of the Urban and Racial Crisis, 25 November 1968, at Ann Arbor, Michigan: University of Michigan.

Georgetown Law Journal. 1969. From private enterprise to public entity: the role of the community development corporation. 57:956-991.

Goodfaster, G. S. 1969. An introduction to the community development corporation. *Journal of Urban Law* 46:603-665.

Grier, W. H. and Cobbs, P. M. 1968. *Black rage.* New York: Bantam.

Hampden-Turner, C. 1969. Black power: a blueprint for psychosocial development? In *Social innovation in the city, new enterprises for community development,* eds. R. Rosenbloom and R. Marris. Cambridge: Harvard.

Harvard Law Review. 1969. Community development corporations: a new approach to the poverty problem, 82:644-667.

Kanter, R. M. 1968. Some social issues in the 'community development corporations' proposal. Waltham, Mass.: Brandeis University Department of Sociology. Unpublished mimeograph.

Kennedy, R. F. 1967. *To seek a newer world.* New York: Bantam.

Kotler, M. 1969. *Neighborhood government.* New York: Bobbs.

——————. 1969. The road to neighborhood government. *New Generation* 51:7-12.

Kozol, J. 1967. *Death at an early age.* Boston: Houghton §.

Lawrence, P. R. 1969. Organization development in the black ghetto. In *Social innovation in the city, new enterprises for community development,* eds. R. Rosenbloom and R. Marris. Cambridge: Harvard.

Lewis, O. 1966. The culture of poverty. *Scient. American* 215:19-25.

Llorens, D. 1967. Apostle of economics. *Ebony* Aug.

Miller, K. H. 1969. Community capitalism and the community self-determination act. *Harvard Journal of Legislation* 6:413-461. Cambridge: Harvard Student Legislative Research Bureau.

—————. 1969. Community organizations in the ghetto. In *Social innovation in the city, new enterprises for community development*, eds. R. Rosenbloom and R. Marris. Cambridge: Harvard.

National Advisory Commission on Civil Disorders. 1968. *Report of the National Advisory Commission on Civil Disorders.* New York: Bantam.

Northwestern University School of Business. 1967. *Eastman Kodak and FIGHT.* Intercollegiate Case Clearing House Case No. ICH 12H68.

Pinderhughes, C. A. 1966. Pathogenic social structure: a prime target for preventive psychiatric intervention. *J. Natl. Med. Assoc.* 58:424-429.

—————. 1968. The psychodynamics of dissent. In *The dynamics of dissent.* New York: Grune.

—————. 1968. Understanding black power: processes and proposals. Preliminary pre-publication copy of paper presented at the American Psychiatric Society Meeting, 15 May 1968, at Boston, Mass.

Playboy. 1969. Playboy interview: Jesse Jackson, Nov.

Poussaint, A. F. 1966. The Negro American: his self-image and integration. *J. Natl. Med. Assoc.* 58:419-423.

—————. 1967. A Negro psychiatrist explains the Negro psyche. *New York Times Magazine* Aug. 20.

Ridgeway, J. 1967. Attack on Kodak. *The New Republic* Jan. 21.

Rosenbloom, R. S. 1969. Corporations for urban development. In *Social innovation in the city, new enterprises for community development*, eds. R. Rosenbloom and R. Marris. Cambridge: Harvard.

Silberman, C. E. 1964. *Crisis in black and white.* New York: Random.

Sullivan, L. H. 1969. *Build brother build.* Phila.: Macrae Smith Company.

Tobier, A. 1968. Bedford-Stuyvesant after Kennedy. *New York Advocate.*

U.S. Department of Commerce, Bureau of the Census. 1969. *Trends in social and economic conditions in metropolitan areas*, Current Population Reports, Series P-23, No. 27, Feb. 7.

U.S. Department of Labor.

    1967. *Social and economic conditions of Negroes in the United States*, Bureau of Labor Statistics Report No. 332.

    1968a Sub-employment in the slums of Cleveland (Multilith, n. d.).

    1968b Sub-employment in the slums of New York (Multilith, n. d.).

    1968c Sub-employment in the slums of Philadelphia (Multilith, n. d.).

    1969a Perspectives on poverty. *Monthly Labor Review* Feb.

    1969b Employment situation in poverty areas of six cities, July 1968-June 1969. Bureau of Labor Statistics Report No. 370.

    1970. The employment situation in urban poverty neighborhoods: fourth quarter 1969.

Virginia Law Review. 1969. The inner city development corporation 55:872-908.

Emotional Disorder as a Social Problem:
Implications for Mental Health Programs*
William Ryan

The overriding problems in the mental health field
are manifold, well documented, and, at this point, one
hopes, well known. As a beginning point, I will do no
more than list them—the manpower shortages, the
maldistribution of care, the deprivation of care suffered
by the poor and the black, the fragmentation of services
and lack of coordination in programming, and the
continuing uncertainty as to how well, in fact, the
services provided meet the needs of those who are in
distress.

The community mental health center, to the extent
that it is a new kind of institution, is a social invention
designed to solve these problems and, to a substantial
and encouraging extent, it is beginning to do so. There is
some reason, then, to be optimistic. But there are other
reasons to be pessimistic that are, at least to me, more
compelling and persuasive. For every new center program
that is creative and innovative, there are, I fear, a half
dozen that are being assimilated to past practices, that
are, in fact, merely providing more of the same. For
every community mental health professional who is
approaching these problems in an imaginative and in-
ventive way, there are several who are too bound by
their professional identities and ideologies to do much

*This essay appeared in the *American Journal of Orthopsychiatry*
41:638-645 © 1971 in slightly revised form. Reprinted by permission.

more than spruce up and put a fresh coat of paint on their old-model methods.

I would suggest that the difficulty in solving these problems is not so much rooted in what we do, how often we do it, how many of us do it, or in how many places we do it, but rather in the basic shape of our thought processes, in how we *think about* the problems we are concerned about.

We think about and speak of all the new programs we are creating, all the new centers springing up across the land like a new chain of motels; we generate great excitement and heated discussion. Heat, however, is often a danger sign, as well as a source of soothing comfort. And one particularly dangerous source of heat is a short circuit. I propose that there is a short circuit in our thinking about mental health issues. Our thinking and planning is too often based on an equation, with needs on one side and services on the other, but in the hasty calculation there is often a short circuit in the process of translating problems into needs. In other words, when we are confronted with a person or a family whose life situation is stressful or disrupted, and, within that constellation, we detect the telltale signs of anxiety, distress, depression, and emotional turmoil, we make the assumption that we have identified a need for mental health services, an incipient or active case of mental illness, and we leap to the other side of the equation to correct the balance by somehow increasing the quantity of services.

I would like to make several points that bear on this issue. First, I would suggest that we are handicapped and blocked in confronting the basic problems of the mental health field by ideological barriers, by distortions and deficiencies in our viewpoint, our way of thinking, our assumptions about the phenomena with which we are supposedly dealing. Second, I will propose that it is more fruitful and effective to think about mental health under the category of social problems than under the category of medical diseases. And finally, I would like to summarize an ideological analysis of the problem of the mental health of the poor in some detail as an example of how our thinking about issues is deficient and how this deficiency hampers us in the development of appropriate programs.

Defining a social problem is not so simple as it may seem, as John Seeley has pointed out in his essay "The problem of social problems" (1967). To ask, "What is a social problem?" may seem to be posing an ingenuous question, until one confronts its opposite: "What human problem is *not* a social problem?" Since any problem in which people are involved is social, why do we reserve the label for some problems and withhold it from others? To use Seeley's example, why is crime called a social problem and why is university administration not? The phenomenon we study is bound by the act of definition. It becomes a social problem only by being so considered —in Seeley's words, *"naming* it as a problem, after naming it as a *problem."*

It is only recently, for example, that we have begun to *name* the rather large quantity of people on earth as the *problem* of overpopulation, or the population explosion. Before the 1930s, the most anti-Semitic German was unaware that Germany had a "Jewish problem." It took the Nazis to *name* the simple existence of Jews in the Third Reich as a "social problem," and the act of naming, that definition, carried inexorably within its terms the shape of the final solution.

We have removed "immigration" from our list of social problems (after executing the inherent solution of choking off the flow of immigrants) and have added "urbanization." Nowadays, we define men out of work as the social problem of "unemployment," rather than, as in Elizabethan times, as "idleness." In the near future, if we are to credit the prophets of automation technology, the label "unemployment" will fade away and "idleness" will begin again to raise its lazy head, now renamed as the "leisure-time problem."

In addition to the first issue of what is and what is not a social problem, there are additional issues of what *causes* social problems and, then, perhaps most important, what do we do about them. Generally speaking, in American social thought, the cause is attributed to special, individual characteristics, and the proposed cure usually involves changing the individual affected. For example, C. Wright Mills has analyzed the ideology of those who write about social problems and demonstrated its relationship to class interest and the preservation of the existent social order (1943). By sifting the material in thirty-one widely used textbooks on "social problems," "social pathology," and "social disorganization," Mills was able to demonstrate a pervasive, coherent ideology with a number of common characteristics. First, the textbooks present material about these problems in simple, descriptive terms, each problem unrelated to the others, and none related in any meaningful way to other aspects of the social environment. Second, the problems are selected and described largely in relation to predetermined norms. Poverty is a problem in that it deviates from the standard of economic self-sufficiency; divorce is a problem because the family is supposed to remain intact. The norms themselves are taken as givens, and no effort is made to examine them, nor is there any thought given to the manner in which norms might themselves contribute to the development of the problems. In a society in which everyone is assumed and expected to be economically self-sufficient, as an example, doesn't economic dependence almost automatically mean poverty? No attention is given to such issues. Within such a framework, then, deviation from norms and standards comes to be defined as failed or incomplete socialization—individuals haven't learned the standards and rules or haven't learned how to keep them. A final, variant theme is that of adjustment or adaptation. Those with social problems are viewed as unable or unwilling to adjust to society's standards, which are narrowly conceived of as the standards of what Mills calls "independent middle class persons verbally living out Protestant ideas in small town America." This is, of course, a precise description of the social origins and status of almost every one of the authors of these textbooks.

By defining social problems in this way, the social pathologists are, of course, ignoring a whole set of factors that might ordinarily be considered as relevant, such as income differences, social stratification, political struggle, ethnic and racial group conflict, and inequality of power. This ideology concentrates almost exclusively on the failure of the deviant. To the extent that society plays any part in social problems, it is said somehow to have failed to socialize the individual, to teach him how to adjust to circumstances, which, though far from perfect, are gradually changing for the better.

This ideology, identified by Mills as the predominant tool used in *analyzing* social problems, also saturates the majority of programs that have been developed to *solve* social problems in America. These programs are based on the assumption that *individuals* "have" social problems as a result of some kind of unusual circumstances—accident, illness, personal defect or handicap, character flaw or maladjustment—that exclude them from the ordinary mechanisms for maintaining and advancing themselves. For example, the prevalent belief in America is that, under ordinary circumstances, everyone can obtain sufficient income for the necessities of life. Those who are unable to do so are special, deviant cases—persons who, for one reason or another, are unable to adapt themselves to the generally satisfactory income-producing system.

In America, health care, too, has been predominantly a matter of particular remedial attention provided individually to the more or less random group of persons who have become ill, whose bodily functioning has become deviant and abnormal. In the field of mental health, the same approach has been, and continues to be, dominant. The social problem of mental disease has been viewed as a collection of individual cases of deviants, persons who—through unusual hereditary taint, or exceptional distortion of character—have become unfit for the normal activities of ordinary life.

It has been the dominant style in American social welfare and health thinking, then, to treat what we call social problems, such as poverty, disease, and mental illness, in terms of the individual deviance of the special, unusual groups of persons who have those problems. There has also been a competing style, much less common, however, not at all congruent with the prevalent ideology, subordinate, but continually developing parallel to the dominant style. Adherents of this approach tend to search for causes in the community and the environment rather than for individual defects, to emphasize predictability and usualness rather than random deviance, to think about preventing rather than merely repairing or treating, to see social problems, in a word, as social.

In the field of disease, we have the public health approach, whose practitioners sought the cause of disease in environmental factors such as the water supply, the sewage system, and the quality of housing conditions. They set out to prevent disease, not in individuals, but in the total population, through improved sanitation, inoculation against communicable disease, and the policing of housing conditions. In the field of income maintenance, this secondary style of solving social problems focused on poverty as a predictable event, on continual income deficiency, and on the development of usual, generalized programs affecting total groups. Rather than trying to fit the aged worker ending his occupational career into some kind of special case, those who practiced this secondary style assumed that a 65-year-old man should expect to retire from the world of work and have the security of an old-age pension. This was viewed as usual and normal—something to be arranged through governmental activity in the social field.

These two approaches to the solution of social problems have existed side by side, the former always dominant, but the latter gradually expanding, slowly becoming more and more prevalent.

Elsewhere (Ryan 1969, 1970), I have proposed the dimension of *exceptionalism-universalism* as the ideological underpinning for these two contrasting approaches to the analysis and solution of social problems. The *exceptionalist* viewpoint is reflected in arrangements that are private, voluntary, remedial, special, local, and exclusive. Such arrangements imply that problems occur to specially-defined categories of persons in an unpredictable manner. The problems are unusual, even unique; they are exceptions to the rule; they occur as a result of individual defect, accident, or unfortunate circumstance, and must be remedied by means that are particular and, as it were, tailored to the individual case.

The *universalistic* viewpoint, on the other hand, is reflected in arrangements that are public, legislated, promotive or preventive, general, national, and inclusive. Inherent in such a viewpoint is the idea that social problems are a function of the social arrangements of the community or the society and that, since these social arrangements are quite imperfect and inequitable, such problems are both predictable, and, more important, preventable through public action. They are not unique to the individual, and their encompassing of individual persons does not imply that those persons are themselves defective or abnormal.

Fluoridation is universalistic; it is aimed at preventing

caries in the total population; oral surgery is exceptionalistic, designed to remedy the special cases of infection or neglect that damage the teeth of an individual. Birth control is universalistic; abortion exceptionalistic. It has been said that, in ocean travel, navigational aids have saved far more lives than have rescue devices, no matter how refined. The compass, then, is universalistic, while the lifeboat is exceptionalistic.

The similarity between exceptionalism and what Mills called the "ideology of social pathologists" is readily apparent. Indeed, the ideological potential of the exceptionalist viewpoint is unusually great. If one is inclined to explain all instances of deviance, all social problems, all occasions for providing help to others as the result of unusual circumstances, defect, or accident, one is unlikely to pursue any generalized inquiries about social inequalities.

This is not to devalue valid exceptionalistic services. Despite fluoridation, there will be instances of caries and gum disease that require attention; despite excellent prenatal care, handicapped children will occasionally be born; husbands will doubtless continue to die suddenly at early ages, leaving widows and orphans in need. And at any given moment, the end products of society's malfunctioning—the miseducated teenager, the unskilled adult laborer, the child who is brain-damaged as a result of prenatal neglect—will require service that is predominantly exceptionalistic in nature.

Generally speaking, mental health services have, in the past, been organized and arranged in an exceptionalistic fashion. This would be perfectly appropriate if we considered mental illness an illness—a genuine disease—and further, viewed it as a disease of mysterious and unpredictable proportions. Given the tremendous quantities of evidence amassed in recent years that suggest the conclusion that emotional disorder is, rather, a social problem, with a relatively predictable pattern of incidence, one would argue that mental health services should be organized in a universalistic fashion. What would that mean?

First, it would mean less and less reliance on the private, voluntary sector, and much heavier emphasis on public programs based on clear legislative sanctions. Second, it would require an expansion of scope so that mental health programs would concern themselves not merely with remedial treatment activities directed toward a special, unusual, deviant population, but rather with preventive efforts directed toward an entire population. It would also mean that the group taking responsibility for planning and decision-making with respect to the organization of services would be expanded in a parallel fashion so that the community as a whole, through some type of representative mechanism, would have the responsibility and the power to decide the form, structure, and priorities of mental health programs.

In summary, mental health services must be carried out with a substantial—and dominant—role being played by the public agency. They must be carried out within a framework of clearly defined planning structures strongly rooted in relevant and effective legislation. They must be carried out with the explicit aim of providing a coverage program to a total population rather than simply giving isolated services to small, special subgroups suffering from specific disorders. They must be planned and implemented with the involvement and participation of ever-increasing segments of the total population, particularly those from low-income and minority neighborhoods and those who have been, or might expect to be, consumers of the services. They must be oriented more toward preventive activities rather than being limited to remedial and rehabilitative programs for those who have already fallen victim to mental illness.

The greatest degree of readiness to view emotional disorder as a social problem is found among those who have concerned themselves with the mental health of the poor. In observing the growing interest in the relationship between poverty and mental health, which has been particularly evident over the past seven or eight years, my own mood has ranged from exhilarated gratification, through puzzlement, to a growing sense of concern and dismay. I see signs that the mental health approach to the problems of the poor is being gradually fitted into the same mold that contains and cripples most other approaches to the poor. The central event in this constraining and crippling process is conceptual or, rather, ideological, what I have called elsewhere "blaming the victim."

Briefly, "blaming the victim" is an intellectual process whereby a social problem is analyzed in such a way that the causation is found to be in the qualities and characteristics of the victim rather than in any deficiencies or structural defects in his environment. However, it is usually found that these characteristics are not inherent or genetic, but are, rather, socially determined. They are stigmas of social origin and are, therefore, no fault of the victim himself. He is to be pitied, not censured; nevertheless, his problems are to be defined as rooted basically in his own characteristics. Some of the common stigmas of social origin that are used to blame the victim are the concept of cultural deprivation as an explanation for the failures of ghetto schools to educate poor and black children, and the concept of the crumbling Negro family as a basic explanation of the persistence of inequality between blacks and whites in America today. "Blaming the victim" is differentiated from old-fashioned conservative ideological formulations, such as Social Darwinism, racial inferiority, and quasi-Calvinist notions of the prospering elect. It is a liberal ideology.

The theoretical—or, more properly, ideological—formulations that are beginning to attain dominance in considerations of the mental health of the poor, show unmistakable family resemblances to the culture of poverty cult and the other victim-blaming ideologies.

Consider this statement attempting to formulate a rational for the relationship between low social class and high rates of emotional disturbance:

> the low SES* has (1) a weak superego, (2) a weak ego, with lack of control or frustration tolerence, (3) a negative, distrustful, suspicious character with poor interpersonal relationships, (4) strong feelings of inferiority, low self-esteem, fear of ridicule and (5) a tendency to act out problems, with violent expression of hostility and extrapunitive tendencies. [Langner and Michaels 1963, p. 438]

> *SES=socioeconomic status.

Another important element in this ideology is the assumption that it is the early experiences of the poor, the failures of mothering, the inconsistent patterns of discipline, the exposure to deviant values and behavior patterns that account for their apparent excessive vulnerability to emotional disorder.

These assumptions, this ideology, boils down to a process of relating mental disorder to social class by relating psychosexual development to presumed cultural features of a subgroup of the population. It derives from the extreme and continuing influence of W. Lloyd Warner in American thinking about social class, in which social class is defined largely in terms of prestige, life style, social honor.

There are other views about social stratification that have been far less influential, but that might, in the long run, prove more fruitful for understanding the complexities of the relationship between class and distress. Max Weber's conception of stratification, for example, which is followed rather closely by C. Wright Mills and others, maintains that there is not one but three dimensions of social ordering (Weber 1958). These are—

1. *class*—the extent to which one controls property and financial resources and maintains a favorable position in the marketplace;
2. *status*—the manner in which one consumes resources and the extent to which one is accorded social honor (this is the predominant element in Warner's view of social class);
3. *power*—the extent to which one (or, more commonly, a group of persons, a "party") is able to control and influence the community's decisions.

Now, if one limits one's thinking about relationships between social stratification and emotional disorder to status questions (largely disregarding class and power issues)—and this has certainly been the dominant tendency in the Warnerian type of thinking about this relationship—one starts seeking explanations in terms of status elements, such as child-rearing practices, values, and life style. One is inclined to conclude that the poor are more subject to emotional disorder than the affluent because their patterns of parenting are deficient, their values are different, their time orientation is different and they cannot defer need-gratification, their life styles emphasize violence and sexual promiscuity, they have ego deficiencies as a result of their childhood experiences in the culture of poverty, etc.

One hears and sees these kinds of formulations more and more frequently in mental health settings. I fear that an ideology is developing in which the mental health problems of the poor (which one might reasonably have expected would be related to poverty) are being analyzed through status-oriented formulations of class differences, with the result that these problems are being conceptually transformed into one more category of intrapsychic disorder. The consequences of such transformations are predictable. The evidence that appears to relate disorder to environmental circumstances is being rapidly assimilated into pre-existing patterns of intrapsychic theorizing, and maintaining the status quo—which, after all, is the purpose of ideology.

When one focuses on status and life style as explanatory variables, one omits at the same time the other elements that determine social stratification—power and money. Lack of money as a cause of emotional disorder can be conceptualized through the mediating concept of stress. Stresses relating to lack of money—poor and crowded housing, nutritional deficiencies, medical neglect, unemployment, and similar events—rather regularly have been found as correlates of disorder. Moreover, there is evidence that certain kinds of stressful events, such as illness, which can be merely inconvenient for the well-to-do, are often disastrous for the poor. Some of Dohrenwend's recent work contains some intriguing ideas on the possible relationship between poverty, stress, and emotional disorder (1967). He sets forth the hypothesis that reaction to stress is ordinarily cyclical and time-limited and that most emotional symptomatology evidences in such reaction is temporary. A prevalence study at a given point in time would tend to include substantial numbers of such temporary stress reactions. If one assumes that stresses in the lives of the poor are both more prevalent and more severe than those in the lives of the more prosperous, one would expect that, at a given point in time, the poor as a group would exhibit more stress reactions and would therefore demonstrate a higher prevalence of emotional disorder. This is one example of the way in which the class-oriented method of dealing with stratification—which is to say the money-oriented way—can be introduced into the process of theorizing about the relationship between poverty and mental health.

The third leg of the stratification stool—power—can be dealt with principally through the concept of self-esteem. There is an overwhelming array of theoretical and empirical literature suggesting that self-esteem is a vital element in mental health and, further, that self-esteem is based on a sense of competence, an ability to influence one's environment, a sense of mastery and control over events and circumstances that affect one's life. These are psychological terms that are readily translatable into the sociological concept of power as used by Weber. To the extent that a person is powerful, then, he is more likely to be what we call mentally healthy; to the extent that he is powerless, he is likely to be lacking in this characteristic.

The functional relationship between the exercise of power, feelings of self-esteem, and mental health has been empirically observed in a number of settings—civil rights demonstrations, block organization projects, and even, according to some, in ghetto disorders.

There are, then, relationships to be found between mental health phenomena and issues of money and power that are direct—more direct than the secondary kinds of relationships hypothesized between mental health and social status and life style. The major difference, however, is in program implications. If one makes the assumption that the relevant variable is status, one tends to work on changing the characteristics of the individual—his life style, his values, his child-rearing practices, or the effects of the child-rearing practices of his parents. If, on the other hand, one makes the assumption that the relevant variables are money and power, one tends to work toward changing the environment, toward developing programs of social change rather than individual change.

I am dismayed and concerned that we in the mental health field are moving more and more toward a narrow view of status issues, which will permit us to conduct business as usual—focusing on changing the person—and avoid the broader view of class and power issues that would oblige us to alter our methods and start putting our resources into the business of social change.

If we did make such a shift, such a change in our

ideology and our assumptions about what is wrong, what alterations would there be in our style of doing business? How might we translate the problems we confront into different kinds of needs? And what kinds of services would we develop to meet those needs?

We would, first of all, turn our attention to the patterns of social inequity and injustice that play such a major role in producing the casualties who come to us for attention. Just as, in years gone by, the pioneers of public health spoke up and cried out for change in housing, sanitation, and factory conditions, so would we be required to cry out about our society's basic injustices in the distribution of money and power. In the councils of professional activity, in the councils of social welfare, and in the councils of government, ours would be a voice agitating for equality as a fundamental prerequisite for mental health.

Second, as we encounter and evaluate—or, as we used to say in the good old days, "diagnose"—our clients, we would necessarily find ourselves including in our thoughts and our repertoire of labels and categories, redevelopment as well as repression, superhighways as well as superegos, police training as well as toilet training, discrimination as well as displacement, and racism as well as autism.

It would also follow that in our interactions with clients drawn from low-income and black neighborhoods, our services would have to be at least partially geared toward the fundamental issues of money and power. We would have to act to increase our clients' resources— through training and referral services to help them get jobs, or better jobs, through encouragement of the development of unions in unorganized settings to help them get more money, through advocating more public funds for such matters as assured minimum income and public assistance, public housing, subsidized medical care, better education, increased day-care facilities, etc.

And we would have to act to increase our clients'

power in the community—primarily through community organization efforts in the low-income neighborhoods of our specific catchment areas, but also through our own political, lobbying, and public educational activities.

An indispensable element in, and touchstone of, our commitment to increase the power of our constituency is the way we deal with the issue of decision-making in our own centers. Power-sharing—like charity—begins at home, which means citizen involvement and participation in shaping the programs and priorities of the mental health center. In a word, community control. If powerlessness gives rise to pathology, and the only cure for powerlessness is power, and we have the occasion to relinquish power to the citizens we profess to serve, the consequences are obvious. We must put our money where our mouth is.

An unexpected byproduct of such a shift in orientation, that is, a reconceptualization of the great majority of mental health problems as *social* problems, flowing from structural and environmental distortions on the axis of money and the axis of power, would be the possibility of some easing of the acute shortage of manpower in the psychiatric professions. On the one hand, the mental health center would become one agency among several in an alliance of equals that could attack these problems jointly. (I say alliance of equals deliberately, to distinguish this hypothetical situation from the present case, in which a psychiatric facility is seen as a dominant agency collaborating condescendingly with a group of ancillary or paramedical agencies.) And the appropriate manpower to engage in such a preventive, social, universalistic program would not have to include any substantial number of trained mental health professionals.

The latter—the psychiatrists, clinical psychologists, nurses, and social workers—could then turn their attention more vigorously to the minority of mental health problems that may be considered more accurately as *medical* or *quasi-medical* in nature—the psychosomatic disorders, the metabolic disorders, the major and minor brain dysfunctions and the most acute and refractory of the disorders that are characterized by disorientation, thought and mood disruption for which there is some evidence for genetic or other physical causation.

In summary, I am suggesting that the mental health center can fulfill its promise only if those of us in the field consciously undertake to revamp and expand our ideological framework to include the disorder of the community as well as the dysfunction of the individual. We must learn that the emotionally disturbed individual is not an unusual, abnormal, unexpectable "case," but is rather a usual, highly predictable index of the distortion and injustice that pervades our society. Only after such ideological transformation can the community mental health center become what it must become—a committed instrument for social change and social justice.

Bibliography

Dohnrenwend, B. 1967. Social status, stress and psychological symptoms. *Am. J. Pub. Health* 57:625-632.

Langner, T. and Michaels, S. 1963. *Life stress and mental health.* New York: Free Press.

Mills, C. 1943. The professional ideology of social pathologists. *Amer. J. Sociol.* 49:165-180.

Ryan, W. 1969. Community care in historical perspective: implications for mental health services and perspectives. *Canada's Mental Health* Supplement No. 60.

——————. 1969. *Distress in the city.* Cleveland: Press of Case Western Reserve University.

——————. 1971. *Blaming the victim.* New York: Pantheon Books, Random.

Seeley, J. 1967. *The Americanization of the unconscious,* pp. 142-148. New York: International Science Press. (Material originally appeared in the *Indian Sociol. Bull.* Vol. 2. 1965.)

Weber, M. 1958. Class, status and party. In *Max Weber: essays in sociology,* H. H. Gerth and C. W. Mills, trans. New York: Oxford University Press.

III. roles and goals

New Role Problems in Neighborhood Legal Services
John C. Cratsley

Historical information

Neighborhood law offices.

In late 1964, with the advent of the "neighborhood law office," the legal profession took a major step out into the community. Pushed by an active group of service-oriented attorneys, most of the legal profession came to the whole-hearted support of the concept of neighborhood legal services for the poor. In essence, this idea called for the decentralization of the traditional downtown legal aid program. Its basic premise was that poor people, living in ghettos and other outlying neighborhoods, had legal problems which never came to the attention of the few lawyers available to help them. It also held that the availability of young, aggressive advocates in the neighborhood would better serve the legal needs of the low-income community. This initial idea was strongly oriented toward comprehensive service at the neighborhood level. The need for legal services for the poor was known to be great—bar association leaders as well as legal commentators had long acknowledged this. Two classic studies of the legal needs of the poor done thirty-two years apart but reaching similar conclusions are Smith (1919) and Brownell (1951). A more recent report, written in the early days of concern with establishing federally funded neighborhood legal services is Wald (1965). Consequently, with the help of federal funds from the Office of Economic Opportunity, most large American cities began legal services programs emphasizing neighborhood law offices and de-emphasizing the downtown legal aid office. The neighborhood offices were open to all low-income persons and were designed to handle a large volume of clients.

In fact, the volume of clients in the neighborhood offices proved to be overwhelming. It was not long before many such offices became deluged by their caseloads. In reaction to this problem, as well as in recognition of the limited achievement of a case-by-case approach, neighborhood legal services attorneys began to ask how to make more sweeping changes in the social and legal system. Soon the concept of "law reform" became stylish. Law reform is based on the premise that individual cases help only individual clients and do not change the living conditions, or social and economic relationships, of large numbers of people. This approach seeks to identify legal, economic, or political barriers affecting large groups of poor people. It is thought that by bringing one "test case" attacking a particularly burdensome rule, regulation, or practice, hundreds of thousands of people will benefit from a court victory (Johnson 1967). In a subsequent speech, Johnson (1970) estimated that three important test cases—the welfare residency case, *Shapiro* v. *Thompson,* 394 U.S. 618 (1969); the man-in-the-house case, *King* v. *Smith,* 392 U.S. 309 (1968), and the California Medi-Cal case, *Morris* v. *Williams,* 67 Cal. 2d. 733, 433 P. 2d. 697 (1967)—had resulted in an income transfer of approximately $600 million dollars to the lower one-fifth of society. This idea captured the imagination of many young legal services attorneys. Certain of these attorneys, hard at work in neighborhood offices, tried to limit their caseloads and to do more law reform work; others sought to establish special law reform units within their programs to undertake test case litigation.

Service versus law reform.

It was not long before a tension developed among legal services attorneys, between those interested in providing neighborhood-oriented legal services to individual clients, and those anxious to bring up important test cases. The organized bar, which was generally pleased to see low-income persons represented in court on their individual matters, was not as happy to see the state welfare department, or the city housing authority, or large banking and consumer interests, sued on behalf of the poor. It is fair to say that much of the political opposition to legal services programs then and today stems from the aggressive work of certain law reform oriented attorneys. Threats of a number of state and local officials (in California, Illinois, and Missouri) to terminate legal services programs are directly related to these programs' litigation against governmental agencies (e.g., welfare, school, and police departments) and against vested economic interests (e.g., landlords, merchants, and farm owners) (Pearson 1971, p. 646). The California Rural Legal Assistance (CRLA) was finally vetoed by Governor Reagan in late 1970, despite its record of victories in over 80 percent of the cases they initiated on behalf of the poor (Pearson 1971, p. 647). Although the federal government did continue to fund CRLA, its future now seems to rest with the politicians, not the people (Hiestand 1971).

Other new themes in legal services.

After the rise of the law reform concept, two other themes developed in legal services work. First, there was a movement among certain legal services attorneys toward emphasizing local economic development and neighborhood-based corporations. These persons took the position that even law reform did not achieve significant social and economic changes for the poor. They felt that the organization of the poor into economic units, such as co-ops, neighborhood credit unions, and community corporations to operate private enterprises, would provide a more viable means for change. A second theme which developed out of the first is the concept of legal services attorneys working for neighborhood "political" organizations. Basically, this work began at the organizing level. Its results are best seen in tenants' unions, consumer rights organizations, and welfare rights organizations. The view of these attorneys is that community groups must struggle for their own political gains, and that no amount of litigation, courtroom representation, or entrepreneurial activity will gain what voting power and direct political confrontation can obtain.

These various themes in legal services all are expressive of one dominant theme—to be effective advocates for the poor, lawyers have to be involved in the community at the neighborhood level in activities of neighborhood significance. This is a radical change—first, from the traditional, downtown, charitable legal aid society; and second, from the idea that a handful of idealistic private attorneys could provide legal assistance to the poor in their spare time. Each theme is, then, on the part of members of the legal profession, a bold statement of an active desire to assist poor persons with their problems. One approach insists on individual assistance, another on the use of political power; but each approach is an expression of the essential role of the lawyer as an advocate for an unpopular cause. The unpopular cause, however, is not a foreign ideology, or an anti-religious view but is simply the democratic notion that poor as well as rich are entitled to participate in government and to receive equal treatment before the law.

Role problems in working with neighborhood groups

<u>Leader versus general counsel.</u>
As a result of the expansion of legal services for the poor and the various themes and approaches undertaken in this field, special problems have arisen with respect to working with neighborhood groups. Although these problems are most significant for those attorneys who seek to play the role of "political organizer," the same difficulties exist for the neighborhood lawyer who works with a group of mothers interested in a day-care center, or a group of parents interested in school problems. The basic difficulty is the conflict between the role of the neighborhood legal services attorney as a leader or dominant force in a group and the role of the attorney as legal counsel for the group. In the former role, he is making policy and guiding all of the decisions of the group; in the latter role, he provides technical assistance when his help is specifically requested by the group. Occasionally, a legal services attorney cannot help but play a dominant role in the early days of the organization. Some neighborhood attorneys have withdrawn from this dominant role after the group gained strength. The temptation, however, is to continue to hold power once it has been obtained and used.

The importance of an attorney serving only as legal counsel to the neighborhood group, and not as policy maker, should be obvious. If the goal is for the neighborhood group to wield effective political power or to articulate its own policies for its own best ends, that group should make all of its own decisions. The neighborhood attorney, who unfortunately is almost always *not* from the low-income community, simply does not have a legitimate role, either by way of birth or experience, to dictate policy to the group. If the group is to rise in self-esteem and community impact, it must do so on its own.

Giving legal advice.

A much harder problem for the neighborhood lawyer in his work with community groups is that of defining his legal role. Once he has undertaken the role described above, he still must be careful in how he offers his "counsel." There remains a very fine line between legal advice and personal coercion. In keeping that line clearly defined, it is essential that the legal services attorney take a back-seat role in all community meetings and respond with legal memoranda or legal opinion only when he is asked. But, as any good attorney knows, legal advice affects policy decisions. Consequently, the effective neighborhood lawyer will outline for his clients his legal advice regarding a range of alternative actions, describing how each alternative affects certain policy goals of the community organization. A capable neighborhood lawyer should be able to communicate his legal advice in as clear and understandable a manner as possible, so that the policy decisions that are logically tied to the legal opinions can be easily made. Often, this "art of explanation" will require some detailed development of certain legal concepts. An attorney who is active and interested in community work should find it well worth his time to try to turn textbook legal jargon into understandable community phrases.

A related problem in working with community groups occurs on that predictable day when a community group directs an issue to the neighborhood lawyer to resolve. An example is the client who tells his attorney, "You make the decision; you're my lawyer." The community group simply throws up its hands and asks the lawyer to guide it through what appears to be a tricky decision involving many legal ramifications. It is in this situation that the neighborhood lawyer who has trouble articulating legal doctrine in an understandable way so that the community group can make its own decisions has failed. It may also be, however, that the community group simply cannot reach a decision, or that it feels the legal consequences of the decision are beyond its comprehension. In this case, the neighborhood lawyer may have to render the requested decision simply to preserve the on-going operations of the neighborhood group or his relations with it. It would certainly be a mistake for the neighborhood lawyer to feel that the concept of community control was so pure that it could not be violated by certain decision making on his part on appropriate occasions. In fact, it is not at all inconsistent with the traditional role of "general counsel" to make those decisions that are viewed by the client as being so tied up in law that no one else is competent to render them. At the same time, it is on these unusual occasions when the neighborhood attorney risks his credibility. If his decision is wrong and/or has adverse repercussions, he is probably finished with the community group, and perhaps in the neighborhood in which he has been working. If he is right, or his decision is met with further successful results, he will be pressured to do more of the same in the future.

As an example, let me describe one type of neighborhood lawyer-community organization relationship that has been going on in our neighborhood law office for some time now. Our office has been counsel for over a year to a citizens' committee interested in establishing rent control in Cambridge. The ground rules for our work were carefully established by our client when our help was first sought. It was made clear to us that we were only to provide legal advice and legislative draftsmanship, and to play no other role in the meetings of the committee. We were placed in the unusual position for attorneys of drafting into "legalese" only what we were told to draft, and of bringing each individual product back to the committee for approval, rather than being given a general drafting task and told to return with a final, finished product. As one downtown Boston attorney said to me, "You're terribly brave to try this, but you're doing it all wrong as a lawyer." As a matter of fact, I found the experience most exciting. Both the law students who worked on the project and I were hard pressed to articulate legal doctrines in terms that could be dealt with during citizen discussions. As each policy issue in rent control was discussed and certain relevant legal concepts were analyzed, the committee voted as to what results they wanted in their bill. Section by section we drafted a bill which reflected the citizens' wishes. At times, the citizens respected our legal opinions and either deleted or modified certain of their own wishes. At other times, they rejected our legal opinions outright in favor of what they felt was a more intelligent and humane policy approach. The most striking example of this was their vote to entirely alter the state eviction laws in one section of their proposed rent-control ordinance. An added advantage which resulted from our close work with the citizens' committee was that when the proposed ordinance reached the city council, and the question of compromise came up, the citizens were well aware of all of the legal issues being raised by their opponents. Our work had not only been advisory, it had also been educational; and it created an improved capacity for the "politics" of legislation during the final weeks of amendment and clarification.

Role problems in working with other professionals

The attorney as advocate.
Another area of special concern to the neighborhood

legal services attorney as he works with individual clients and community groups is his relationship with other professionals. This problem is particularly pressing because of the extension of other professional services into the same client community. As neighborhood mental health centers, neighborhood planning teams, and other new forms of neighborhood service and action develop, the neighborhood lawyer is hard pressed to relate to each. His primary difficulty in this regard is that of interpreting his role in the neighborhood to these other professionals. This is because the neighborhood lawyer, true to his professional ethics, is an advocate for a client, whether that client be right or wrong. The other professionals see themselves simply as helpers or providers of services, who are free to make a range of moral and social judgments about the character and situation of their clients. The neighborhood lawyer, on the other hand, is obligated to serve his client's wishes. He is an advocate for his client's cause.

This conflict in professional roles is most forcefully seen by contrasting the neighborhood lawyer with the neighborhood mental health worker. The neighborhood attorney is frequently trying to keep his client on the street, to win custody of his client's child, or to get an extra welfare check for his client. He is seeking these results not because they represent "the best" or "what is right," but because they are his client's wishes. The neighborhood mental health aides, social workers, and psychiatrists, however, seem to the neighborhood attorney to be singularly concerned about "the best interests" of the client. While a lawyer may want the mental health worker to testify on behalf of his client so that his client can win his case, the worker may feel that a professional evaluation of the client prevents him from giving favorable testimony. And while a lawyer would never ask a psychiatrist or social worker to lie, and while the psychiatrist or social worker should never offer any evaluation but a professionally valid one, both parties seem unable to understand the position of the other. The mental health staff feels suspicious of being "used" by the attorney, and the attorney feels, in turn, that the mental health staff is completely uncooperative in helping his client.

Breaking barriers in communication.

The barriers in communication between those professions which are now reaching into the community stem largely from a lack of understanding of each other's role. Unfortunately, they pose significant problems for the future of such neighborhood work. If neighborhood legal services attorneys cannot obtain the help of those in other professions undertaking similar work because of the suspicions previously described, and if the other professions find attorneys difficult to work with, most of the impact of these professions at the neighborhood level will be destroyed.

One solution, of course, is to ask the other professions to become "advocates" for their clients. There is much talk these days of "advocate planners," or "advocate social workers." I suspect that the more traditionally minded in these other professions will reject this suggestion as being inconsistent with their obligation to render independent, professional judgment. On the other hand, neighborhood law offices have been successful in recent years in the use of certain types of nonlegal professional skills in the adversary context. Both city planners and social workers have been added to the staffs of neighborhood law offices to work on particular cases and to develop particular materials for one side of a piece of litigation. In this context, it would seem that the nonlegal professional can carry out his work for a client; i.e., for the attorney, and participate with the attorney in a free and confidential evaluation of the work product. If the attorney finds it useful for his case, he will accept and use it; if the information developed is not useful, the attorney will reject its use. Hopefully, the professional will feel somewhat pressed by the neighborhood attorney to come up with the data, materials, or opinions which the particular adversary position of the attorney requires. This close association between professionals is best done in association with the neighborhood law office, and, when properly done, it can result in a much freer use of nonlegal professional skills at the neighborhood level. What is significant is that the professional has become part of the adversary process, not because he, himself, is an advocate, but because he has devoted his skills to the needs of an attorney who is always an advocate, and who is much more comfortable in that role.

The foregoing plea for greater advocacy by those who have the needed professional skills, and who are compassionate enough to be using them at the neighborhood level, is not to say that this is the only form of cooperation between these professionals. Rather, it is suggested as one solution to the obvious communication gap between the various professionals now active and available in the community. It is also obviously a self-serving plan to enhance the ability of neighborhood lawyers to serve their clients. There remains ample opportunity and need for the professions (such as social work, the ministry, city planning, and mental health) to develop and carry out new and imaginative neighborhood-oriented programs. Many of these programs can be carried out by one of the professions using its special area of expertise, such as architecture, city planning, psychological counseling, etc. But when coordination is needed, and advocacy for a particular cause is required, it is suggested that all of the professional skills ally under the guiding hand of the neighborhood legal services attorney. He is comfortable in the adversary role and better able to marshal the professional data for presentation than any of his other skilled counterparts. It may also be that because of his prior adversary work with community groups, he is the first to learn of new neighborhood problems and needs, and the first to be asked to solve them. Consequently, the neighborhood attorney is in a better position to take the lead in seeking out other relevant professions and asking for their contributions.

Bibliography

Brownell, E. A. 1951. *Legal aid in the United States.* Rochester: Lawyers Co-operative Pub. Co.

Hiestand, F. J. 1971. The politics of poverty law. In *With justice for some,* eds. M. J. Green and B. Wasserstein, pp. 160-189. Boston: Beacon Press.

Johnson, E. 1967. Introductory address at the Harvard Conference on Law and Poverty, 17-19 March 1967, at Harvard Law School, Cambridge, Mass.

————. 1970. Law as an instrument of social change. Speech at the 47th Annual Meeting of the American Orthopsychiatric Association, 25 March 1970, in San Francisco, Calif.

Pearson, J. B. 1971. To protect the rights of the poor: The Legal Services Corporation Act of 1971. *University of Kansas Law Review* 19:641-650.

Smith, R. H. 1919. *Justice and the poor.* The Carnegie Foundation for the Advancement of Teaching, Bulletin Number 13. Boston: Merrymount Press.

Wald, P. M. 1965. Law and poverty: 1965. Prepared as a working paper for the National Conference on Law and Poverty, 23-25 June 1965, at Washington, D.C.

Professionals' Participation in Community Activities: Is It Part of the Job?*
Irving N. Berlin

With the advent of community mental health centers, it has become much more "professional" for workers in the mental health field to participate in community activities (Cowen et al. 1967). For some time now, a number of schools of social work have been teaching courses in community organization and have provided a variety of field-work placements in the community (Ibid.; Lippitt et al. 1958). Courses in social and community psychiatry are increasingly part of the training of psychiatrists, nurses, and psychologists (Berlin 1964, 1967, 1969; Caplan 1961, 1963; Newman 1967; Sarason et al. 1966).

It has become clear from the community mental health center movement—especially in or near ghetto areas—that unless the mental health professionals become part of their community by participating in some of its activities and understanding its needs, priorities, and values, the center may function in a way that will restrict its usefulness to the community (Webster 1966). To insure the success of such community mental health centers, potential staff members must be versed in the workings of community life. Where should such training occur, who should do the training, and how should it be done?

*This essay appeared in the *American Journal of Orthopsychiatry* 41:494-500 © 1971 in slightly revised form, under the title "Professional Participation in Community Activities: Is it Part of the Job?" Reprinted by permission.

Currently, teaching in most schools of social work provides few guidelines for certain problems inherent in community mental health work: how to participate personally, how, through direct involvement, to provide models and help in problem solving, and how to recognize that the community no longer requires one's help in a particular area.

The reality is that mental health workers view their participation in the community and its political activities as something extraprofessional or as a phase in the process of becoming known and trusted in the community.

The critical issue is that few, if any, professional schools prepare students for community activities having political implications. The workers are therefore no more sophisticated in the political process than are the members of the community with whom they work, and they are often less reality-based. Although generally looked upon as experts, they are in fact usually inexpert in the political process. They may be familiar with the hierarchy of local agency and governmental structures, group processes, and interacting systems, but they rarely know how to go about getting things done, where the leverage is, who can cut the red tape, etc.

Ghetto-area mental health centers and family counseling agencies are often under pressure to become involved in the community's political issues. They are asked to help the community exercise political power to obtain critical health and mental health needs. In one ghetto community, for example, the schools found themselves in an estranged situation. The community viewed the public schools as an agency that, by default, helped their children fail. Community members believed that their youngsters would never be educated enough to compete on the open market. The community as a whole was angry, and the schools were seen as the Siberia of the total school system. It was undeniable that the most ineffective and rigid teachers and administrators were sent there to live out their days. Children with learning problems that required very clear evaluations of their capacities did not receive any special attention. Parents were frustrated by the unresponsive school system, their children were frustrated by the poor quality of instruction—clearly, effective education was impossible.

The pupil-personnel workers, primarily four social workers, felt it was their function to become involved with the community through several aspects of community participation. First, they attended and participated in community council meetings, trying to help the community understand the nature of sources of the pressures faced by the superintendent and thus learn how he might be influenced. The hope was that the community council might more effectively make their needs known and be able to effect change.

Second, the mental health professionals, using mental health consultation techniques and consultation with their psychiatric consultant, worked with school personnel to help them become more flexible and attuned to student and community needs. They posed this community's concerns as a unique challenge to evolve a kind of participant and relevant education not yet possible elsewhere in the city. For example, it was suggested that the school allow concerned parents to work as volunteer school aides. They could be trained in a volunteer program, and their reliability and effectiveness were almost assured, because they were aware of their children's problems in school.

The third task undertaken by the mental health workers was to become directly involved with parents of disturbed children. Over coffee and doughnuts on a regular open-house basis, they got groups of parents together to discuss their children's problems. Small groups of parents who had children in need of help were involved in activities with groups of children to learn

241

about the helping process, first by observing and later by participating as aides in children's activity groups. In addition, the mental health workers asked the part-time school psychologist to evaluate some of these youngsters, so that teachers became more clearly aware of the children's needs and of ways they might start helping them.

Effects of actual participation in the community

The workers viewed their involvement in the community with mixed pleasure in the beginning and then with more professional satisfaction as they saw uninvolved, hostile, or helpless parents become more effective human beings.

One of the most effective, although unplanned, activities was the creation of a preschool program by a private philanthropic organization, which hired an experienced and talented preschool teacher and several aides (teachers) from the community. With parent participation as part of the contract for admission of a child, the school was established for three- and four-year-olds. This organization had one advantage over the local Head Start program—it had no connection with an official body, either OEO or the public schools. This meant that its direction *had to be* determined by the teacher, teacher's aides, and parents.

This small program served to augment the inadequately funded Head Start program. While the public school pupil-personnel services had no officially designated role, they functioned in a liaison role to identify children, and refer them, and participated with parents and teachers in planning. The need for this was so great that fathers and mothers were immediately very involved in doing the necessary building, painting, and making of equipment. Thus, a feeling of camaraderie and investment developed early. Fathers participated eagerly, much more than had been expected.

The first crisis faced by the new program centered around a difference of philosophy between the preschool teacher and her aides. The teacher felt that the task of three- and four-year-olds was to play, learn to verbalize effectively, and become involved in exploratory and creative collaborative play activities. The aides believed that greater benefit would come from introducing the children to the basics of reading, writing, and working with numbers. One of the teacher's aides, a black woman who was a very effective disciplinarian, felt that the only way black children could make it was to learn immediately all the skills necessary for kindergarten and first grade. The other aide, who was of Mexican-American descent, also had some strong question as to whether play itself would really be helpful to the children, although she could effectively involve herself with children in play activities. The parents very much supported the black teacher's aide because they recognized that unless their children could read, write, and become effective learners very early, they had no chance to make it in school.

At this point, the mental health professionals were drawn in. They tended to support the preschool teacher. They pointed out how play can be utilized to develop curiosity and interest in learning—skills necessary for learning reading and writing. Because the parents were confronted with the very real problem of recurrent failure of their children in the elementary schools, they did not buy this concept. The question then raised was: Should the elementary schools be changed so that they would provide all youngsters with the necessary educational opportunities, or should the preschool be geared to fit in with an outmoded elementary education methodology?

Parents were now critically concerned with learning more about the total educational process. They asked the teacher and mental health professionals to organize a series of meetings to help them more effectively assess both the preschool and the primary school educational processes, and to provide them with reading materials (Kohl 1967; Lewis 1967; Webster 1966; Zax and Cowen 1967).

Discussion at each meeting was active. Because parents were deeply involved, they sometimes became volatile. The speakers found they were required to present their particular points of view with clear facts and illustrations. A number of parents, both mothers and fathers, did their homework very thoroughly, read the material, and presented their interpretations of the articles.

One of the child development experts described with vividness the developmental process from a maturational point of view, emphasizing how learning occurred at every step. He showed how concept formation develops, how curiosity is stimulated, and how the schools' emphasis on rote learning can interfere with effective concept formation and critical thinking.

At the conclusion, the parents decided the preschool teacher's ideas were correct. Their next move had to be to alter the primary neighborhood schools to which their children were assigned. At this point, the mental health professionals indicated that such a reformation was the job of the entire community. The parents agreed to raise the issue at the next community council meeting.

A number of stormy meetings followed, in which these parents militantly presented to the community council what they expected from the primary schools. Some members of the council tried to pacify these parents and were reluctant to bring such issues to the attention of the school board and superintendent because previous meetings had brought no change.

Since school board elections were near, however, one member of the council, who had a child in the preschool and one in the elementary school, offered himself as a candidate for the school board. The concern of most parents for the education of their children was of such magnitude that they were able to swing the council into backing their stand, and obtained a meeting with the superintendent and the school board.

During this meeting, the parents clearly outlined the issues involved in the primary schools and their concern for the education of their children. The president of the school board and the superintendent quickly acknowledged the problems and described how overburdened they were with problems throughout the city. They pleaded for time to alleviate the many problems. The superintendent also called upon some of the mental health professionals who worked for the schools to back up his stand that the elementary school was not "that bad." Caught in the bind between the school that employed them and the community in which they worked, the professionals felt they had to face the issue squarely. Their spokesman was able to define clearly—and in educational terms—why the elementary school's efforts were outmoded and had an adverse impact on the children. The professionals described the kinds of teachers and administrators who had been assigned to these schools and their inflexibility and incapacity to work meaningfully with children, especially those who needed special help. Thus confronted, both the school board and the superintendent said they would do what they could to remedy the situation. The parents' group said they would give the superintendent and the school board several months to make changes. They said if the school system failed, their community council would find other means of effecting change, such as going directly to the city council as well as trying to elect a parent to the board. One of the city councilmen, as the board knew, was a resident of this area. His re-election depended very heavily upon his being able to satisfy his constituents.

The mental health workers were later called into the superintendent's office and asked why they supported the community against the superintendent. They stated that they had long served this particular community, were familiar with the schools, and felt that the requests of the community were both reasonable and justified. As mental health professionals, they had no alternative but to speak the truth. One of them inquired of the superintendent if he would have preferred she speak untruthfully in order to save the face of the school system. The superintendent, of course, remarked that he would not want anybody to do this; however, it was clear he was extremely disturbed. He asked several workers if they had tenure.

The snowballing effect

Having become involved with the school and the school board over the issue of the education of their children, the community council, led by some of the parents, also became very much concerned with the way in which they were being treated by the welfare and health departments. They focused on two problems. First, because there was no welfare agency in their area, thay had to travel a considerable distance to rectify errors or to make inquiries or complaints. Second, the public health well-child clinic in their area was inadequately staffed and equipped. Mothers and babies had to wait interminably. The community council began to meet with the director of public welfare, as well as with the director of public health.

Participation in community action led parents who were never previously involved in activities on their own behalf to become aware of their potency as they learned the methods and strategies required to gain support from other community members and from individuals in power in the community. They became more aware of the political process and how they could use it for their own needs. For the first time, the city councilman who had been elected from this district was asked to help the community council with planning. When he did not reply to a letter, he was directed by a delegation to attend a meeting to help them with their strategies; he complied. The progressive state legislator from this area was asked to participate in the community council strategy meetings for obtaining more and better school, welfare, and public health services. He became an advisor to the council.

During these meetings, the schools' mental health workers began to describe what data was required in the way of evidence to help support their cause. They encouraged parents to monitor all of the classrooms in the elementary school and to actually record, hour by hour and day by day, the teaching and learning that was going on. Parents were also encouraged to note in diary form the welfare problems that were occurring, and also the service provided and the number of people who attended the well-child clinics. They accumulated data on the length of time it took for them to be served and the number of young mothers who had to walk out unserved. In addition, they gathered information on the number of police harassments of young people in the community.

An interesting and now well-known phenomenon began to occur as the preschool parents and the members of the council began to get a sense of their potential power and effectiveness. Having utilized the mental health professionals to help them discover how they might become effective on their own behalf, and having gone through the data gathering process that helped them reach some of their objectives, they next experienced a period of unease and a sense that they no longer needed help from the mental health professionals. This period of strain and uncertainty about the role of the mental health professionals was bridged in two ways. First, it became clear to the parents in the preschool that they still needed expert guidance in the education of their youngsters and help with some of the more disturbed youngsters and their troubled parents. Second, in one of the negotiation sessions with the police department, they called upon one of the black mental health professionals to participate. Her very skillful intercession clarified the issues, especially the actual examples of the kind of provocation by the police that resulted in retaliatory behavior by the young people. This led to an experimental period in which some of the officers were relieved of their duties. An effort was made to see what would happen if police officers who had better attitudes toward the youths in the area were provided.

The community leaders realized that improved schools and welfare and public health services were only a beginning, that there would be other ways to effectively utilize the professionals' skills.

In another area of the same city, a similar undertaking failed. Both the community council and concerned parents in this ghetto area as well as the teachers and mental health professionals were at constant loggerheads about their mutual objectives. When we examined the issues in this second instance, it became clear that the mental health professionals and educators, though professionally competent, had no expertise or training in helping parents become effective in the community.

Only a new, concerned school administrator was able to help this community organization clarify the issues. His single-minded concern to obtain better education for the students helped mobilize the community to effective action.

Summary and conclusions

It is evident that the present training, per se, of the mental health professional puts him in a position to be helpful to the community only if he is used primarily to provide mental health services to individual children and parents. Those who have been trained in community mental health and consultation learn early that they must establish their worth in a situation. They do this through their commitment to collaborate in a variety of ways with the community organizations—to learn about, identify, and perform needed services required by the community organizations. They utilize their expertise in mental health to further the objectives of the community. It is clear that their psychodynamic understanding of individuals, while helpful in individual work, cannot be applied to the community in undigested form. Some of the omniscience characteristic of mental health professionals is clearly designed to turn off any community organization with whom they might be involved.

The first group's initial success depended upon their willingness and capacity to be useful to the community. Their sense of commitment to community priorities helped them live through the period of disenchantment. They continued to be willing to be useful in a variety of ways designated by the community, and to face their own system's threat to them as employees through their professional clarity about the importance and validity of their position. Their unique role was to use professionally every avenue within their reach to enhance the integrative goals of the community organizations in terms of the community priorities as they evolved.

Bibliography

Berlin, I. 1964. Learning mental health consultation: history and problems. *Ment. Hyg.* 48:257-266.

——————. 1967. Preventive aspects of mental health consultation to schools. *Ment. Hyg.* 51:34-40.

——————. 1969. Mental health consultation for school social workers: a conceptual model. *Community Mental Health Journal* 5:280-288.

Caplan, G. 1961. *An approach to community mental health.* New York: Grune.

——————. 1963. Types of mental health consultation. *Amer. J. Orthopsychiat.* 33:470-481.

Clarizio, H. 1969. *Mental health and the educative process: selected readings.* New York: Rand McNally.

Cowen, E. et al. 1967. *Emergent approaches to mental health problems.* New York: Appleton.

Katz, D. and Kahn, R. 1966. *The social psychology of organizations.* New York: Wiley.

Kohl, H. 1967. *36 Children.* New York: New Am. Lib.

Lewis, W. 1967. Project re-ed: educational intervention in discordant child rearing systems. In *Emergent approaches to mental health problems,* eds. E. Cowen et al. New York: Appleton.

Lippit, R. et al. 1958. *The dynamics of planned change.* New York: Harcourt.

Newman, R. 1967. *Psychological consultation in the schools.* New York: Basic Books.

Sarason, S. et al. 1966. *Psychology in community settings.* New York: Wiley.

Webster, S., ed. 1966. Understanding the education problems of the disadvantaged child. In *The disadvantaged learner.* San Francisco: Chandler Pub.

Zax, M. and Cowen, E. 1967. Early identification and prevention of emotional disturbances in public schools. In *Emergent approaches to mental health problems,* eds. E. Cowen et al. New York: Appleton.

The Supply-Demand Dilemma in Community Mental Health Centers*
Catherine Kohler Riessman

It has been widely assumed in the last decade that underutilization of various community services by the poor reflected some subjective inadequacy in the reluctant clients. The poor, it was believed, didn't plan for the future, or were culturally or medically deprived, or were not able to defer gratification (Lewis 1959; Rainwater 1960; Suchman 1963). However, with the advent of neighborhood-based services, staffed in part by community workers, it is becoming increasingly apparent that the poor rapidly come to utilize health services, family planning services, mental health services, and social services.

It is interesting, for example, that historically most family planning clinics were grossly underutilized by low-income people (Freedman, Whelpton and Campbell 1959; Rainwater 1960); but when these services were reorganized and delivered in a humane, neighborhood-based fashion, the demand for services rose rapidly (Riessman 1968; Polgar 1966). In fact, Planned Parenthood now estimates that there is need for between 5,000 and 13,000 paraprofessional workers, as well as for many thousands of professional workers, to serve the family planning demands of the poor in the United States (Dryfoos and Manisoff 1969).

*This essay appeared in the *American Journal of Orthopsychiatry* 40:858-869 © 1970 in slightly revised form. Reprinted by permission.

Another illustration is offered by James Carl Stewart (1967), who reports that while 3 public health nurses brought in an average of 200 persons a month to an immunization clinic in Oklahoma, 7 indigenous paraprofessional workers serving the same areas during the following year brought in 2,000 persons a month.

The tendency has been for demand to outstrip the supply of these services. Hence, the current problem is not to persuade the poor to utilize services, but rather to find ways of organizing the services to meet the galloping demand.*

This recent experience leads us to three simple propositions:

1. If a service is underutilized by the target population, there is something wrong either with the service or with the way it is being offered;
2. If the service is overutilized by the population in need, this is an indication that the program is successful;
3. If the supply of a service does expand in response to rising demand, this in turn will lead to an even further increase in demand.

Strangely enough, the only ways to reduce the demand for a relatively *free* service are to lower the quality, or to offer the service inappropriately (that is, make it difficult to obtain). In other words, demand is reduced only by returning to the first proposition. This is the heart of the supply-demand dilemma.

*There is now considerable literature on the rapid expansion of demand associated with new practices: Sidney Garfield, founder of the Kaiser Permanente Plan, observes that prepayment plans "flood our delivery system." (Address by Garfield to Group Health Association of America, November 12, 1969); the advent of open enrollment promises to do the same in the colleges; and the burgeoning literature of neighborhood service centers indicates a similar rapid growth of demand for services. (See Kirschner Associates, "A Description and Evaluation of Neighborhood Centers," OEO, December, 1966.)

Traditionally, in a free market economy, supply and demand should adjust through the mechanism of price. But many of the human services offered to the poor are either free or provided at nominal cost. In the circumstance of a vast unfilled reservoir of need, demand will accelerate rapidly if a needed service is offered humanely.

Until such time as a large-scale, hitherto unknown input of resources takes place, this supply-demand dilemma will be with us.

The supply-demand dilemma and mental health

It has been argued that mental health centers would encounter the special resistance of the poor to treatment of "mental" disorders, or "craziness" (Star 1955). The poor supposedly are not "psychologically minded" (Brill and Storrow 1960). Hence, it might be presumed that the clinical services offered by community mental health centers in low-income neighborhoods would be underutilized. In general, this appears not to be the case; on the contrary, as community mental health programs proceeded in contacting the community and establishing a receptive image, the demand for services rapidly outstripped the supply of currently organized therapeutic modalities, as we will show later in this article more specifically with regard to the Sound View Throgs Neck Community Mental Health Center.

There are at least three reasons for this:

1. As Srole et al. (1962), Hollingshead and Redlich (1958), and Pasamanick et al. (1959) document, there is much undiagnosed mental illness in urban centers. When clinics are located directly in urban ghetto communities, accessible and responsive to the urban poor who hitherto have been ignored or "cooled out" (Adams and McDonald 1968) by the traditional service-giving agencies, these unidentified

patients quickly come into the treatment system.

2. Effective work with community caretakers leads to casefinding (secondary prevention) and referral for treatment. The unidentified social agencies of the community—such first aid stations as churches, school guidance offices, etc.—can easily double to triple the caseloads of mental health workers in community mental health centers.

3. Successful outreach techniques that keep services free from stigma lead to rapidly increased *self-referral*. Not only is this true for the unidentified patients with severe mental illness but also, and perhaps more importantly, for individuals and low-income families who are experiencing problems but who usually never get to social agencies, let alone psychiatric clinics.

Hence, the community mental health centers now face, or are about to face, a continually increasing demand for their services.

Let us briefly review how various programs attempt to cope with this problem. These approaches, of course, are not mutually exclusive; in practice, various approaches are combined. We will highlight the advantages and disadvantages of each approach, touching on the paradoxes and contradictions inherent in each.

Typical response strategies

The restrictive intake policy.

What occurs here is a subtle "brush off" for all but bona fide psychiatric emergencies. The community mental health center maintains a stance as a *psychiatric* facility, and rejects requests for direct service from those individuals who do not meet the criteria *it* selects as appropriate.

The paradox inherent in this approach is obvious. The community mental health center risks becoming like the traditional agencies and hospitals in the eyes of the community: you must have the right disease, come from the right geographic area, or provide interesting teaching material, etc., in order to be served. Of course, there are very real issues at stake for the community mental health center if the reverse of this practice becomes the norm, that is, if all who apply for service are accepted. Feldman and Jacobson (1969) argue that a restrictive intake policy, sensitively implemented, has the potential of mobilizing the community care apparatus.

The waiting list.

In many programs, this approach to the increased demand is still common, the rationale being that in order to assure high quality of care to some, others must wait. This approach is surrounded by a mystique of tradition, and functions often for the convenience of staff rather than to meet the needs of the patient or the community. It is obvious that the disequilibrium created by a crisis is a powerful therapeutic tool that is lost if the situation is allowed to degenerate, through postponement, into a chronic, long-term problem. On the other hand, spontaneous remissions occur, and as the community mental health worker learns to spot these, and to use a waiting list resourcefully, this approach may expand supply somewhat.

The referral route.

Here, the community mental health center acts as a "clearing house" for all applicants—screening, diagnosing, and referring to the appropriate agency in the community all or most of the patients who apply for services. This approach rests on the myth of available resources elsewhere. Numerous investigations have documented the fallacy of this assumption and have revealed the course of the referred patient (Teele and Levine 1957). Many agencies are organized largely for diagnostic work, and resources for treatment are scant, if not nonexistent, in most low-income areas. Referral, then, most often means no service. On the other side, the judicious use of the referral route with adequate follow-up to check that patients are actually being treated elsewhere could expand supply. As a major strategy, however, this approach appears limited.

The use of auxiliary manpower (paraprofessionals and volunteers).

The community mental health center employs paraprofessionals to provide "psychosocial first aid" to patients (Grosser and Kelley 1961; Hallowitz 1968; Rioch et al. 1963). This is coming to be the most widely utilized approach to the supply-demand dilemma in community mental health settings. However, some argue that service is compromised, that psychiatric care is diluted, that the poor are given second-class service by paraprofessionals, while a middle-class applicant can negotiate his way through the system and see a psychiatrist. Another danger is that the service offered will be determined by what this less expensive manpower is able to provide, rather than by client need. Thus, the service offered is likely to be concrete social service, less psychiatrically relevant than may sometimes be needed. However, mental health technicians, being used increasingly by community mental health centers around the country, can be trained to provide a variety of appropriate, psychiatrically relevant services. And to the extent that it is recognized that sociotherapeutic approaches are crucial to a broadbased approach to mental health, indigenous paraprofessionals are a valuable community resource.

The reorganization of service.

Here, new approaches and new treatment methods are tried in order to make services more relevant to the expectations of poor people, and more suitable to their life styles. Such new treatment modalities as brief therapy, short-term group approaches, and crisis intervention are considered more effective and economical than the long-term, intensive, analytically oriented approach. However, it is argued that long-term situational problems and primarily personality or neurotic disorders are not amenable to such brief treatment, and are therefore inappropriately treated, referred, or screened out. Some practitioners compare such brief approaches to applying a band-aid to a cancer. Also, individuals who expect long-term treatment (often the middle-class applicants) will continue to demand psychotherapy and be dissatisfied with brief therapy. Then, referral becomes the second line of defense. In actuality, these clients get no services, or the quality of care is compromised. Clearly, the patient often receives treatment different from what he bargained for. Again, a treatment strategy determined by lack of resources is rationalized in therapeutic terms.

The development of community caretakers.

In this approach, the center attempts to identify, support, and upgrade the efforts of the community's informal caretakers—the school guidance personnel, the ministers, general practitioners, et al. Here, the primary thrust is to develop the community's capacity to "treat" its own mentally ill.

The community mental health center provides back-up services, psychiatric consultation as necessary, case consultation, and ongoing support to these caretakers (Caplan 1961, 1964). This approach is aimed at expanding supply in the community. Carried to its extreme, the community mental health center consciously refrains from the direct treatment of patients whenever possible. Many schools and established agencies react to this approach with anger, and accuse the community mental health center of "passing the buck." Communities may then feel that the center is like the other agencies that give the client the "run around," rather than assuming direct treatment responsibility for individuals with problems.

The use of sociotherapy and treatment at a distance.

Here, the approach is broadly to "treat" community ills, such as poor housing, lack of job opportunities, sanitation, etc., rather than to treat the products of these large social disorders. The public health model maintains that improving the conditions of life can reduce rates of illness. While this is generally viewed as primary prevention, it is here being viewed in its therapeutic context. This can be called "treatment at a distance." Leighton's classic study (1965) suggests that changes in the social integration or social cohesion of a community markedly affect rates of pathology. This is perhaps the best illustration of treatment at a distance, and may provide the model for the social action wing of the community mental health movement.

The sociotherapeutic approach involves the population in developing its own resources, competencies, and power through participation and social action as needed (Poston 1963).

Focusing on improving positive mental health, as this approach does, however, may leave untouched those mentally ill people who require direct treatment to maintain themselves outside of hospitals. In addition, the critics argue that mental health professionals should not attempt this sociotherapeutic task, as it is not within their area of expertise, and has little to do with psychiatry. Moreover, programs, such as Mobilization For Youth

(M.F.Y.), which have attempted basic community development, appear to be far short of reaching their goal. Yet, one must be mindful of treating "cases" and leaving untouched the large and very real urban problems that may cause and certainly exacerbate illness. In addition, as we indicated above, the social approach can function as a powerful treatment modality.

The neighborhood service center model.

Here, concrete services provided by paraprofessionals are often provided in lieu of psychotherapy. In this approach, it is argued that what the urban communities need is not psychotherapy, or diagnosis of "inadequate personality," but concrete help and extensive social services to make life more tolerable in the urban ghetto. The mental health worker focuses his efforts on procuring services from the established health and welfare agencies, which may be unresponsive to the client's needs. The mental health worker becomes the mediator, sometimes the advocate of the client (Hallowitz 1968; Peck and Kaplan 1969). Again, this approach is accused of having little relation to psychiatry, of providing for patch-up efforts, and treating symptoms rather than uncovering causes. It can perpetuate the practice of providing psychotherapy for the middle class and concrete services to the poor, as though the latter do not require psychiatric assistance as well.

We have reviewed briefly the major strategies used by community mental health centers to resolve or reduce the supply-demand dilemma in their programs. In practice, these approaches are not applied in isolation, but more often in combination. All have advantages and disadvantages, some clearly more than others. Each presupposes a point of view regarding the primary goals of a community mental health center.

Now, let us look concretely at how one center has

attempted to cope with the supply-demand dilemma it has encountered in practice. It should be clear that by no means is it suggested that the program to be discussed has resolved the dilemma.

A concrete case

Sound View Throgs Neck Community Mental Health Center (SVTN CMHC) is currently in its third year of operation in the southeast Bronx. This center is part of Albert Einstein College of Medicine, Yeshiva University, and serves a total catchment area of 186,000 in an area eight square miles. The population is mixed economically and ethnically, ranging from lower middle-class Italians and Jews to poor blacks and Puerto Ricans. The center has 200 employees, including psychiatrists and the usual clinical professionals, community organizers, an urban planner, and paraprofessionals. SVTN CMHC is funded under federal legislation and contains all the elements required of a community mental health center (inpatient day hospital, outpatient, consultant and education, community services, etc.). The center has experienced a demand for its outpatient clinical services that might quickly outstrip the supply as currently organized. When two of the outpatient units moved into community-based facilities, one in a local shopping center, applications for services vastly increased. When mental health workers spoke at schools, parents' associations, or other community meetings, individuals, many in serious distress, sought out the workers to request appointments. Because adequate supply was not available, the initial stance of the workers and the agency was to "hide out," as it were, thus defeating the very purpose of the program.

Aside from the quantity of services requested, as the outpatient units moved into the community, the types of requests underwent a change as well. Individuals on public assistance came seeking help in finding jobs; old ladies came to "talk to someone" because they were lonely and their families and communities had little use for them. Sometimes, these individuals displayed some *psychiatric symptomatology*—they were depressed, anxious, often labeled "inadequate personalities" by the social workers and psychiatrists who saw them. They were treated as psychiatric patients because this was the nature of the service being offered, and was the "set" used by the mental health professional to define the problem.

The staff wrestled with the problem of expanded utilization of services in a variety of the ways described: restricting intake policy, using paraprofessionals to provide direct clinical services to patients, etc. The response strategies were essentially reactive to the phenomenon of increased utilization. Slowly, a more deliberately planned approach is emerging.

The telephone

The center has explored the use of the telephone to increase supply. It is used selectively for intake evaluation of applicants for service; background data is obtained and a relationship is established so that the first face-to-face interview may be more profitable. (It appears that the drop-out rate is lower after extensive phone contact.) The suicide prevention centers have made extensive use of the telephone, and SVTN CMHC is attempting to explore further and modify its use to add to its resources.

A telephone information service, modeled on HELP, Help Line Center, and other programs, utilizes indigenous paraprofessionals to man a phone twenty-four hours a day. The telephone number is widely circulated in the community and residents are encouraged to call for help with *any* problems, not just psychiatric ones. The paraprofessional examines the request, and connects the person with an appropriate resource in the community, including the outpatient units of the center. Numerous possibilities exist here: forming the callers into self-help, or social action groups, documenting community need for special programs, etc.

Experimental group approaches

The individual, therapist-patient relationship is of necessity giving way to extensive and experimental group and family approaches. Many different types of groups have been tried. Socialization groups for chronically disabled patients appear to be successful in preventing many repeated hospitalizations. These groups are run by paraprofessionals and utilize activities and largely non-verbal tools with these severely disturbed patients. Often, these groups assume a life of their own. One has named itself the "Friendship Club," and between-session visiting and companionship between patients are encouraged. The goal is to have a community center in the catchment area assume primary responsibility for the leadership of these groups, with backup, medication, and consultation from the community mental health center. In this way, these patients can begin to re-enter the "normal" community, the community can provide for their treatment, and the community mental health center can use its resources to initiate other, similar groups.

Other innovations have been tried, such as flexible use of group therapies, including group screening of patients. (These groups can be seen as treatment modalities in themselves and not merely as diagnostic tools.) Clearly, the modality of time-limited group therapy offers one answer to the extreme demand for service in a community mental health center. Experience has shown, however, that the traditionally trained professionals often resist the use of groups, feel uncomfortable with this modality, at least initially, and evaluate the experience as less helpful than do the patients (Behrens, Riessman and Wood study in process).

Extensive use is being made of time-limited, goal-specific groups. Here, patients, of similar age range but with vastly different diagnoses, are placed in a group after careful preparation. Specific but realistic goals for each patient are discussed and worked on in the group; for instance, the return to school for a high school drop-out who is schizophrenic. These groups focus on the unique life tasks that need to be accomplished by the members, and members help one another in very specific ways. In a late-adolescent group, for example, one patient accompanied and assisted another boy while he registered for a high school equivalency program, a task the boy had been unable to undertake himself. Eventually, the plan could include the training of community caretakers to co-lead these groups. At a later point, a co-leader might assume primary responsibility, with the backup of the community mental health center.

Community and school programs

The center devotes a portion of its resources to community development work. It has helped to organize block associations and tenant associations, and has the goal of creating a community council that can enable the community to grapple more effectively with its problems, and develop its social competencies in so doing. We have seen in practice the therapeutic effects of these organizations on individuals as well as on the community at large. Former patients have made use of these groups, often with surprisingly beneficial effect on their symptomatology. For example: "Mrs. W., a 40-year-old, married, Negro woman with six children, supported partially by welfare, called requesting help for her 15-year-old son, who was acting out in school. Mrs. W. had made one suicide gesture in the past, but had no previous treatment. After exploration, and work with the school and a local youth-serving agency so that they could better serve the child, numerous family problems emerged. The husband refused to become involved in marital counseling, and shortly after left the home.

"Mrs. W. became involved in a short-term therapy group, and her passive dependent approach to family difficulties gradually gave way to a more active effort. The group recommended and supported her while she attempted to reestablish some social relationships for herself. She related that the group meant a great deal to her in easing her loneliness and giving her practice in relating to others again. Mrs. W. became angry at the termination of the group—therapeutically a significant step for this patient. She was encouraged to utilize the gains made and to contact the community mental health center in the future should the need arise.

"Several weeks later she called to say that she had become involved in a tenants' league being organized by one of our community workers. She stated the first meeting had taken place in the same room in which the group had met and this had upset her. The worker helped her sort out her feelings in relation to termination, confidentiality, and supported her efforts to become involved in the community group. We learned that she had become one of the officers in the association."

In this case, the community group became the "after care" for this patient.

An extensive school consultation program, guided by a community advisory group, and with strong parental involvement, is an integral part of the community services. It aims at improving the guidance and educational service offered by selected schools in the catchment area. Case, program, and organizational consultation are offered to school staff. Teachers and other personnel here have been trained in group approaches and group guidance that help them to deal with the acute needs they face in the shores. Again, the focus should be on using the resources available in the community to increase supply rather than to substitute the resources of the community mental health center.

Human service network

SVTN CMHC sees as one of its primary purposes the creation of an effective human service network. The center consults with community centers, churches, senior citizens' centers and other service-giving agencies in an effort to improve and extend its services, enable agencies to identify community needs, and work together to meet those needs. The center is working toward the creation of a collaborative service network, in which the community mental health center will be only a small part.

A case example illustrates how this approach multiplies supply: "Three years ago, a preschool program requested help from the community mental health center to lead therapy groups for parents. Staff was provided by the center, and the agency felt this to be a beneficial service. Much case finding was done through these groups, and many parents became patients at the center. After an evaluation of this relationship in light of the goals of the Human Service Network, a new approach was taken. The community mental health center said it could no longer continue to provide a staff leader. In order to continue the group program, the consultant offered to train an agency staff member and co-lead a group with her for a limited time. This was done systematically, and the following year the agency staff member, a paraprofessional, led a similar group herself, with only consultation from the community mental health center.

"The parents volunteered in increased numbers for

this 'discussion group,' as it was called, and decided to alternate activities with the discussion of problems. One group continued to meet without the staff member during the summer. Fewer referrals for service came from this agency as the program progressed, for the parents were urged to use the group." These are some of the approaches one community mental health center has adopted in its struggle with the supply-demand dilemma, which of course it has not resolved. It is apparent that many of the demand-meeting mechanisms proposed can also increase demand; for example, the telephone information service.

Other approaches to the dilemma, not attempted by SVTN CMHC, might include the following—

1. professionally-led therapy groups started in the clinical setting, moving into the community with trained volunteers, community caretakers, or patient leaders, supported by "intermittent reinforcement" and consultation from the professional staff;

2. a thorough investigation of the self-help approaches might be integrated selectively in a community mental health center. Possibilities here include a network of self-help groups located in the community, modeled on A.A., Recovery Inc., but with clearly established professional liaison. The basic principle here is that individuals with problems may be able to play a crucial role in aiding others with problems, thereby increasing the supply of services. In a sense, suppliers of services might be created from among the demanders of service, thus multiplying resources in a unique fashion;

3. social action groups pressuring existing agencies and the larger institutional forces to provide more and different kinds of service, directed at expanding supply in the community.

Conclusion

From these experiences, several implications emerge:

1. Community mental health planners must be *aware of the supply-demand dilemma* and develop some frustration-tolerance for its existence, in order to avoid suppressing demand by introducing waiting lists, restricting intake policy, making the service difficult to obtain, etc.

2. *A "proactive" planned approach*, rather than a reactive posture to cope with the problem is essential, otherwise ad hoc, piecemeal stopgaps develop. For example, the community mental health center can respond to the accelerating demand for service by expanding direct services, allocating a larger share of its budget for individuals in need, with only token payment for consultation and education services, community development, and primary prevention approaches. Rather, we would propose a planned distribution of community mental health center resources based on a thorough understanding of the dilemma and a conscious ordering of priorities.

3. An additional dilemma faces the community mental health movement today, one related to its multiple mandates and multiple roles. The mental health worker becomes the mediator, the catalyst, the service giver, the advocate, the consultant, the social diagnostician, to name but a few roles. This dilemma still further compounds the supply-demand dilemma. It may mean spreading services too thin, diluting service, and the approaches are often difficult to integrate. It may be argued that this dilemma reflects the imperialism of community mental health—it is a field that tries to do everything. In a sense, mental health is affected by everything,

and needs to address itself to the fabric of systems, both internal and external, to which the individual relates.

4. From sharing the supply-demand dilemma with our communities, rather than providing *solutions from above*, a new process is started, new competencies can emerge, and alternatives may develop that are not to be found within the repertoire of intervention as traditionally practiced by the professional.

Such an approach represents a new stance for the professional. He would become less remote, and the mask of "professional mystique" would give way to a genuine participatory process with increased accountability to the consumer. The professional would honestly admit both the lack of resources and his limited technology to do completely the community mental health job; he would admit his vulnerability. The effect could be that, rather than attempting only to treat illness, the community mental health center would stimulate the emergence of therapeutic processes (Gendlin 1968) in the community itself, and in the "patient."

It is important to recognize that there is massive institutional resistance to the vast expansion of resources needed to deal with the problem, and this resistance lies at the base of the dilemma. It may be that *only with a massive influx of supplies can the dilemma really be resolved.* More jobs, housing, recreational facilities require money and national commitment. The stance that the community mental health center takes in relation to this reality may determine whether mental health services will indeed be a pacification program (Statman 1970)*,

*Elsewhere in this volume.

a patchwork of remedial efforts that leaves institutional inequities in the social system of the country untouched. The attitude of the community mental health center regarding social action in behalf of communities to increase the resources available to individuals cannot be bypassed or ignored.

To some extent, the entire supply-demand dilemma is framed by the basically limited resources directed toward human needs in our society. In this context, it is natural that relative improvements in the way services are offered will stimulate more of the vast untapped demand.

In essence, the supply-demand dilemma is historically conditioned. In a society abundant with human services, it may disappear rapidly, just as the underutilization of services, so salient a decade ago, is becoming historically irrelevant in the current period.

Summary

The paradox facing community mental health programs is that as the program proceeds successfully in contacting the community and establishing a positive, receptive image, the demand for services rapidly outstrips the supply of currently organized therapeutic modalities.

Experience with the supply-demand problem indicates that typical response strategies to handle the increased demand have been—

1. restrictive intake policy—subtle brush-off for all but bona-fide psychiatric emergencies;
2. the waiting list;
3. the referral route;
4. the use of auxiliary manpower (paraprofessionals) to provide "psychosocial first aid";
5. reorganization of service—use of different treatment modalities (crisis intervention, phone screening

and treatment, brief psychotherapy);

6. development of community caretakers as auxiliary treatment supports;

7. sociotherapy—treatment at a distance;

8. neighborhood service center model—providing services in lieu of psychotherapy.

The supply-demand dilemma cannot be faced by the professional alone, with solutions from above; the consumers of the service, and the community in general, need to join the professional as partners in sharing the problem and establishing priorities, keeping in mind the fundamental paradox: a properly offered service produces a new order of demand which cannot be met by our present allocation of resources.

Bibliography

Adams, P. and McDonald, N. 1968. Clinical cooling out of poor people. *Amer. J. Orthopsychiat.* 38:457-463.

Behrens, M. 1969. Clinical services in a community mental health program. *Current psychiatric therapies* 9:224-233.

Behrens, M., Riessman, C. K., and Wood, M. Short term therapy as total treatment. (In preparation.)

Brill, N. and Storrow, H. 1960. Social class and psychiatric treatment. *Arch. Gen. Psychiat.* 3:340-344.

Caplan, G. 1961. *An approach to community mental health,* pp. 205-231. New York: Grune.

——————. 1964. *Principles of preventive psychiatry,* pp. 212-266. New York: Basic Books.

Dryfoos, J. and Manisoff, M. 1969. Estimated manpower needs for a national family planning program. *Perspectives* 1:40-41.

Feldman, S. and Jacobson, M. 1969. Intake policy as a community organization tool. *Community Mental Health Journal* 5:75-83.

Freedman, R., Whelpton, P. and Campbell, A. 1959. *Family planning, sterility & population growth,* p. 40. New York: McGraw-Hill.

Gendlin, E. 1968. Psychotherapy & community psychology. *Psychotherapy: Theory, Research & Practice* 5:72.

Grosser, C., Henry, W., and Kelley, J., eds. 1961. *Nonprofessionals in the human services.* San Francisco: Jossey-Bass.

Hollingshead, A. and Redlich, F. 1958. *Social class and mental illness.* New York: Wiley.

Hallowitz, E. 1968. The role of a neighborhood service center in community mental health. *Amer. J. Orthopsychiat.* 38:705-714.

Leighton, A. 1965. Poverty and social change. *Scient. American* 212:21-27.

Lewis, O. 1959. *Five families: Mexican case studies in the culture of poverty.* New York: Basic Books.

Pasamanick, B. et al. 1959. A survey of mental disease in an urban population: prevalence by race and income. In *Epidemiology of mental disorder,* ed. H. Massbaum, pp. 183-196. Washington, D.C.: American Association for Advancement of Science.

Peck, H. and Kaplan, S. 1969. A mental health program for the urban multiservice center, In *Mental health and the community,* eds. M. Shore and F. Mennino, pp. 130-133. New York: Behavioral Publications.

Polgar, S. 1966. United States: The PPFA mobile service project in New York City. *Studies in Family Planning* 15:9-15.

Poston, R. 1963. Comparative community organization. In *The urban condition,* ed. L. Duhl. New York: Basic Books.

Rainwater, L. 1960. *And the poor get children,* p. 24. Chicago: Quadrangle.

Riessman, C. 1968. Birth control, culture and the poor. *Amer. J. Orthopsychiat.* 38:693-699.

Rioch, M. et al. 1963. NIMH pilot study in training mental health counselors. *Amer. J. Orthopsychiat.* 33:678-689.

Srole, I. et al. 1962. *Mental health in the metropolis: The Midtown Manhattan Study,* Vol. 1. New York: McGraw-Hill.

Star, S. 1955. The public's ideas about mental illness. Paper presented at annual meeting of the National Association for Mental Health, at Indianapolis, Ind.

—————. 1957. The place of psychiatry in popular thinking. Paper presented at annual meeting of the American Association for Public Opinion Research, at Washington, D.C.

Statman, J. 1970. Community mental health as a pacification program. Paper presented at 47th annual meeting of the American Orthopsychiatric Association, at San Francisco, Calif.

Stewart, J. C. 1967. Employment of indigenous personnel as a strategy for increasing immunization rates in "hard core" areas. Doctoral dissertation, University of Oklahoma.

Suchman, E. 1963. *Sociology and the field of public health.* New York: Russell Sage.

Teele, J. and Levine, S. 1957. The acceptance of children by psychiatric agencies. In *Controlling delinquents,* ed. Stanton Wheeler. New York: Wiley.

Wilder, J., Levin, G., and Zwerling, I. 1970. Planning and developing the locus of care. In *Community psychiatry,* ed. H. Grunebaum. New York: Little.

271

HEW's Inner-City Training Program:
An Experiment in Change
Natalie Davis Spingarn

In the spring of 1968, the last of 6 groups of about 35 top-level federal officials departed from an unusual experimental Baltimore live-in. For 2½ days they had been immersed in the flesh and blood lives of the inner-city poor.

Almost all were from the Department of Health, Education, and Welfare, with formidable titles which denoted responsibility for programs like Medical Assistance, Hill-Burton, or Elementary and Secondary School Education. Directors, deputies and branch chiefs had followed the ground rules carefully: wear sensible shoes; walk or use public transportation; visit 3 out of 4 or 5 programs offered in your discipline; spend no more than 33 cents for lunch (then a third of the daily public welfare allotment in Baltimore) and carry no brief cases or other badges of bureaucracy. Armed only with the basic facts about Baltimore, a map of the city and a bus schedule, they set out singly or in pairs.

There were few meetings. The excursion focused on HEW and the closely-related programs of such agencies as OEO—how they affected their ultimate recipients and the field office troops who deliver services on the frontlines. The idea was not to look *at* poverty, but to produce what one trainee described later as "a kaleidoscope of images which has destroyed the comfort of intellectual rationalization . . ." With such images simmering in their minds, it was hoped that government leaders would arrive at new, and perhaps better, ways of running their own programs, and meshing them more effectively.

Many such live-in, plunge, or immersion sessions have sprung up over the past years. Some are day long, others last two or more weeks. Some give participants a dollar or two and let them shift for themselves; some involve considerable role playing; others are just bus tours through the slums. This paper is presented so that those who work in large bureaucratic organizations—in and out of government—might benefit from our experiences, both good and bad, in planning such a training approach.

Tooling up

The Center for Community Planning which was assigned the management of the program, was organized in 1967 by Secretary John Gardner as the federal government's largest domestic department, strove to grapple with the urban crisis. It dealt with interdepartmental programs like Model Cities; internally within HEW, its mandate was to focus the resources of the department on the problems of the cities. This meant that HEW, with its $50 billion budget, 250 socially oriented programs, and 110,000 staff members, was seeking to serve American cities more effectively.

A very early focus of this effort was the deeper involvement in inner-city programs of HEW officials who ran hospital, school, or vocational rehabilitation programs—and made daily decisions affecting the "guts" of inner-city life. We knew that they were usually well trained and highly motivated. But for the most part, they were deskbound and paper focused.

Living in a slum—smelling it, tasting it, suffering with it—is quite different from looking at it from a taxi window. As one distinguished physician high up in the manpower hierarchy put it, while picking up a plastic garbage pail full of rat holes: "I haven't seen a rat for 30 years." He and the rest of us learned from the dynamic Baltimore rat eradication program chief, John Childs (who wore a tie clasp in the shape of a rat), when he explained the key to success in his vigorous war on rats: hire neighborhood young people to help in cleanups rather than sending in your own people.

Baltimore: 1701 West Pratt

We named our project "The Inner-City Training Program," avoiding the more condescending words "sensitivity training," and chose Baltimore as our training site. It was a city with urban-oriented leadership, which we judged would be sympathetic to an influx of federal officials. It was also only an hour away (from Washington, D.C.), easy to reach by train, automobile, and bus. Statistics we later included in our Training Kit showed Baltimore as a typical American City with typical inner-city problems—sixth largest city in the country, with 2 million people, the twelfth largest labor force and the third highest unemployment rate in the nation. Between 1950 and 1964, its suburban population increased 89.9 percent; 144,590 white people moved out of the city, and 133,500 nonwhite people moved in.

Mayor Theodore Roosevelt McKeldin, a Republican with populist views, was, as we had hoped, delighted at the prospect the program presented. He proved the validity of our theory that, when working in a city—even when observing its faults—it's wise to start at city hall. He came to the point immediately: "Mrs. Spingarn," he said, "I like federal money. Just tell me what you want. And when you're finished, tell us what's wrong." We ran six sessions over a eight-month period in Baltimore, and we had to explain constantly to the city officials that we were not there to evaluate—or even to suggest—what was right or wrong, but to learn and thus try to improve our own performance as public officials.

In every big city hall these days, there is a human resource office or human relations person and Mayor McKeldin assigned this man to us as our contact. The practice was continued by Mayor Thomas D'Alesandro III when he was elected the following fall. The city department heads met with us and we asked them for lists of programs our trainees might visit and in which they might participate.

Our first day in Baltimore we touched base with Daniel Thursz, who was just about to be named Dean of the University of Maryland's School of Social Work (now the School of Social Work and Community Planning). He offered us the use of the school's VISTA Training Center as a training base. The center was ideally located at 1701 West Pratt Street in the heart of a poor white neighborhood, mostly blue collar workers of Irish and Eastern European background, with all the problems one would expect, including a rising delinquency rate, and the highest mental illness rate in the city. Two blocks north ran Baltimore Street, separating the black ghetto from the white; and three blocks east lay the beginning of the Model Cities area.

The center consisted of an old, small convent and an adjoining school house which had been closed by the Archdiocese when the parish refused to integrate with an adjoining parish some years back. It had the advantage not only of location (even Bill's Bar across the street was a realistic white poverty laboratory), but of providing exactly the amount of discomfort middle-aged physicians, administrators and social workers might be asked to bear: the army cots; the community toilets; the dirty alleys; the hordes of little children chalking obscenities on the front doors; and the noise, above all the noise—roaring in from the streets when you opened the windows at night, or causing you to shut the windows and suffocate. Still, it was our home away from home; if to learn, one needs both confrontation and support, 1701 West Pratt helped supply both.

Program design: orientation

Through Social Security Commissioner Robert Ball, we acquired the part-time services of an able, community relations worker from the Social Security Administration, Mrs. June Williams Greene. Mrs. Greene, a young social worker who had been on the Baltimore Public Welfare Department staff, knew the inner city and the Baltimore agencies well. She handled liaison with Baltimore agencies, a detail-heavy job which involved much time and legwork before each of the six program sessions. Once a trainee had decided what activities he wished to visit, she carried the ball, arranging all scheduling, phoning agency personnel, and mollifying local officials when trainees canceled, or switched program choices.

Such choices were made at an hour-long orientation meeting, ten days or two weeks before the actual training began. At this orientation, we explained the program and its intent, and gave trainees a kit containing—

1. *a fact sheet* outlining the schedule for the 2½ days in Baltimore, and describing living arrangements;

2. *a list of program choices,* divided into three columns: the first column—"If you are interested in this program," (i.e., *Family Living*); the second column, "which offer these services," (supplements to welfare payments for rents and other services to selected families consisting of a mother and at least four children); the third column, "you could" (go with caseworkers or aides to visit the families);

3. *a city map and bus schedule* to help find the way;

4. *a fact sheet* about Baltimore, emphasizing inner-city problems and a *copy of a newspaper article* on HEW-funded programs in Baltimore;

5. *a roster of fellow participants.*

Of the 40 programs offered, prospective trainees chose the 6 in which they were most interested; of these they would be assigned 3, 4, or even 5 according to their preference. Some asked to be worked hard and scheduled themselves rigorously, others preferred fewer, more intensive visits. We tried to see that at least one experience got them into a client's home and gave them the chance to accompany and talk with a case worker, sanitarian, or public health nurse making routine rounds.

We also asked them to choose one evening visit, and to have a look at a variety of program areas rather than just concentrating on their own. In the first summer of 1967 we allayed fears by stipulating that women trainees should not go out alone on evening visits. We also checked with the city and its police officials before each visit. Our understanding was that they were to be frank with us about conditions in the city. If there was real danger, or if our presence would interfere with their duties in any way, we would cancel. We never had to.

We explained the ground rules: that trainees were to be living in the inner city; that they were to use public transportation only; that they were to eat at least one lunch for 33 cents. We also explained that if they could be comfortable doing so, they should act as participant observers, assisting as much as they could in their program visits. For a few, this might mean actual role playing in specific situations, for instance, acting the part of a patient or client. For others, it might mean being paired with a nurse on her slum rounds; for still others, sitting and listening at a clinic intake desk. Generally, we precluded mandatory role playing, feeling we should not ask high officials to dress in old clothes and pretend to be something they were not.

Program design: Baltimore

Usually, the program began on a Monday with a 5 p.m. reception at city hall. (If the mayor's schedule

precluded this, we ended the program in his office.)
D'Alesandro, a direct, young mayor, used to look us in
the eye, and put it bluntly: "We need help. We're in bad
shape here. There's a tremendous amount of unrest down
in the street. We're fighting a delaying action and we're
fighting it without tools. We've got to come up with
some bread." He got straight to the core of the matter:
the steady exodus of tax paying, middle-income families
to the suburbs; spiraling school and other social needs
demanding more funds; and increased welfare rolls. It
was no wonder he felt "like I'm walking on quicksand."

Trainees next went to the VISTA center for supper
and first program visits. There were facilities for heating
food at the center; we had our meals catered. The
Baltimore Welfare Department was still using surplus
foods during the first program (it later switched to food
stamps) and we arranged with Esther Lazarus, the vigorous, sympathetic welfare director, to use this food in the
meals. This proved futile: the caterer took the raisins and
dressed them up in a carrot and raisin salad; dry milk
was made into an elegant dessert. When we complained,
the culture gap asserted itself: "These foods are good,"
he explained. *"Those* people just don't know how to use
them."

The program visits were, of course, the core of the
program. The discussions with the mayor, and later with
Baltimore officials, came alive when participants tried to
follow a typical route of a welfare client: facing the
countless forms to be completed; and seemingly endless
travel back and forth for help; going to a legal service
center and seeing a lawyer help a middle-aged AFDC
(welfare) complainant; or when others pretended they
were patients in a community mental health program; or
it might be a parent involvement program where mothers
(and some fathers) of school-age children got a free
breakfast and two hours of instruction in basic education, home economics, and general cultural background.

One of the few non-HEW trainees, HUD's Jim King, evaluating the program, wrote:

> My notion is that we think too big to meet the needs of little people when we concentrate on changing the system. The system obviously turns out a product that relieves pain—at least in the short run—and should be not only retained, but improved and expanded. On the other hand we need to take a look at the system . . . Are welfare and legal aid part of the same system? If so why does legal aid have three important legal suits against the Department of Public Welfare? What would be the situation under a "block grant" to the city? Better or worse?

After an early breakfast the next morning, the trainees embarked on their second program visit. They were due back at the training center at 3:30 for a discussion of coordination problems with the Baltimore agency staff. This seminar grew out of the HEW leadership's desire to somehow achieve better coordination among HEW programs to give the different branches of the HEW empire the chance to know each other's programs and problems better. We invited first line workers, nurses, teachers and social workers to our first session, but found they had few managerial insights into coordination problems: They were as confounded as anyone else by the school program that didn't report a child who was falling behind for lack of food or eyeglasses. So we switched to the supervisory personnel.

These men and women spoke of overlapping functions, duplication of efforts, and lack of money. We heard people like Gerry Aronin, Chief of Community Relations for the City Department of Welfare, tell us that people who plan programs don't think. She gave us the example of a slum child hurt in an accident, who was fitted with an expensive heavy appliance. His mother was told to bring him twice a week to a suburban hospital. But even if she had 50 cents bus fare for herself, and 50 cents for her child (which the welfare department didn't provide), she couldn't lift the child onto the bus. If she took him to the hospital, she left four kids behind. If she didn't take him, she was neglectful. If she took the other kids, that cost money, and if they ran around the hospital, she was considered a woman who couldn't control her own children.

That evening we had dinner in the center with neighborhood residents recruited through the mayor's human relations office—a highlight for some, unsettling to most. Several welfare mothers, for instance, gave the bureaucrats a reading of the high temperature of the ghetto. One welfare leader told the people at her table: "When we ask for jobs, we have to ask a lot of questions. What kind of jobs? Will they benefit my kids later on or will they be overcome with automation? I don't have to demonstrate for no elevator job, because I can get that now. Talk about guaranteed income, sure, but for whom, how much, how long?" A member of the Maryland Council for Interracial Justice told the visitors that "black people are tired of the double standard, of white Ph.D.'s writing books about us, and giving us Negro leaders." And, a civics and history teacher held: "The white people don't care about us. I worked at Bethlehem Steel for eight years, and I saw hundreds of white people promoted over me who didn't have any-where near my qualifications."

There were 2 more program visits: an optional one that night for the energetic and a final visit the next morning. The program ended with a 1 p.m. wrap-up session. We had hoped at first to recruit a nationally known urbanist to lead this two-hour meeting—lifting the trainees' experiences out of one city, Baltimore, and applying them to the broader social and political scene. Anxious, as befits a community-minded school of social work, to participate in the program, the University of Maryland School of Social Work head asked to participate more fully. HEW granted a small contract, under which the school took responsibility for the coordination, gave us staff support, and provided Dean Thursz to lead the wrap-up session.

To sum up, the program design included at least 3 program visits, and as many as 5 for the energetic, a session with the mayor, a seminar on coordination, a dinner meeting with neighborhood residents and a final wrap-up session.

Resistances: the pilot

We ran our own center staff of about 20 people, including a representative of each of the HEW agencies, through the program in August, 1967. This may not have been a true test, for our staff was smaller, younger, possibly more flexible and "with" community problems different than those of officials running big programs. But it went well. We had not wanted press coverage because it's hard to talk naturally with a welfare client or school child in the presence of a reporter. However, the story did leak and several reporters attended; they wrote sympathetic stories with pictures of bureaucrats among slum clildren. This publicity increased the popularity of the program in the department.

Our popularity badly needed a lift, though Secretary Gardner approved the program and gave it his strong support. Resistance surprised the bureaucratically naïve among us. We failed to gain the involvement of the personnel people in the office of the secretary; one personnel officer who planned to attend the pilot program backed off because she feared ghetto uprisings. So we went ahead alone. Each participant paid his own living costs (about $18 for room and board) to the training center. He was reimbursed on a per diem basis, at $18 a day for 2½ days; using public transportation and eating a 33-cent lunch, he came out a little ahead.

More important was the resistance that came from prospective trainees themselves. Comparisons are odious, but we did find that those people we had expected to be most sympathetic with the experiment—the welfare staff—seemed to resent it, feeling they *knew* the ghetto, understood its problems and hardly needed a refresher exercise which might prove extraneous to their work. (Later they turned into some of the most responsive trainees.) The commissioned public health officers, on the other hand, seemed to react most favorably, perhaps because they were used to taking military-type orders. Some of our most excited, involved trainees were distinguished physicians running multi-million dollar programs like Hill-Burton. The office of education people, for the most part, regarded their nomination as something to negotiate.

The system we evolved was to ask the commissioners, or agency heads, to submit lists of decision-maker nominees; later we asked that some young people be included, to bring us a fresh point of view. Working from these lists, I spent endless hours contacting people, telling them they had been nominated and pinning down the time of their visit. We had hoped at first to schedule the programs at bi-weekly intervals. This proved impossible for various reasons, most important of which was the extraordinary difficulty of persuading real decision-makers to come. Persuasion cannot be done by someone low on the bureaucratic totem pole, however capable he may be. One needs the boss's clout.

Again people varied in their responses according to personality and agency. Resistance faded as the program became more prestigious. But we always counted on an attrition of ten or more due to illness, pressing business, secretarial or congressional calls, and so forth. And once we were in Baltimore, a wild assortment of events and unheard of calamities summoned people home: family crises, bosses with questions, and the need to prepare for congressional hearings.

Contrasted with the federal resistance, municipal resistance was negligible. The cooperation of the city itself, and its institutions, including the University of Maryland School of Social Work, was generous and enthusiastic. Occasionally, we had to remind city agencies not to treat our trainees to royal tours, but either to ignore them, let them listen to what was going on, or invite them in as active participants. Early in the program, a fourth-hand rumor was heard from the streets: the militants resented our coming into the inner city to look *at* them and they might picket us. We reacted by inviting the neighborhood residents to be our guests for dinner and give us their point of view about our programs. If a picket line had formed, we would have asked it in, too. But it never did.

Impact

Six sessions produced a multitude of impressions. There was the emergency clinic of a hospital, which serves as the doctor to the inner-city poor. Four trainees ended up working desperately hard at the intake desk helping the volunteer lady who had come to help five days and stayed five years. The clinic was understaffed and ill-managed, with crowds of people packed on poorly arranged benches, waiting for hours to be seen. We called the doctor's attention to a little girl who had fallen off her bike that afternoon and was sitting there with an ugly, swollen eye. We had to turn away a couple who wanted birth control pills (the planned parenthood clinic was closed; the doctors brushed them off). We shuffled Medicaid cards and countless other papers; it was rumored that one doctor thought it was worse than a clinic in Thailand.

There were those 33-cent lunches. That sum doesn't cover a hamburger and coffee, or even a plain 35-cent hot dog. One trainee bought a bowl of soup with it and then was so hungry he ate saltines buttered with ketchup! As for public transportation, it gets you there, but the ride is bumpy and it takes the sort of time most two-car families don't have (in 1967, 79 percent of American households owned one car; and 25 percent owned two cars or more). The rides to the welfare department across Baltimore take about 40 minutes, and in the summer you get hot waiting for transfers; in winter, cold; in the rain, wet. . . . There was the police officer who showed our trainees, while driving together through the streets at night, a glue sniffing street gang. Because of insurance technicalities, the city could not let us ride in patrol cars; but it supplied us with two "community relations" officers and cars to drive us about. . . . There was the mother of ten illegitimate children in the pioneer family living program who wanted to find a job and was trying to find the way with help from her earnest young social worker.

Trainees, as might be expected, reacted differently. The impact varied with the extent a person could participate. Some threw themselves into the program and were absorbed by it. A young woman played the role of a patient, went through a maternal and child health clinic, with its teenage mothers and 15-year-old putative fathers, got sick to her stomach and had to leave. Another became involved with a little girl and her family in The Johns Hopkins Hospital and stuck with her into the night until her problem was solved. The department's assistant general counsel asked so many good questions at the welfare department that he almost brought it to a standstill. A research chief in the welfare department saw vocational rehabilitation programs in action for the first time. A rehabilitation worker, who obviously hadn't wanted to come, was genuinely hostile. He spent the night in a motel and then left.

We handed out evaluation forms to the 200 trainees. The first question, *Did you get sufficient information at the orientation sessions?* was answered affirmatively, though some wanted more facts about their program choices which, we felt, would have taken the program from the sensory to the intellectual level. The answer to the second question, *Were the program visits a positive experience for you?* was an almost unanimous "yes" with a few exceptions—those to whom "it was nothing new." For the most part, the positive experience was a result of the opportunity to experience HEW programs at first hand: "No amount of reading," said one, "could convey the personal impact of seeing for myself."

Comments in the answer to the third question, *What did you find out about HEW programs and the way they affect people?* generally reflected dismay at fragmented services and inadequate funds. Agency personnel were seen as dedicated, but working with too little and too late. Clients were seen as needing help, appreciative for what they got, and confused about overlapping services: "The history of their life seems to be one referral after another," said one of the program participants.

The *panel discussion on coordination* turned out to be the weakest part of the program. One trainee described it as a "pointless game called 'who's to blame' " and indeed one of the hallmarks of the discussions seemed to be an unwillingness to accept responsibility for programs. People would say "Oh, if only the secretary would come," or "If only senator 'so and so' would come." Working in the legislative branch, one finds a similar tendency to feel that the executive can solve problems; in the secretary's office, that the bureaucracy must do so, and vice versa. Overwhelmed by the flesh-and-blood reality of the inner city, everyone feels helpless.

The *evening with residents* was, for most, extremely rewarding. The most frequent criticism was that the activist militants among them were not typical of the ghetto poor they were meeting out in the city during daytime visits: the militants were performing. But it was an opportunity to meet people who "could not be reached in reasonable argument." Some felt we should have included more of the silent majority of middle-class Negroes. The *final seminar,* led by Dean Thursz, was for some, "classroomish," but for most it was worthwhile.

Another question we asked was *How did the whole experience suggest new approaches to your program concerns?* and the responses varied. Some questioned the federal practice of funding demonstration or pilot programs which communities cannot continue. Some stressed the inclusion of the community in planning. Some saw the need to review priorities.

We also asked *what participants learned about programs other than their own.* Many welcomed the opportunity to meet people from other than their own bailiwicks, and realized they all had the same problems. We asked *what they learned about other programs.* Many were impressed with the OEO contribution. Though, as one trainee put it, "OEO and HEW seem to be walking down the lane hand in hand, but their hands aren't touching." (The OEO role has changed considerably since this time.)

Specific questions about *using public transportation* and *the 33-cent lunch,* which some thought "gimmicky," brought specific and some unrealistic suggestions: "give us money for the day—breakfast, lunch and dinner—and let us struggle," or "have participants purchase food and live in the ghetto for one week to a month."

More than half of the participants felt that *the program gave thorough first-hand exposure to the ways HEW-funded programs affect* the lives of inner-city people to a *great degree*; almost all the rest felt it did so *moderately.* Most *would have made no structural changes* but the most frequent suggestion was more personal contact with clients and other residents. Though several asked for more time in the inner city, most felt the 2½ days enough to make an impact (and realistically, it was the longest we could keep them in Baltimore). While a few felt the program should be restricted to policy-makers, others felt it should be available to all HEW employees.

We asked the participants to *rate the program on a scale* "as a learning experience to you as an HEW official." Nineteen rated it 100; two rated it 30; the largest number, 45, rated it 80; the average was 76. Since participants were asked to rate the program as a "learning experience," the strongest ratings come from those with little previous exposure in the field. In each group, a few gave the program a relatively low score because they felt they had seen it all before. A few participants gave the program a lower score because they were asked to rate it as *HEW officials*; they said the program was extremely valuable as a personal experience but not directly job-related.

We asked for other comments and these were pungent and varied. There is space for only a few here:

"My chief impression (of HEW programs in the inner city) was of some very able highly motivated and articulate mice trying to attack a bull elephant."

"I do not believe that the use of professional time in this manner is appropriate or economical."

"I felt that I had been out of the field only three years and had not forgotten what it was like to be 'in the market place.' I am very pleased that I participated. I had forgotten what it was really like for the caseworker to walk the dirty streets with broken beer bottles and other litter . . . it was enlightening for me to observe the frustration of a dedicated caseworker who recognized the many needs of the family yet has available so few resources."

"All in all, the two days made a tremendous impact on me, and left me shaken and disturbed . . ."

Although more than 200 people experienced the Inner-City Training Program, we have no hard data on how we changed HEW performance. We have the evaluations and we have impressions: A doctor who helped handle a crucial Newark situation seemed to do so with increased insight. A nursing official recommended counseling for future LPN's trying to adjust their busy training schedules to their patients' harassed lives—an idea, she explained, realized as a result of her Baltimore experience. All health manpower staff was asked to reevaluate their programs, and did. Public information people concluded that despite hundreds of HEW publicity experts, there was little communication with the inner city. For example, even in HEW-funded clinics, the free literature racks were filled with industry throwaways picturing smiling Gerber babies and *Good Housekeeping* ladies. They formed a task force to take action on this matter. Rehabilitation, welfare, and education executives all told us their attitudes toward grant applications had changed. They began to see things less from the point of view of the institution whose applications they were reading, than that of the ultimate recipient of services.

Still, we failed to fit the program into the ongoing administrative scheme so that it could have a continuing effect on program management. There was a great deal of interest in it in other agencies—HUD, labor, Civil Service, justice, and officials from these other agencies were briefed at their request. HEW's Kansas City region staged an inner-city program following our format, with trainees, unfortunately, going home to their spouses and good dinners at night. New Jersey's Department of Community Affairs worked with our design to put on a striking, short-lived program in Trenton, which aimed to include important institutional volunteer board members as trainees with state officials.

Since the Center for Community Planning's mission was to spark new programs, not to run them, we suggested to the new Secretary, Wilbur J. Cohen, that the Inner-City Training Program belonged in the Office of the Deputy Assistant Secretary for Personnel or in the Civil Service Commission's Training Section. Negotiations were started, with the secretary's approval, and there was discussion of a sizeable contract with the University of Maryland School of Social Work under which the school would staff and run this program for the government.

With the change in administration, the natural inclination of the new people to follow their own bent, and ever tightening restrictions on program funding, the inner-city program has been lost in the shuffle. True, priorities have to be set; programs have to compete for their slice of the federal pie. The other side of the coin is that increased coordination and more expert management based on incisive understanding can cut costs, as well as increase human happiness.

Summary

A major federal department undertook an inner-city training program in 1967-68 with considerable success. More than 200 decision-making Department of Health, Education and Welfare officials participated in 6 sessions of this innovative program. Evaluations and empirical judgment showed that great impact on such official trainees can be made through their experiencing inner-city life, without, necessarily, any in-depth self-examination or classical sensitivity training.

contributors

Charles W. Archibald is a mental health consultant, Indian Health Service, Health Services and Mental Health Administration, Albuquerque, New Mexico.

Harold M. Baron is currently on the staff of the Urban Studies Program, Associated Colleges of the Midwest located in Chicago. He is an historian who has spent many years as a professional in the civil rights movement. He is now writing a book on racism in modern America, under a grant from the Russell Sage Foundation.

Irving N. Berlin is professor of psychiatry and pediatrics, head of the Division of Child Psychiatry, and co-director of social and community psychiatry, University of Washington School of Medicine. In addition to his many professional activities, Dr. Berlin has written extensively for scholarly publications.

Harvey Bluestone is currently director of the Department of Psychiatry at the Bronx Lebanon Hospital Center. In addition to his professional affiliations, he has contributed frequently to publications in the fields of psychiatry and mental health.

Michael Brower currently is a lecturer in the Florence Heller Graduate School of Advanced Studies in Social Welfare at Brandeis University. Dr. Brower is a political economist who studies development—human, social and economic.

John C. Cratsley is a staff attorney with Cambridge and Somerville Legal Services in Cambridge, Massachusetts, and a teaching fellow in law and clinical practice at Harvard Law School.

Joseph P. Fitzpatrick currently is professor of sociology at Fordham University and chairman of the Department of Sociology and Anthropology. He is the author of *Puerto Rican Americans: The Meaning of Migration to the Mainland* (1971), and co-author with John M. Martin and Robert E. Gould of *The Analysis of Delinquent Behavior* (1969).

Sarah Flores is a mental health aide at the Bronx Lebanon Hospital Center, Department of Psychiatry and is studying for her R.N. degree. Previous publications include a paper on spiritism in *The Bulletin: New York State District Branch, American Psychiatric Association* (Oct. 1969).

Robert E. Gould is associate professor of psychiatry at New York University Medical Center and director of adolescent psychiatry at Bellevue Psychiatric Hospital. He is co-author with John M. Martin and Joseph P. Fitzpatrick of *The Analysis of Delinquent Behavior* (1969).

Alan E. Guskin is currently provost at Clark University, Worcester, Massachusetts. He is the co-author of a text on the social psychology of education.

Elizabeth Herzog is project director, Social Research Group, at George Washington University, Washington, D.C. She has written numerous articles and is co-author of *Life is with People* (1952). Her most recent book is *About the Poor: Some Facts and Some Fictions* (1968).

Carl L. Kline is clinical assistant professor of psychiatry, University of British Columbia, Vancouver, British Columbia. In addition to a private practice in child, adolescent, and family psychiatry, he is Canadian editor of *Excerpta Medica,* and he serves on the editorial board of the Bulletin of the Orton Society.

Morton Levitt is professor of psychology and associate dean for academic affairs at the University of California, Davis School of Medicine.

Renee Pellman is currently a family therapist with the Family Mental Health Clinic of Jewish Family Service of New York and is in private practice. She has also worked in the field of child psychology and is author of several publications.

Beatrice Purdy currently is chief psychiatric social worker at the Bronx Lebanon Hospital Center's Department of Psychiatry. Prior to this, she had extensive experience in family and child welfare agencies both in Michigan and New York.

Katherine Weavers Rider became director of staff development for the Children's Aid Society of Vancouver, British Columbia, upon emigration to Canada in 1967.

Although Mrs. Rider has worked in nearly every social work setting, her primary interest has been in children and their families.

Catherine K. Riessman currently is co-ordinator of Community Consultation Service, Mental Hygiene Clinic, Albert Einstein College of Medicine, Bronx, New York.

Robert Ross is a research associate at the Center for Research on Utilization of Scientific Knowledge, and is completing doctoral work in sociology at the University of Chicago. He has written articles on the welfare state and social problems and is currently doing research on advocacy planning and the politics of environmental regulation.

Ben Rubenstein is a lecturer at Marlboro College in Vermont.

William Ryan is chairman of the Department of Psychology at Boston College and director of the Ph.D. program in community social psychology. His professional activities and publications have been in the field of community mental health, urban problems, and social planning. His books include *Distress in the City* (1969) and *Blaming the Victim* (1971).

Natalie Davis Spingarn is a writer and consultant on urban affairs and a former HEW official and executive assistant to Senator Abraham Ribicoff (D/Conn.). She has written extensively on human service problems and issues.

James M. Statman is currently assistant professor and assistant chairman of the Department of Psychology at Catholic University of America, in Washington, D.C. In addition to teaching and research, he is also involved in radical consciousness raising and political action groups.

Gary L. Tischler is now associate professor of clinical psychiatry, Yale University School of Medicine, and acting director of the Hill-West Haven Division, Connecticut Mental Health Center.

E. Fuller Torrey currently works in the National Institute of Mental Health in Washington as a special assistant to the director for international activities. He is author of over 40 professional publications, including *The Mind Game: Witchdoctors and Psychiatrists*, and the editor of *Ethical Issues in Medicine: The Role of the Physician in Today's Society*.

Sheila W. Wellington is a research associate in psychiatry and public health, Yale University School of Medicine. She is also associate director of administration for the Hill-West Haven Division, Connecticut Mental Health Center.

index

This manuscript was prepared for publication by Alice Nigoghosian. The book was designed by Helene Skora. The typeface for the text is Linotype Baskerville originally designed in the eighteenth century; and display face is Univers.

The text is printed on Allied natural text paper and the book is bound in Columbia Mills' Atlantic Vellum cloth over boards. Manufactured in the United States of America.